Communications in Computer and Information Science 1807

Rationale

The CCIS series is devoted to the publication of proceedings of computer science conferences. Its aim is to efficiently disseminate original research results in informatics in printed and electronic form. While the focus is on publication of peer-reviewed full papers presenting mature work, inclusion of reviewed short papers reporting on work in progress is welcome, too. Besides globally relevant meetings with internationally representative program committees guaranteeing a strict peer-reviewing and paper selection process, conferences run by societies or of high regional or national relevance are also considered for publication.

Topics

The topical scope of CCIS spans the entire spectrum of informatics ranging from foundational topics in the theory of computing to information and communications science and technology and a broad variety of interdisciplinary application fields.

Information for Volume Editors and Authors

Publication in CCIS is free of charge. No royalties are paid, however, we offer registered conference participants temporary free access to the online version of the conference proceedings on SpringerLink (http://link.springer.com) by means of an http referrer from the conference website and/or a number of complimentary printed copies, as specified in the official acceptance email of the event.

CCIS proceedings can be published in time for distribution at conferences or as post-proceedings, and delivered in the form of printed books and/or electronically as USBs and/or e-content licenses for accessing proceedings at SpringerLink. Furthermore, CCIS proceedings are included in the CCIS electronic book series hosted in the SpringerLink digital library at http://link.springer.com/bookseries/7899. Conferences publishing in CCIS are allowed to use Online Conference Service (OCS) for managing the whole proceedings lifecycle (from submission and reviewing to preparing for publication) free of charge.

Publication process

The language of publication is exclusively English. Authors publishing in CCIS have to sign the Springer CCIS copyright transfer form, however, they are free to use their material published in CCIS for substantially changed, more elaborate subsequent publications elsewhere. For the preparation of the camera-ready papers/files, authors have to strictly adhere to the Springer CCIS Authors' Instructions and are strongly encouraged to use the CCIS LaTeX style files or templates.

Abstracting/Indexing

CCIS is abstracted/indexed in DBLP, Google Scholar, EI-Compendex, Mathematical Reviews, SCImago, Scopus. CCIS volumes are also submitted for the inclusion in ISI Proceedings.

How to start

To start the evaluation of your proposal for inclusion in the CCIS series, please send an e-mail to ccis@springer.com.

Antonio Skarmeta · Daniele Canavese ·
Antonio Lioy · Sara Matheu
Editors

Digital Sovereignty in Cyber Security: New Challenges in Future Vision

First International Workshop, CyberSec4Europe 2022
Venice, Italy, April 17–21, 2022
Revised Selected Papers

Editors
Antonio Skarmeta
University of Murcia
Murcia, Spain

Antonio Lioy
Politecnico di Torino
Turin, Italy

Daniele Canavese
Politecnico di Torino
Turin, Italy

Sara Matheu
University of Murcia
Murcia, Spain

ISSN 1865-0929 ISSN 1865-0937 (electronic)
Communications in Computer and Information Science
ISBN 978-3-031-36095-4 ISBN 978-3-031-36096-1 (eBook)
https://doi.org/10.1007/978-3-031-36096-1

This Springer imprint is published by the registered company Springer Nature Switzerland AG
The registered company address is: Gewerbestrasse 11, 6330 Cham, Switzerland

Preface

CyberSec4Europe (Cyber Security Network of Competence Centres for Europe) is a European research project whose main goal is to explore and drive the future of cybersecurity for securing and maintaining European democracy and the integrity of the Digital Single Market. The CyberSec4Europe consortium consists of 43 partners, both academic and industrial ones, and is fueled by more than 100 cybersecurity projects and initiatives. CyberSec4Europe is one of the 4 pilot projects approved to design, test, and demonstrate potential governance structures for a future European Cybersecurity Competence Network and the creation of a European cybersecurity community. CyberSec4Europe aims to lead the next generation of challenges and innovations related to cybersecurity. In particular, it wants to strengthen the research and innovative competencies and capacities at the national and European level. It comprises public and private research centers and universities, which collaboration will help to investigate the needs of the present to propose competitive solutions for the future.

Amongst the ambitious objectives of CyberSec4Europe, Work Package 3 Blueprint Design and Common Research, has been a technical-oriented work package whose goals were to define and research new strategies and directions in the next-generation cybersecurity European landscape. WP3 explored a variety of cutting-edge cybersecurity technologies in a number of critical sectors, such as finance, energy, and transport.

As part of WP3's focus, one ambition has been to analyze the current state of the art, new trends, and emerging technologies in the cybersecurity field. In that sense one of the objectives has been to collect findings, conclusions, research, and recommendations in various security-related areas, from highly technical ones (e.g., software and network security) to law and human-centric ones (e.g., governance and cybersecurity awareness). In that sense it was proposed in the context of the Privacy Symposium to organize the 1st Workshop on Digital Sovereignty in Cyber Security: New Challenges in Future Vision and a Call for Papers was launched to produce the book you are reading now, with the goal of pushing even further the investigation of advanced cybersecurity innovations to support European solutions for privacy and security. Although originally spurred by the activities of Task 3.9 Continuous Scouting, the Call for Papers was extended to the entire CyberSec4Europe project and the other pilots and saw great participation from multiple partners. The goal of the Call for Papers was to study new cutting-edge cybersecurity technologies, trends, and their possible impact on society. We asked the authors to investigate only very recent subjects and provide updated references, ideally in the last couple of years.

We received 13 submissions on various cybersecurity-related topics. On April 7th, 2022, we held a session titled "CyberSec4Europe - Research to Innovation: Common Research Framework on Security and Privacy" during the Privacy Symposium hosted by Università Ca' Foscari in Venice (Italy). The event was very well received, quite interactive, and with participation of multiple people from various European countries with different technical backgrounds and from different projects too.

After the conference, we asked the authors to write a full paper of at least 12 pages about the topic they presented, with each submitted article reviewed by three reviewers. The reviewers were asked to examine the meaningfulness of the investigations, their quality level, whether the paper was technically sound, and whether the references were appropriate. After the round of revisions, eleven papers were accepted and modified according to the suggestions provided by the reviewers.

This book collects all these papers and tries to provide a scouting analysis of the field of cybersecurity, privacy, and Digital Sovereignty in Cyber Security, to stimulate cooperation and synergies between research and industry communities to develop and deploy technology in cybersecurity and complement the capacity-building efforts in this area at the EU and national level.

We would like to sincerely thank all the papers' authors for their submissions, investigations, and participation, and the reviewers for their work. Our gratitude also goes to the Privacy Symposium committee for hosting our session in Venice.

Finally, we hope these proceedings will be of interest to future researchers and that they might provide some food for thought for both academic and industrial experts in the cybersecurity field.

April 2023

Antonio Skarmeta
Daniele Canavese
Antonio Lioy
Sara Matheu

Organization

General Chair

Antonio Skarmeta	University of Murcia, Spain

Program Committee Chairs

Daniele Canavese	Politecnico di Torino, Italy
Antonio Lioy	Politecnico di Torino, Italy
Sara Matheu	University of Murcia, Spain

Reviewers

Abdelmalek Benzekri	Université Paul Sabatier, France
Afonso Ferreira	CNRS, France
Aljosa Pasic	ATOS, Spain
Angelica Liguori	University of Calabria, Italy
Antonio Lioy	Politecnico di Torino, Italy
Antonio Skarmeta	University of Murcia, Spain
Carlos Esteban Budde	University of Trento, Italy
Christina von Wintzingerode	Goethe University Frankfurt am Main, Germany
Daniele Canavese	Politecnico di Torino, Italy
Dirk Müllmann	Goethe University Frankfurt am Main, Germany
Elvire Prochilo	Pragma-Consult, France
Erica Coppolillo	University of Calabria, Italy
Fabio Massacci	Vrije Universiteit Amsterdam, The Netherlands
Francesco Ciclosi	University of Trento, Italy
Francesco Sergio Pisani	CNR, Italy
Gencer Erdogan	SINTEF Digital, Norway
Giuseppe Manco	CNR, Italy
Indra Spiecker gen. Döhmann	Goethe University Frankfurt am Main, Germany
Jorge Bernal Bernabé	University of Murcia, Spain
Juan Francisco Martìnez Gil	University of Murcia, Spain
Leonardo Regano	Politecnico di Torino, Italy
Luca Durante	CNR, Italy
Manuel Cheminod	CNR, Italy

Massimo Guarascio	CNR, Italy
Narges Arastouei	Goethe University Frankfurt am Main, Germany
Pablo Fernández Saura	University of Murcia, Spain
Pierre-Henri Cros	Université Paul Sabatier, France
Shukun Tokas	SINTEF Digital, Norway
Silvia Vidor	University of Trento, Italy
Sunil Chaudhary	Maastricht University, The Netherlands
Vasileios Gkioulos	Norwegian University of Science and Technology, Norway

Contents

Software Security

Computer-Aided Reverse Engineering of Protected Software

Daniele Canavese(✉), Leonardo Regano, and Antonio Lioy

Dipartimento di Automatica e Informatica, Politecnico di Torino, Torino, Italy
{daniele.canavese,leonardo.regano,antonio.lioy}@polito.it

Abstract. Reverse engineering is undoing or circumventing the protections deployed on a code region. Software crackers perform this to remove license checks in commercial applications and video games, but it can also be done for legitimate purposes. Many software houses perform a security assessment phase by reverse engineering their protected software before releasing it to the market. Furthermore, anti-virus experts need to reverse engineering malware (e.g., viruses and ransomware) to understand how it works and spreads. Typically, reverse engineering is performed by hand with minimal computer support with debuggers, decompilers, and disassemblers. Nevertheless, in recent years, new research directions have proposed various promising automatic methods, primarily based on machine learning and symbolic execution techniques.

Keywords: reverse engineering · software protection · software obfuscation · machine learning · natural language processing · symbolic execution · concolic execution

1 Introduction

Software protection techniques are one of the cornerstones of modern (commercial) applications. Their flexibility and applicability are endless. Commercial software frequently uses them to fight piracy and to delay the release of cracks that can significantly reduce the monetary gain of software houses. Several video games are also protected to avoid cheaters. In addition, these techniques are also frequently used by various malware to fool anti-viruses.

Among the vast plethora of protection techniques, obfuscation techniques are the most widely used ones. The key idea of these algorithms is to boost the code complexity so that the effort necessary by an attacker to remove it is so high that it becomes impractical or economically unworthy. Many research papers showed that obfuscations, and software protection techniques, in general, increase the attack time by using empirical human studies [4,7,22,23]. Increasing the code complexity can be performed in various ways, such as rewriting mathematical expressions with bigger ones, introducing fake branches and convoluted loops, or leveraging odd pointer arithmetics to perform computations.

A. Skarmeta et al. (Eds.): CyberSec4Europe 2022, CCIS 1807, pp. 3–15, 2023.
https://doi.org/10.1007/978-3-031-36096-1_1

With the term *reverse engineering*, we indicate removing or bypassing the protections applied to a piece of code. This is usually done at the binary level by inspecting the assembly instructions. Attackers reverse engineer software for piracy-related purposes, such as cracking a commercial application or a video game. On the other hand, these techniques can also be used for defensive purposes. For instance, several software houses, before releasing a new protected software on the market, frequently perform several reserve engineering tests to assess the strength of its protections. Furthermore, several malware uses various protection techniques to thwart anti-virus detection.

Currently, the job of the reverse engineer is performed mainly by hand, with minimal automated support. Binaries are usually dissected via disassemblers and debuggers, at most with some custom scripts, and this process requires a high level of expertise and a long time. In the last few years, a new trend has started to appear gradually: automating most, if not all, the operations performed by a reverse engineer. Even if this area is still in its infancy, recent progress in machine learning and symbolic execution has already started to provide promising results. In the following sections, a variety of recent papers, patents, technologies, and tools will be studied. The goal of this paper is twofold. On one side, it is an interesting survey on the most recent automatic reverse engineering trends. On the other, it may serve as food for thought for researchers and experts willing to enter this fascinating area of cybersecurity.

The works presented in the following paragraphs suggests that replacing (for the most part) the human being in performing this kind of analysis is very feasible. Shortly, it is very likely that we will see a large adoption of AI-based techniques to speed up the protected area identification of released applications and libraries. It is foreseeable that machine-learning approaches will be prime citizens in this field, especially based on natural language processing techniques.

2 Protected Region Identification

When reverse engineering a binary file (e.g., an application, a plug-in, or a library), the first step is usually to identify the protected areas, as this is a strong indication that they may be the resources the attacker is looking for (for example, a license check function that needs to be cracked). This is traditionally performed by hand with the aid of disassemblers and debuggers, making it a time-consuming and labor-intensive operation. However, recent developments have shown that AI-powered methods can be used successfully to parse a binary file and detect protected regions quickly.

The critical idea in being able to identify a protected area is that software protections tend to change the code by leaving a consistent and recognizable pattern known as a *fingerprint* [16]. For instance, Fig. 1 shows an example of a simple function written in the C programming language protected with the control flow graph flattening obfuscation technique [12]. This technique transforms the code into a giant while loop with several nested branches, which can be identified by inspecting the (source and assembly) code or other representations such as the control flow graph.

```
x = y + z;
if (x < 0 || x > 100)
    w = c1;
else
    w = c2;
```

(a) Pre-protection code.

```
i = 0;
while (1) {
    if (i == 0) {
        x = y + z;
        i = 1;
    } else if (i == 1) {
        if (x < 0 || x > 100)
            i = 2;
        else
            i = 3;
    } else if (i == 2) {
        w = c1;
        i = 4;
    } else if (i == 3) {
        w = c2;
        i = 4;
    } else if (i == 4) {
        break;
    }
}
```

(b) Post-protection code.

Fig. 1. Control flow flattening obfuscation example.

2.1 Security Assessment

The software protection field research mainly focuses on the strength guaranteed by a protection technique once it is located. However, the invisibility of a protected asset, that is, its ability to blend with the other non-protected areas, can significantly impact the attack time, thus increasing the security of the application.

Neural networks seem particularly promising in this context due to their ability to detect very well-hidden patterns, even in complex and long collections of data. The current state-of-the-art works seem to favor two main techniques in this regard:

- NLP (Natural Language Processing) approaches: although NLP was born to deal with human languages (e.g., English, Spanish, or Italian), it can also be used to reason on programming statements and assembly instructions since they are languages too;
- CNNs (Convolutional Neural Networks): these deep neural networks are commonly used to analyze images and videos. However, due to their flexibility, they can also be used to perform various time-sequences analyses.

Kim et al. [10] proposed using a neural network to detect obfuscated functions in Intel binaries. Their work focuses on some protection techniques offered by Obfuscator-LLVM[1]. After disassembling the binary, the proposed approach involves counting the occurrence of some specific mnemonics (e.g., `add`, `mov`). This information is then given as input to a fully-connect neural work for classifying the code regions.

This approach showed good accuracy of 91% when a single obfuscation technique is used. However, when two protections are applied to the same code region, it drops to 85%.

In 2021, Canavese, Regano, and Basile [3] patented a methodology for identifying functions and assembly snippets protected with various protection tools on ARM and Intel architectures. Their approach uses state-of-the-art NLP neural networks and custom embeddings for the assembly instructions to locate obfuscated code regions. They experimentally showed that their system was able to detect functions protected with several well-known obfuscators, such as Obfuscator-LLVM, Tigress[2], and Diablo[3]. They reported that the accuracy for identifying a function obfuscated with a single protection technique is about 97% for both Intel and ARM architectures. In comparison, the accuracy slightly drops to 92% when the proposed system is used to pinpoint functions protected with two obfuscations.

In the same year, Jiang et al. [9] proposed a method based on LSTMs[4] [8] to identify functions on Intel and ARM architecture protected with Obfuscator-LLVM. Their approach consists of three several features for each basic block[5] and their adjacency matrix to model the control flow graph. This information is then given as input to an LSTM for the final classification of the functions. Their tests showed an accuracy of 95% for Intel applications and 99 % for Android binaries in detecting functions obfuscated with a single protection technique.

Zhao et al. [27] proposed a more complex approach based on a mix of CNNs and NLP techniques for identifying functions protected with Obfuscator-LLVM or Tigress on Intel architectures. Their procedure consisted of four steps:

1. disassembling the binary;
2. encoding the basic blocks using a custom embedding scheme;
3. performing a second encoding of the basic blocks embeddings with a CNN;
4. feeding an LSTM with the CNN output for the final classification of the function.

The tests showed that this approach could detect a function protected with a single protection with an accuracy of 91% and functions safeguarded by two protections with an average accuracy of 88%.

---

1 https://github.com/obfuscator-llvm/obfuscator.

2 https://tigress.wtf/.

3 https://github.com/csl-ugent/diablo.

4 LSTMs (Long-Short Term Memory) are a family of neural networks used to investigate time-sequences. They represent one of the modern key technologies to perform NLP, and several commercial products utilize them (e.g., Google Translator, Alexa).

5 A basic block is a sequence of instructions with exactly one execution flow ingress point (the first instruction) and one egress point (the last instruction).

2.2 Malware Analysis

Another important application in automatically detecting protected code regions is to perform malware analysis. Modern viruses, worms, and ransomware frequently obfuscate parts of their code to fool anti-viruses and anti-malware products. A common obfuscation technique used by malware is *packing*, which compresses the executable code. For instance, UPX[6] (Ultimate Packer for eXecutables) is a well-known packer, also used by many viruses. When an application wants to execute its code, it unpacks (decompress) the code into memory and then launches it. While this kind of malware can evade static analysis, it cannot fool dynamic analysis since the executable code must be put into the memory to be run. Static analysis, however, is safer since it does not require running some potentially malicious code. The research efforts are particularly active in this context, especially in detecting malware on mobile devices such as Android smartphones and tablets.

Tang et al. [21] proposed an interesting approach based on a mix of classic NLP techniques and CNNs to identify obfuscated malware on Android systems. The first step in their process is to analyze the opcodes of the function under scrutiny and extract several features based on the TF-IDF (Term Frequency-Inverse Document Frequency) [17] technique. This algorithm computes various frequency-based metrics of the opcodes in a binary and creates a numerical vector for each opcode. These numbers are then combined to form a sort of grayscale image fed to a CNN for the classification of the function. They tested the effectiveness of their approach on a variety of Android malware applications obfuscated with the AVPASS tool[7]. They proved experimentally that their accuracy was respectively 96% and 95% for detecting the unobfuscated and obfuscated malware.

BLADE [19] is a tool proposed in 2021 by Sihag et al. able to detect obfuscated malware by analyzing the Dalvik bytecode of the Android OS. The key idea of this tool is to transform the malware classification problem into a document classification problem. The first phase in the authors' approach is to simplify the bytecode by grouping similar instructions into several categories. Then, several metrics (e.g., occurrence counts) are computed to transform the simplified bytecode into a numerical vector. This vector is then fed into a traditional machine-learning classifier to detect the presence of some malware. The authors tested various classic machine-learning models, such as random forests and k-NN, on multiple data sets containing a variety of obfuscated malware and experimentally found that their accuracy was about 96%.

Zhang et al. [26] compiled an interesting survey on various obfuscation detection (and deobfuscation) tools and techniques for forensic investigations of Android devices, focusing on malware analysis. For obfuscation detection, they examined eight publicly available tools. Most of the investigated tools use a similar approach: computing some numeric feature on the bytecode (e.g., counting

[6] https://upx.github.io/.

[7] https://github.com/sslab-gatech/avpass.

the number of specific instructions) and then using some (machine-learning-based or not) classifier to detect the presence of some protected code automatically. They concluded that although several research papers are available in this area, most of the tools are not publicly available, thus prohibiting the improvement of their detection capabilities.

3 Code Understanding

After identifying an interesting area of code, potentially an asset, the attacker must first be able to understand the code's inner workings before circumventing the protection applied to the target code successfully. To understand the code, the attacker must first obtain an intelligible representation of it. This is typically achieved by disassembling or decompiling the code, getting respectively the assembly code (in the format of the binary's target machine, e.g., x86-64 or ARM), or a reconstructed version of the source code (with varying degrees of accuracy w.r.t. the original source code). Many disassemblers are available, including commercial solutions (e.g., IDA Pro, Binary Ninja, OBJ2ASM) and open-source ones (e.g., Capstone, objdump, gdb). Indeed, this task may take a non-negligible time, proportional to the skills and experience of the attacker and the tools at his disposal. Similarly, various decompilers are available, both commercial (e.g., Hex-Rays Decompiler) and free (e.g., Ghidra, RetDec). After obtaining an understandable representation of the code, the attacker may comprehend the target code statically or dynamically. In the first case, the attacker does not execute the code and tries to understand it, either by reading it directly or leveraging more user-friendly representations of it (e.g., Control Flow Graph, Data Dependency Graph). In the second case, the attacker observes the program at run-time, typically executing the target application with a debugger attached. Typically, dynamic code analysis is more straightforward and faster w.r.t. static analysis. However, it should be noted that protections able to prevent debugging are available [1]. Thus, the second option is not always viable.

Symbolic execution is a static program analysis technique that may be used to speed up the process of code understanding. This technique resorts to a mathematical representation of the code, typically modeling the latter via a graph-like state model. Using this mathematical representation, it is possible to prove mathematically the values that, given in input to the target application, will result in the execution of the target code. Furthermore, this will result in the list of instructions that will be executed given a specific set of inputs. In this way, it is possible to emulate the execution of the application without actually running it, thus circumventing anti-debugging protection. The idea in itself is not new; however, it has been gaining traction in the last years due to the increased available computational power in commodity hardware (thus enabling the more complex programs to be emulated). Also, an interesting application of this technique is the possibility of analyzing malware without resorting to sandboxed execution since many malicious applications can understand if they are executed in a sandboxed environment and consequently alter their run-time behavior to confuse security experts analyzing them.

One of the main problems of symbolic execution is path explosion since there is an exponential relation between the SLOC of the target application and the number of possible execution paths. This may render this technique unfeasible for large programs, notwithstanding the aforementioned increase in computational power in recent years. Concolic (i.e., Concrete-symbolic) execution tries to resolve this limitation by mixing static and dynamic code analysis. In particular, symbolic execution is still used for the main parts of the application that must be analyzed. However, other code areas are executed (i.e., concretely), driving their input with the results of symbolic execution to avoid their emulation. In this way, path explosion can be limited. Typical targets for run-time execution are standard libraries and system calls since they can be executed in isolation. This technique may still be used for malware analysis and on programs protected with anti-debugging techniques. Overall, this technique permits us to obtain in a faster way the same results of symbolic execution.

The works presented in the remainder of the section show applications of symbolic and concolic execution to two relevant cybersecurity problems: automated identification of vulnerabilities leading to information leakage and malware analysis. Indeed, these works prove that symbolic and concolic execution may be successfully used to automate tasks usually carried on by cybersecurity analysts, reducing the space for human error and increasing the efficiency of both vulnerability and malware detection. Future advancements in both these techniques may lead to an even greater amount of automation, thus leading to the widespread adoption of these approaches in commercial solutions.

3.1 Automated Identification of Information Leakage Vulnerabilities

A recent application of symbolic/concolic execution in this context is the automated identification of vulnerabilities leading to secret leakage during execution. A well-known example of such vulnerabilities is the Spectre family of attacks. These vulnerabilities exploit the speculative execution systems used by Intel CPUs to increase program execution speed. In particular, when a branch execution must be executed, the branch condition should usually be evaluated to select the branch where execution should continue. However, with speculative execution, a CPU component, named branch predictor, will try to guess the branch that must be executed, continuing program flow without actually evaluating the condition, which is postponed to increase efficiency. If the guess is deemed correct, the program execution usually continues. Instead, if the guess is incorrect, the program state is reversed, and the instructions of the right branch are executed. Unfortunately, wrong branch guesses may lead to side effects (e.g., on the contents of CPU caches) that attackers may leverage to recover application secrets. Applications of this attack family to recover cryptographic secrets have been demonstrated[8].

Daniel, Bardin, and Rezk [5] adapted binary symbolic execution to consider the effects of speculative execution. They employed pruning techniques

[8] https://spectreattack.com/spectre.pdf.

of the code graph representation used by symbolic execution, crafted for specific attacks in the Spectre family, to keep complexity at bay. They developed a Haunted RelSE tool to demonstrate their approach's effectiveness. They successfully identified Spectre vulnerabilities in various cryptographic libraries, including OpenSSL. Furthermore, their tests lead to an interesting finding: defense techniques developed to mitigate Spectre vulnerabilities may introduce other vulnerabilities of the same family in the protected code.

Guo et al. [24] developed a plugin for KLEE, a concolic execution framework based on the LLVM compiler. This plugin, called SpecuSym, can detect cache side effects that may lead to information leaks by programmatically exploring all program states. They developed an ad-hoc model of speculative execution to assist concolic execution in taking into account the cache side effects during path exploration. Similarly, Wan et al. proposed KLEESpectre [15], another plugin for KLEE based on similar ideas of SpecuSym, but specifically developed to identify vulnerabilities of the Spectre family.

Borzacchiello, Coppa, and Demetrescu [2] introduced FUZZOLIC, a concolic analysis framework. In particular, they combine concolic execution with fuzzing. In this dynamic analysis technique, the application is executed many times with varying input, to detect bugs by observing if a particular set of inputs lead to unexpected run-time behaviors or program crashes. Since FUZZOLIC runs under QEMU, a well-known software emulation solution, it supports binaries developed for many CPU architectures. They have found various software bugs by combining such techniques and applying them to a set of Linux command-line tools, including memory leakage vulnerabilities.

3.2 Malware Analysis with Symbolic and Concolic Execution

As previously stated, one interesting application of symbolic and concolic execution is the possibility of securely analyzing malware without actually executing it, without resorting to sandboxed approaches that may be hampered by the sandbox detection included in advanced malware.

Sebastio et al. [18] introduced a framework for symbolic/concolic analysis of obfuscated malware. In particular, the authors leverage angr[9], a binary analysis tool, to analyze the binary. The tool parameters are carefully selected to speed up the code analysis. Then, malware system calls are identified to populate an SCDG (System Call Dependency Graph) structure. This permits an accurate representation of the run-time behavior of the malware. Using gSpan7, a graph mining solution, the analyzed malware can be classified in one of the various families (e.g., , worm, ransomware, crypto-miner), with a 97% classification accuracy.

Van Ouytsel et al. proposed SEMA, a symbolic execution toolchain specialized in the detection of polymorphic malware, i.e., malware that can hinder classical static analysis solutions by dynamically changing the virus code at each execution while preserving its business logic. SEMA leverages an ad-hoc angr

[9] https://angr.io/.

extension to obtain from the target malware the SCDG, with optimizations for frequent API calls to hasten the analysis. Then, classification of the malware may be performed through two different approaches, one based on graph mining and the other on deep learning. An interesting addition is the adoption of federated learning, where multiple devices may remotely collaborate to train and update the malware detection classifier base on deep learning.

Namani and Khan [14] leverage concolic execution to analyze malware, again for identification and classification purposes. The analysis is performed by first disassembling the malware to obtain both the binary header and calls to external libraries. A subsequent concolic execution is targeted on the code areas containing API calls. This results in a feature vector that can be fed to a machine-learning classifier. In particular, the author tested three different machine learning approaches (decision trees, random forests, and fully connected neural networks), with a resulting accuracy ranging from 92% to 97%.

Park et al. [15] introduced BDHunter, an automated system for the identification of malware behavior dispatchers, i.e., groups of branch instructions that lead to the execution of malicious actions. The system first identifies candidate behavior dispatchers with two different approaches based on identifying patterns in the target binary control flow graph and weighted API calls. The candidates are confirmed or disproven by analyzing run-time behavior via concolic execution. Indeed, malware typically checks various run-time conditiocode's inner workings before receiving commands from a C2 server.

4 Protection Removal or Bypass

After locating promising code areas in the target application and understanding the program's internal workings, the attacker may need to remove or bypass protections applied to the target code areas to be able to perform attacks ultimately. This step is typically done manually, editing or rewriting the binary code directly or using ad-hoc scripts to bypass a specific protection technique. Thus, only a sufficiently motivated and expert attacker can typically remove non-trivial software protections. However, the latest research in the field has been directed at automating this complex and time-consuming process, leveraging the possibilities given by the new findings in the machine learning and AI area. The work has been focused on obfuscation since it is the most common family technique and is typically employed by malware to escape classical identification mechanisms implemented by anti-malware solutions.

Menguy et al. [13] introduced a framework for deobfuscation based on a black-box approach called Xyntia. In particular, this framework performs deobfuscation by defining an optimization problem to generate a code that preserves the business logic of the target code while minimizing its complexity. The optimization problem solution is carried on with a variation of a well-known heuristic, ILS (Iterated Local Search). The authors provided experimental proofs of successful reconstruction of code obfuscated with various techniques, including opaque predicates, an obfuscation approach able to increase code size by inserting branches to add dead code to the target area, and Mixed-Boolean Arithmetic (MBA), which increases the complexity of arithmetic expressions.

David, Coniglio, and Ceccato [6] proposed an approach to thwart various obfuscation techniques such as data encoding, MBA, and virtualization. The latter is a protection technique that translates the target code using a custom bytecode, which is interpreted at run-time by a VM included in the distributed protected application. The proposed tool performs deobfuscation in two phases, the first resorting to concolic execution to analyze the program and extract an abstract syntax tree representation of the target application and the second performing a top-down breadth-width search of the AST to obtain a deobfuscated version of the protected code.

A systematic literature review by Kochberger et al. [11] enumerates different solutions to thwart virtualization obfuscation. In their experiment, they deobfuscated various applications previously protected with virtualization, using 15 automatic deobfuscators, to assess their performance in understanding the virtualized bytecode. Furthermore, they organized deobfuscation techniques in state of the art into a taxonomy based on the analysis type performed by the deobfuscators (e.g., static, dynamic, or hybrid), the artifacts used to perform such analysis (e.g., traces, control flow graphs), and the level of automation achieved (fully or partially automated).

Suk, Bi, and Lee [20] developed SCORE, a tool for reversing Control Flow Flattening, one of the most used code obfuscation techniques. The tool starts by executing the code to recover information needed to perform the actual deobfuscation, such as the order of execution of instructions of obfuscated code areas and patterns of execution of program functions. Deobfuscation is then performed with a three-step process. First, the instructions are rearranged in the order of execution. Then, dead code elimination is achieved, given the prior results of code execution. Finally, various source code optimization techniques are performed to improve the readability of the obtained deobfuscated code.

You et al. [25] performed a study of two different code optimization and deobfuscation tools for Android applications, ReDex[10] and Deguard[11]. In particular, they generated a set of obfuscated Android applications using two different obfuscation tools (R8 and Obfuscapk) on three vanilla Android applications. They then performed deobfuscation on the applications using an ad-hoc tool for Android apps and compared the resulting source codes with the original unobfuscated ones to evaluate deobfuscation accuracy.

The works presented show that it is indeed possible to automate the task of reverse engineers since automatic deobfuscators have been successfully developed. Since code obfuscation is the most common technique employed to protect software, these advancements will certainly boost the research in the field, possibly leading to the development of completely new protection techniques and

[10] https://fbredex.com.
[11] https://apk-deguard.com.

improvements of existing ob techniques to improve their resilience against automatic deobfuscation.

5 Conclusions

Reverse engineering a software application is inherently challenging and requires expertise, time, and patience. Even more so if the code to analyze is protected. Attackers typically crack software applications for illegal purposes, such as removing or bypassing license checks in commercial software and video games. However, software houses also frequently use reverse engineering techniques for defensive purposes, such as assessing the security of a protected application before its release or helping anti-viruses detect new and more advanced forms of malware.

Even in our technocentric world, this task is performed primarily manually via tools such as debuggers, decompilers, and disassemblers with minimal automatized support. In the last few years, however, the surfacing of new techniques has started to change this trend.

In our analysis, two families of techniques will dominate the scenes in the reverse engineering field: machine learning techniques based on neural networks and symbolic/concolic execution approaches. None of these techniques is new: in fact, neural networks were born in the 1950s, and symbolic execution has been known since the 1970s. However, recent advancements in computation power have unleashed the ability to use more complex and demanding analyses that were prohibitive before.

Successfully automatizing the reverse engineering process will greatly impact the future of the software protection world in many different ways. First, it is foreseeable that companies will start using AI and symbolic execution-based techniques to aid their expert in releasing more secure and protected commercial software (and their patches) while significantly reducing their time-to-market window. On the other hand, anti-viruses and anti-malware programs will also benefit from these advancements. Machine-learning bases analysis can drastically enhance the detection of new breeds of malicious and obfuscated malware.

Acknowledgments. This work has been partly supported by the CyberSec4Europe project (Horizon 2020 proposal no. 830929).

References

1. Abrath, B., Coppens, B., Volckaert, S., Wijnant, J., Bjorn, S.D.: Tightly-coupled self-debugging software protection. In: Proceedings of SSPREW 2016: Workshop on Software Security, Protection, and Reverse Engineering. Los Angeles (USA), pp. 1–10 (2016). https://doi.org/10.1145/3015135.3015142
2. Borzacchiello, L., Coppa, E., Demetrescu, C.: Fuzzolic: mixing fuzzing and concolic execution. Comput. Secur. **108** (2021). https://doi.org/10.1016/j.cose.2021.102368

3. Canavese, D., Regano, L., Basile, C.: Method for the identification of protected assets in software binaries (2021). https://www.knowledgeshare.eu/en/patent/method-for-the-identification-of-protected-assets-in-software-binaries/, application number 102021000012488
4. Ceccato, M., Di Penta, M., Falcarin, P., Ricca, F., Torchiano, M., Tonella, P.: A family of experiments to assess the effectiveness and efficiency of source code obfuscation techniques. Empir. Softw. Eng. **19**(4), 1040–1074 (2013). https://doi.org/10.1007/s10664-013-9248-x
5. Daniel, L.A., Bardin, S., Rezk, T.: Hunting the haunter-efficient relational symbolic execution for spectre with haunted relse. In: Proceedings of NDSS 2021: Network and Distributed System Security Symposium, pp. 1–18. Virtual conference (2021). https://doi.org/10.14722/ndss.2021.24286
6. David, R., Coniglio, L., Ceccato, M.: Qsynth - a program synthesis based approach for binary code deobfuscation. In: Proceedings of BAR 2020: Workshop on Binary Analysis Research. San Diego (USA), pp. 1–12 (2020). https://doi.org/10.14722/bar.2020.23009
7. Hänsch, N., Schankin, A., Protsenko, M., Freiling, F., Benenson, Z.: Programming experience might not help in comprehending obfuscated source code efficiently. In: Proceedings of SOUPS 2018: USENIX Conference on Usable Privacy and Security. Baltimore (USA), pp. 341–356 (2018)
8. Hochreiter, S., Schmidhuber, J.: Long short-term memory. Neural Comput. **9**, 1735–80 (1997). https://doi.org/10.1162/neco.1997.9.8.1735
9. Jiang, S., Hong, Y., Fu, C., Qian, Y., Han, L.: Function-level obfuscation detection method based on graph convolutional networks. J. Inf. Secur. Appl. **61**, 102953 (2021). https://doi.org/10.1016/j.jisa.2021.102953
10. Kim, J., Kang, S., Cho, E.-S., Paik, J.-Y.: LOM: lightweight classifier for obfuscation methods. In: Kim, H. (ed.) WISA 2021. LNCS, vol. 13009, pp. 3–15. Springer, Cham (2021). https://doi.org/10.1007/978-3-030-89432-0_1
11. Kochberger, P., Schrittwieser, S., Schweighofer, S., Kieseberg, P., Weippl, E.: Sok: automatic deobfuscation of virtualization-protected applications. In: Proceedings of ARES 2021: International Conference on Availability, Reliability and Security. Benevento (Italy), pp. 1–15 (2021). https://doi.org/10.1145/3465481.3465772
12. László, T., Kiss, Á.: Obfuscating c++ programs via control flow flattening. Annales Univ. Sci. Budapest **30**, 3–19 (2009)
13. Menguy, G., Bardin, S., Bonichon, R., de Souza Lima, C.: AI-based blackbox code deobfuscation: understand, improve and mitigate. CoRR **abs/2102.04805** (2021). https://arxiv.org/abs/2102.04805
14. Namani, N., Khan, A.: Symbolic execution based feature extraction for detection of malware. In: Proceedings of ICCCS 2020: International Conference on Computing, Communication and Security, pp. 1–6. Virtual Conference (2020). https://doi.org/10.1109/ICCCS49678.2020.9277493
15. Park, K., et al.: Identifying behavior dispatchers for malware analysis. In: Proceedings of ASIACCS 2021: Asia Conference on Computer and Communications Security. Hong Kong (China), pp. 759–773 (2021). https://doi.org/10.1145/3433210.3457894
16. Regano, L., Canavese, D., Basile, C., Lioy, A.: Towards optimally hiding protected assets in software applications. In: Proceedings of QRS 2017: International Conference on Software Quality, Reliability and Security. IEEE, Prague (Czech Republic), pp. 374–385 (2017). https://doi.org/10.1109/QRS.2017.47
17. Salton, G., McGill, M.: Introduction to Modern Information Retrieval. McGraw-Hill (1983)

18. Sebastio, S., et al.: Optimizing symbolic execution for malware behavior classification. Comput. Secur. **93**, 101775 (2020). https://doi.org/10.1016/j.cose.2020.101775
19. Sihag, V., Vardhan, M., Singh, P.: Blade: robust malware detection against obfuscation in android. Forensic Sci. Int. Digit. Investig. **38**, 301176 (2021). https://doi.org/10.1016/j.fsidi.2021.301176
20. Suk, J.H., Lee, Y.B., Lee, D.H.: Score: source code optimization & reconstruction. IEEE Access **8** (2020). https://doi.org/10.1109/ACCESS.2020.3008905
21. Tang, J., Li, R., Jiang, Y., Gu, X., Li, Y.: Android malware obfuscation variants detection method based on multi-granularity opcode features. Futur. Gener. Comput. Syst. **129**, 141–151 (2022). https://doi.org/10.1016/j.future.2021.11.005
22. Viticchié, A., Regano, L., Basile, C., Torchiano, M., Ceccato, M., Tonella, P.: Empirical assessment of the effort needed to attack programs protected with client/server code splitting. Empir. Softw. Eng. **25**(1), 1–48 (2019). https://doi.org/10.1007/s10664-019-09738-1
23. Viticchié, A., et al.: Assessment of source code obfuscation techniques. In: Proceedings of SCAM 2016: International Working Conference on Source Code Analysis and Manipulation, pp. 11–20. IEEE, Raleigh (USA) (2016). https://doi.org/10.1109/SCAM.2016.17
24. Wang, G., Chattopadhyay, S., Biswas, A.K., Mitra, T., Roychoudhury, A.: Kleespectre: detecting information leakage through speculative cache attacks via symbolic execution. Trans. Softw. Eng. Methodol. **29** (2020). https://doi.org/10.1145/3385897
25. You, G., Kim, G., Je Cho, S., Han, H.: A comparative study on optimization, obfuscation, and deobfuscation tools in android. J. Internet Serv. Inf. Secur. **11** (2021)
26. Zhang, X., Breitinger, F., Luechinger, E., O'Shaughnessy, S.: Android application forensics: a survey of obfuscation, obfuscation detection and deobfuscation techniques and their impact on investigations. Forensic Sci. Int. Digit. Investig. **39**, 301285 (2021). https://doi.org/10.1016/j.fsidi.2021.301285
27. Zhao, Y., et al.: Semantics-aware obfuscation scheme prediction for binary. Comput. Secur. **99**, 102072 (2020). https://doi.org/10.1016/j.cose.2020.102072

Using Statistical Model Checking for Cybersecurity Analysis

Carlos E. Budde(✉)

Security, University of Trento, Trento, Italy
carlosesteban.budde@unitn.it

Abstract. This work discusses an approach to estimate the likelihood of occurrence and evolution in time of software security issues. First, software vulnerability assessment is revised under the light of recent studies. Then, guidelines are proposed that allow for (formal) modelling stochastic aspects of cybersecurity-relevant scenarios. This opens a connection to the field of formal methods, where automated tools like statistical model checkers can estimate the value of property queries characterising such scenarios. But exploitable vulnerabilities and attacks in cybersecurity are rare events, which calls for specialised tools. In view of this, the work finalises presenting FIG, a statistical model checker specialised on rare event simulation. FIG, an open source software tool freely available at https://git.cs.famaf.unc.edu.ar/dsg/fig, can be used to estimate the probability of an attack within the next release cycle.

Keywords: Statistical model checking · Formal models for safety and security · Cybersecurity analysis · Rare event simulation

1 Introduction

Taken-for-granted technologies in today's digital societies include personal healthcare appliances, assisted-driving cars, AIs that start to chat too well, nightly-build continuous integration/continuous deliveries, etc. Distributed data storage with a *central access point* stands among these feats. In fact, from the digital technologies mentioned, cloud storage is arguably the one with the biggest immediate impact in our everyday lives. Having your account stolen in social media apps is a twenty-first century bonfire story, not to mention the more serious implications of this happening with accounts that contain e.g. your banking data.

These modern dreadful scenarios often portray cybersecurity as the guardian angel that will keep our data safe at all costs. Unfortunately, black and white hats alike have long ago realised that the central access point, that makes cloud technologies so useful for everyone, is often what also makes them prone to

Funded by the EU under GA n.101067199 (*ProSVED*). Views and opinions expressed are those of the author(s) only and do not necessarily reflect those of the European Union or The European Research Executive Agency. Neither the European Union nor the granting authority can be held responsible for them.

A. Skarmeta et al. (Eds.): CyberSec4Europe 2022, CCIS 1807, pp. 16–32, 2023.
https://doi.org/10.1007/978-3-031-36096-1_2

attacks. So much so that cryptography, which is the discipline that studies how to use a user-private password to turn our data into undecipherable mangled bits and back[1], is the most broadly taught subjects across cybersecurity curricula in European countries today—see e.g. recent studies by Dragoni et al. [16].

1.1 Uneducated Mob

The above could sound encouraging. However, cryptography is but one of the many topics that cast a protective mail between our data and its attackers. Interestingly, it is not the weakest link in that mail—rather the opposite. The bigger picture shows several further disciplines which must function in synchrony, in order to deny unauthorised parties access to sensitive digital information.

For instance, [16, Fig. 4] shows the ten best-covered disciplines by European M.Sc. programs. However, a complete education must also include topics in *Component Procurement, Deployment and Maintenance*, *Distributed System Architectures*, compliance to *Policies*, etc. Current higher education and professional training cover these last examples only marginally [16,19].

Perhaps a specially worrying case is human security, also known as the human factor, which is intimately connected to cybersecurity as it concerns how attacks to persons—rather than to machinery, code, or protocols—can compromise the security of individuals and even entire corporations. Human security includes disciplines such as *Identity Management*, *Compliance to Policies and Norms*, and (defence against) *Social Engineering*. And even though these aspects are evidently crucial to keep our data safe—it matters little if our PCs have an AES chip, when a colleague can shoulder-surf us with a latte macchiato—it has been known for over a decade that education is falling behind in these topics [19,31].

As a result, good practices for access and human security which used to be suggestions, such as strong password keys and multi-factor authentication, are now downright enforced into (rather than expected from) users. Unfortunately, not every practice can be enforced, since high-security and ease-of-use typically stand on opposite sides of the user-experience spectrum [34]. Therefore, enforceable user-sided security has limited reach at best, so system administrators (and companies in general) must operate under the assumption that the users will not do the cybersecurity heavy-lifting.

1.2 Fifty Shades of Cybersecurity

The picture appears dire. "*But*"—we tell ourselves—"*this will not happen to*" me "*, whose security hygiene can put the CIA's to shame.*" Things are, of course, not that simple, with a complexity that soars as world-wide distributed servers (that store our data) run on heterogeneous hardware and firmware.

This poses a challenge to backend developers, namely efficiency (and intelligible documentation, one would hope). In turn, frontend developers are in charge

[1] This is rather *encryption*, a sub-field of cryptography. For a more precise (and serious) understanding of cryptography we refer the interested reader to e.g. [4, chs. 1 and 3].

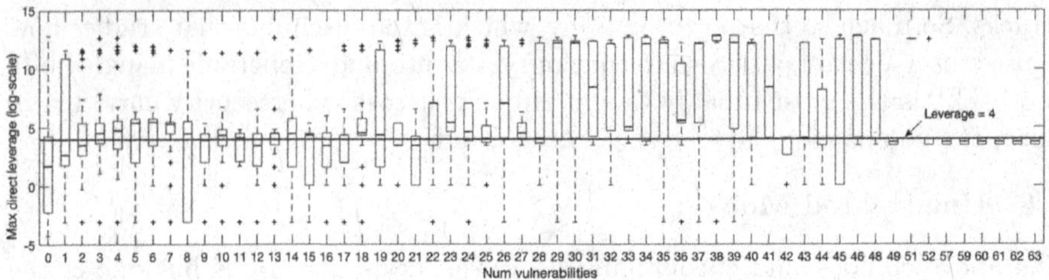

Fig. 1. Higher volume of library dependencies in the owned code (higher max direct leverage in the y-axis) is correlated with higher number of vulnerabilities faced in the lifetime of a software project [28].

of improving user experience, by offering everyone an homogeneous and equally-responsive interface. Cybersecurity appears here as a third layer, whose developers strive to achieve a common minimal *degree of protection*. And maximising this minimum is crucial, since attackers accessing data in the server are effectively bypassing any user-sided cryptographic barrier.

Ideally, system design can achieve good and homogeneous protection in a manner resilient to software heterogeneity and evolution, even in the face of undocumented "efficient" code. Unfortunately, developers seldom have the chance to design a system from scratch. More often than not companies must work with legacy software, so the choices available to developers—already constrained w.r.t. enforceable user-side security—are restricted even more. In fact, it is not uncommon that the only feasible choice is which new library version to update to [33]. The impact in security is apparent, as recent studies show correlations between the use of libraries and the number of security vulnerabilities affecting a software project—see Fig. 1 and related works [28,32,35].

These are practical reasons why cybersecurity cannot be Boolean, e.g. a social media platform is not either cyber-safe or -unsafe. Any software is ultimately susceptible to cyberattacks, which motivates concepts like *cyber resilience*: the ability to continuously deliver a service/product despite adverse cyber events, or to quickly and fully recover from such events [28,33,38].

Therefore, for companies it boils down to investment strategies: how to spend resources in a manner that reduces the risk of cyberharm, viz. the degree of protection mentioned above. Such investments range from buying specialised hardware and software, or implementing security policies, up to training attack-response teams. The ultimate goal is to lower the risk of enduring or recovering from impactful attacks: the more vulnerable the system, the higher the investment needed. Together with the increasing pressure by (inter-) national regulatory treaties—GDPR, HIPPA, PCI DSS, etc.—this has turned the estimation of software vulnerability into an increasingly hot research topic [28,36].

Technically, however, vulnerability estimation comes with many theoretical and practical hurdles. One of the hardest to overcome is the sheer unpredictability of future technologies. In fact, most endeavours take an ostrich approach here and focus on known vulnerabilities, typically zero-day attacks, avoiding to speculate on issues to come. This line of action is mainly chosen due to the complexity of the field, where a seemingly innocuous code fragment can be exploited, but only when accessed via a specific browser with certain plugin installed.

In the face of such complexity, it is extremely difficult to determine from existent code which fragments can become vulnerable in the future, or even how many vulnerabilities one should expect later at project-level (but see [39,46] for time-series approaches that count vulnerabilities in code-agnostic manners).

This work discusses how an abstraction step can be taken to analyse a formalised model of the system's security. This can be used to estimate, with an arbitrary degree of accuracy, the likelihood and time lapse between the exploitation of code-specific vulnerabilities.

Outline. The rest of this paper is structured as follows. First, Sect. 2 briefly revises related work. Then, a minimal introduction to model checking and its statistical variant are given in Sects. 3 and 4, showing why the latter is a feasible approach to estimate (future) security vulnerabilities. However, simulation-based approaches are computationally inefficient when studying rare events, which is the category in which exploited vulnerabilities fall into. That is why Sect. 5 presents FIG: a statistical model checker specialised in rare event simulation, that offers a unique solution to the estimation-by-simulation problem. This work concludes in Sect. 6.

2 Related Work

Studies to find software vulnerabilities date at least from the early 2000's. Most works propose a statistical approach, often demonstrating its capabilities in concrete and complex case studies or large datasets, depending on the specific objective. This has been changing from classic statistical analyses—e.g. confidence interval comparison and hypothesis tests—to modern Machine Learning (ML) approaches, ranging from concrete algorithms (support vector machines, random forests, linear regression, etc.) to full disciplines like deep learning.

For example, works like [3,13,29,30,43] study code and code-activity metrics to either correlate them to reported vulnerabilities, or identify vulnerable code fragments (i.e. the prime suspects of cybersecurity police). The features studied to find these correlations and suspicious code include average length of functions, cyclomatic complexity, nano-patterns, commit code churn, number and seniority of committers, peer comments in code and in commits, etc.

The degree of success of these approaches is variable. While most achieve relatively high sensitivity, precision is a different matter due to the high rate of false positives [2,26,44]. Not to mention the difficulty of extrapolation to different projects and languages—see [35] for a discussion, and [23] for the alternative solution of anti-fragile systems. Interestingly, [35] also reports that in their study of 450 projects written in Java, Python, and Ruby, "*There is no clear relationship between dependency vulnerability count with attributes of the commit including author experience*".

Data mining and ML approaches have been surveyed in [21]. Recent works like [1,7,12,20,27] try to predict vulnerabilities[2] not only from software metrics but also e.g. the dependency tree, the abstract syntax tree (of function call), code cloning, etc. The main disadvantage of these approaches is the black-box models they produce: despite their accuracy, it can be hard for developers to understand why a library dependency is deemed vulnerable. In contrast, white-box models and indicators such as [26,28,33,35] are better in communicating the source of the issue, which helps both developers and managers in making decisions, e.g. which dependencies to adopt, avoid, or simply update—see also [23].

All the works mentioned above attempt to detect vulnerabilities that exist in the code. Instead, the current work proposes a way to generate models that can be used to *foretell vulnerabilities that may occur in the future*. This is in line with the objectives of [39,46], which use time-series analysis akin to those employed in the stock market—e.g. ARIMA—to estimate the number of security issues that a project may eventually face. In that sense, [39,46] suffer from the same critique than ML: the models produced are black-box and cannot explain why is a code vulnerable, or which fix to apply. In contrast, using a formal approach as discussed in Sect. 4 would produce white-box (formal) models that can identify the dependencies from which the estimated vulnerabilities emerge.

3 Model Checking and Cybersecurity

Formal system modelling and analysis is based on mathematical specifications of systems, whose properties are queried using (typically) temporal logic formulae. The field is vast, and a large part of it deals with *model checking* due to its attractive push-button approach, where formal checks can be fully automated [5].

3.1 Model Checking

The fundamental steps for model checking are:

1. defining a model M that describes the system to be analysed;
2. defining a property φ that describes the query to perform;
3. checking whether (or the degree to which) the model satisfies the property, which is typically denoted $M \models \varphi$.

The subsequent formal guarantees on the automatically computed answer have resulted in many success stories of model checking applied to safety analysis—a trend that continues to this day [18,24,37].

For example, in [37], the question from step 3 above is "*what is the probability that the power supply noise of my NoC surpasses the safety threshold*". It is

[2] In ML, *predict* refers to classification, i.e. identify code affected by a CVE or known vulnerable pattern. This is not the same as *foretelling* the occurrence of vulnerabilities in the future, e.g. a yet-to-come CVE. Here we are interested in estimating the latter.

compelling to see the resemblance of such queries to measuring the degree of (cyber-) security resilience. This has in fact started to be noticed, as researchers begin to apply model checking for general cybersecurity studies [17,42].

But there is a zeroth step that precedes modelling and is often assumed:

> Selecting the formalism in which M and φ will be given semantics is crucial, because it determines the type of questions that can be asked.

For example, the semantics on which the model M is interpreted must be able to speak about the passing of time (formally, allow for a continuous state space) if one desires to ask about the duration of events. Also, and quite to the point of attack-resilience, the chosen formalism must allow for probability measures, to query about the likelihood of an event taking place. We now discuss these matters for cybersecurity analysis.

3.2 Semantic Basis

In automata theory, many mathematical formalisms can express either time or probabilities [22]. Arbitrary combinations of these aspects are less common, in part because the complexity of the resulting models quickly reaches undecidability even for reachability properties. That is, if the semantics are chosen to be too expressive, there may be no algorithm that can compute e.g. whether a vulnerable situation is reachable. Computational efficiency is also a factor to consider: the more flexible the model, the more computation steps (and runtime) it will take for an algorithm to find the answer to a query.

Simply put, the modelling formalism must be chosen as expressive as needed—to answer all relevant questions—and as simple as possible.

> For software vulnerabilities we are interested in two types of questions:
> - "*what is the probability of an attack in a defined time window?*",
> - "*what is the expected time between independent attacks?*".

Both questions are stochastic in nature, and the second one requires the estimation of potentially continuous time intervals. The simplest formalism from the literature that can cope with both continuous probability measures and time are *Stochastic Automata*, a subset of STA [14,22].

> A Stochastic Automaton M can encode the occurrence of attacks, according to probability distributions fitted from empirical data coming from real-world measurements. Then, a PCTL-like property φ can query the time-bounded probability of observing relevant events in the foreseeable future.

This regards steps 1 and 2 from the model checking procedure. However, step 3 encounters the extra requirement of verifying *arbitrary* distributions, which come from approximations of the empirical attack information and probabilities observed in the real world. Such typically non-Markovian behaviour rules out traditional (probabilistic) model checking, whose numerical approximation algorithms—e.g. value iteration and its variants—rely on the memoryless property. Workarounds like using face-types to approximate the empirical distributions have short reach, since they increase the number of states to visit, in an already NP-hard problem of known exponential size.

Instead, the analysis of non-Markovian stochastic systems is typically approached with Monte Carlo simulation. Embedded in a formal methods setting this is usually called statistical model checking (SMC [47]).

4 Statistical Model Checking for Cybersecurity

SMC integrates Monte Carlo simulation with formal methods. Via discrete event simulation it generates traces, which are samples of the states that a stochastic model M can visit. Via the generation and analysis of these stochastic samples, SMC estimates the degree to which M satisfies different properties.

4.1 Monte Carlo Simulation: An Informal Primer

Resorting to SMC brings an extra semantic requirement: the model must be fully stochastic and hence be free of nondeterministic behaviour. The following gives an intuition of what this means; formal treatments are e.g. in [5,15,22].

For our purposes it suffices to consider the model M as consisting of a (possibly infinite) set of states $S = \{s_0, s_1, s_2, \ldots\}$, and transitions $s_i \to s_j$ among them. Each state represents a general configuration of the modelled system, so for instance if we are studying how our server processes calls via its web API, s_0 can represent the idle state, s_1 the reception of a message via method `foo()`, s_2 the process of stripping the header from the payload, etc. The transitions in the model represent how the system passes from one state to another; in our example this could be $s_0 \to s_1 \to s_2$.

A simulation trace in the model M is as a sequence of states $\sigma = s_{i_0} s_{i_1} s_{i_2} \cdots$ where for any two consecutive states $s_{i_j} s_{i_{j+1}}$ there exists a transition $s_{i_j} \to s_{i_{j+1}}$ in the model M. The trace σ thus models "a run in the system", describing how it evolves from certain initial state onwards. For simplicity we let s_0 be the initial state, but one could also choose a set of initial states $S_0 \subsetneq S$.

Roughly speaking, a *simulation of Monte Carlo* is the process of generating a trace σ. This is done several times, generating a collection of traces $\{\sigma_j\}_{j=i}^{m}$ that model how the system usually operates. Each trace can then be tested against the property, e.g. $\varphi =$ "sensitive data has been leaked", to see whether the trace makes φ true. This results in a statistical answer to $M \models \varphi$, e.g. "our server leaks data on average 0.0021% of the time, with a standard deviation of 5.2E-4".

Note however that the transitions in our model are not necessarily deterministic. For example, imagine that our web API has a `bar()` method, and let s_{42}

represent the reception of a message via `bar()`. This is modelled by the transition $s_0 \to s_{42}$ in M, which means that from the idle state there are at least two possible choices: $s_0 \to s_1$ (`foo`) vs. $s_0 \to s_{42}$ (`bar`). This is called *branching.*

> To be able to use SMC, all branching in the model must be probabilistic.

In the example above this means that there must be probabilistic weights in the transitions from s_0 to either of its two possible successors. In general, these probabilities need not be discrete: for continuous state spaces one would use stochastic distributions, as Stochastic Automata do. However, the generic definition of Stochastic Automata is not fully probabilistic [14]. Its representation of stochastic time periods via clocks allows nondeterministic behaviour, viz. where branching arises for which there is no quantification whatsoever of which path to follow. Then Monte Carlo cannot generate traces, because when faced with a nondeterministic choice it does not know how to continue.

But there is a subset of Stochastic Automata known to be modular and fully probabilistic: *Input/Output Stochastic Automata*, and its weakly-nondeterministic variant with so-called *urgent actions* (IOSA [15]). This means that IOSA models allow arbitrary distributions, and permit the formal analysis of properties via SMC, to estimate statistical quantities such as the probability of leaking sensitive data via web API calls.

> IOSA models have all desired properties to study cybersecurity via SMC.

4.2 Modelling Considerations and Guidelines

Regarding the design of models for cybersecurity, it is up to the modeller to decide which kind of information is encoded in the states S. The specific choice depends on the behaviour of interest—some straightforward options are: (a) the first-level libraries that a main project depends on, (b) the number of known vulnerabilities for the own codebase and also for these libraries, (c) the criticality of these vulnerabilities, (d) the time since their publication, and (e) whether any of these codebases is currently under attack.

In turn, there are many interfaces to represent the states and transitions of M for (statistical) model checking. To avoid reinventing the wheel, any suitable pre-existent *modelling syntax* must be tried first: cybersecurity is no exception, so syntaxes that can model security-relevant situations should be explored.

Attack trees (ATs) are a simple example [45]: they are structural decompositions of the steps needed to perpetrate a (security) attack, and can be used for cybersecurity. ATs can, for instance, model option (a) above, under the assumption that a security vulnerability in a dependency can also compromise the code that uses it. Technically, the root of the tree would be an `OR` gate that represents the main library, and the leaves would be `BAS`es with relevant information, e.g. the empirical probability distribution of vulnerability disclosure.

```
toplevel "MainLib";
"MainLib" or "own_code" "depend_1" "depend_2";
"own_code" fail~weibull(k=2.3,β=125);
"depend_1" fail~exponential(λ=8.07E-3);
"depend_2" fail~lognormal(μ=30,σ=90);
```

Code 1. Kepler AT for library & dependencies

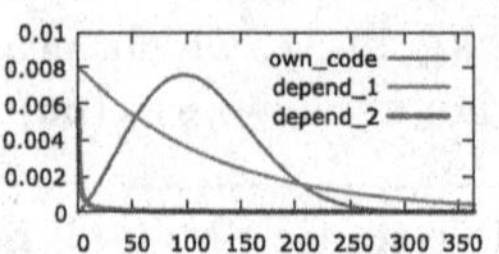

Fig. 2. Attack PDFs

There are modern syntaxes to describe (fault and) attack trees, for instance Kepler [11], that can be re-interpreted to model cybersecurity scenarios. Code 1 shows one such AT for a library with two dependencies, whose hypothesised fitted PDFs for vulnerability disclosure are shown in Fig. 2.

Code 1 proposes a way to declare models for option (a) above. In contrast, option (e) is speculative and defines the goal of the simulations. More precisely, a temporal logic property φ can query the probability of transitioning from the current safe state, to a state in which one or more of the codebases is under attack, before T days have passed. SMC can estimate this value (the step $M \models \varphi$) by generating several samples via Monte Carlo simulation, and computing the proportion of them that suffered an attack before T days.[3] Here, φ is said to characterise a subset of the states $S_\varphi \subset S$, whose reachability we are estimating.

Thus, from M and φ, an SMC analysis yields an estimate $\hat{\gamma} \in [0,1]$ of the actual probability γ with which the model satisfies φ, e.g. the likelihood of an attack. Besides producing $\hat{\gamma}$, SMC can quantify the statistical error incurred via two numbers, $\delta \in (0,1)$ and $\varepsilon > 0$, such that $\hat{\gamma} \in [\gamma-\varepsilon, \gamma+\varepsilon]$ with probability δ. Thus, if $n \in \mathbb{N}$ traces are sampled, the full SMC outcome is the tuple $(n, \hat{\gamma}, \delta, \varepsilon)$.

This statistical quantification is usually returned as a confidence interval (CI) around $\hat{\gamma}$, and conveys an idea of the quality of the estimation. The usual approach is to fix the confidence δ prior to experimentation: then higher quality means smaller ε and thus a narrower CI, achieved by drawing more samples.

4.3 Computational Considerations

Although flexible and automatic, the SMC approach is hindered by rare events. That is, if there is a very low probability γ to satisfy φ, then most traces sampled by SMC will not visit S_φ. The result is then either an incorrect estimate $\hat{\gamma} = 0$ or, if a few traces do visit S_φ, the confidence interval computed is very wide and hence uninformative.

This can affect cybersecurity analyses, since the likelihood of observing an exploit of a vulnerability is quite low in practice. To counter such phenomena, the number of samples n must increase as γ decreases. Unfortunately, for the sample mean, this causes n to increase in inverse proportion to the square of γ, which quickly results in unacceptably-long run times. To tackle this issue, rare event simulation (RES) methods have emerged in many scientific disciplines [40].

[3] Transitions among states are governed by stochastic distributions, that describe the jump probabilities from past evidence. Stochastic Automata encode this via "clocks".

4.4 Rare Event Simulation

Roughly speaking, RES can be divided in importance sampling and importance splitting (ISPLIT). The former modifies the stochastic transitions of the model, in a way that can later be undone when computing the estimate $\hat{\gamma}$. This is not clearly feasible for cybersecurity, where the transition distributions are arbitrary as they come from empirical data.

In contrast, ISPLIT methods are not directly affected by such matters, which makes them more attractive to our purposes. A caveat is that ISPLIT traditionally requires expert knowledge to split the state space S of the model M. This has limited the use of SMC+ISPLIT as an automatic approach in general, and specifically for cybersecurity analysis, since it necessitates (specialised) user input beyond the definition of M.

However, novel theories are emerging to finally automate this step [6,8]. Next and to conclude this work, a statistical model checker that implements automatic RES is briefly presented.

5 The FIG tool

5.1 Main Characteristics

The Finite Improbability Generator, FIG, is an SMC tool publicly available at https://git.cs.famaf.unc.edu.ar/dsg/fig. It uses the formal definitions of M and φ to derive the so-called importance function f and thresholds $\{\ell_i\}_{i=1}^{M}$ [9], which act as an oracle guiding simulation traces towards the rare event in a tractable manner, i.e. keeping a measure of the bias introduced[4]. These are the core components needed by ISPLIT to speed up the statistical convergence for the computation of the estimate $\hat{\gamma}$ [25].

For this, FIG runs a breadth-first search from S_φ on the inverted transitions of M. This computes the number-of-transitions distance from each state to S_φ. The heuristic importance function of FIG, $f^\star$, is the inverse of this distance, stored as an array of size $|S|$. To avoid the state explosion, FIG works on IOSA modules, deriving a local $f_i^\star$ for each M_i whose parallel composition forms M [15]. $f^\star$ is an aggregation of these functions, which in its most basic form adds the local $f_i^\star$ of every M_i whose variables appear explicitly in φ [8,10].

Function $f^\star$ is solely based on the distance measured in number of transitions of M. All stochastic behaviour that is omitted by $f^\star$, such as probabilistic weights in the transitions, is captured in the thresholds ℓ_i. To choose these thresholds automatically, FIG runs dynamic analyses using either Expected Success or a variant of the Sequential Monte Carlo algorithm [10]. In both cases finite-life simulations start from the initial state, to estimate roughly the probability to reach states with higher importance via lightweight statistical analyses.

[4] A more in-depth introduction to the concept of importance function requires to formally define state spaces, nondeterministic vs. probabilistic branching, and simulation traces in formal models—we refer the interested reader to e.g. [8,25].

```
1  module Foo
2      recv : clock;             // receive a call to foo()
3      proc : clock;             // process a call to foo()
4      comm : [0..2];            // communicate with backend
5      busy : [0..2] init 0;     // processing call
6      [rc!] busy==0 @ recv -> 0.1: (recv'=μ)   // package lost
7                            + 0.9: (comm'=1) & (busy'=busy+1);
8      [c??] busy==1        -> (busy'=2) & (proc'=ν); // callback
9      [pc!] busy==2 @ proc -> (comm'=2) & (busy'=0) & (recv'=μ);
10     [b!!] comm==1        -> (comm'=0);  // communicate: busy!!
11     [d!!] comm==2        -> (comm'=0);  // communicate: done!!
12 endmodule
```

Code 2. IOSA module of `foo()` web API call for FIG 1.3

5.2 IOSA Models

FIG is designed to run either crude Monte Carlo or RES simulations on IOSA with urgency [15]. We (briefly) revise the syntax to define these models, as a reference to future cybersecurity implementations—for further details see [9].

Modular Composition. An IOSA model is composed of one or more synchronising modules, which contain local continuous random variables called clocks. Every clock samples a positive value according to its probability distribution. As time evolves, the clocks in all modules count down at the same rate, and the first to reach zero is said to expire. On expiration a clock can trigger (a) local events in its active module—e.g. new sampling of clock values, variables assignment—and (b) synchronisations with other passive modules. The single active module whose clock expired broadcasts an output action, that synchronises with homonymous input actions in the passive modules. IOSA is an input-enabled formalism.

Example. Code 2 shows a simplistic FIG module that represents the reception of a message via the `foo()` method of a web API. It consists of variable declarations (lines 2–5) that define its possible internal states, and transitions (lines 6–11) that define the transitions between these states.

Generally speaking, the different situations in which the model can be (waiting for a message to arrive, expecting the callback, processing the message, etc.) are modelled by the different combination of values of the variables `comm` and `busy`. Instead, the clocks `recv` and `proc` govern the transition between these possible states, i.e. the changes in the values of the variables. This is said to happen "stochastically" by sampling their next expiration times and expiring as described above. The next paragraph gives a sample walk-through of the resulting behaviour for the IOSA model from Code 2.

A simulation starts at state `comm==0,busy==0` and, informally speaking, waits some time until a message is received. This is governed by the expiration of the clock `recv` in lines 6–7, represented by the code "`@ recv`". When this happens, the code to the right of the arrow `->` in line 6 represents a 10% change to lose the message (e.g. due to data corruption), in which case we will repeat the process by waiting until the next message is received. With the remaining 90% chance the model will instead process the package: first it broadcasts a signal (`b!!` in line 10) to indicate that it will be busy for a while; then it waits for the backend to inform that the message is to start being processed (`c??` in line 8). This then makes the model wait for the expiration of clock `proc` (line 9), which indicates the end of the processing. When this happens, a signal is broadcast to indicate that we are done (`d!!` in line 11), after which the full procedure starts over.

Next we give a more technical explanation of the parts that compose the model from Code 2, and any IOSA model that can be simulated by FIG

State variables. IOSA variables in FIG have module-local scope and can be of type `clock`, `bool`, or ranged integer (e.g. `[0..2]`). Constants can also be of type `float`—though not `clock`—and have global-scope. FIG supports array variables and can compute e.g. a-random or the-smallest value from an array.

Transitions. Besides the declaration of state variables, an IOSA module is composed of transitions that describe its behaviour. Each transition is formed by: a (possibly empty) action in square brackets; a Boolean precondition; a clock iff the action is (non-urgent) output; and a postcondition, formed of a probabilistic choice (after `->` and separated by `+`) where single options have probability 1.

Synchronisation Actions. Every transition starts with a (possibly empty) action declaration. Decorators `?/!` at the end of the action name mark it as input or output, e.g. `rc!` in line 6 is an output action. Double decorators are for urgency, e.g. `c??` in line 8 is an urgent input. Output actions (timed or urgent) are emitted by the module, and listened to by other IOSA modules in the system. Input actions (timed or urgent) are received by the module, when another module in the system emits them.

Clock Expiration. Time passes at the same speed for all IOSA modules. Each clock samples a value from its corresponding distribution, e.g. μ for `recv` in Code 2, and counts down (at the global speed of time passage) until its value reaches zero: then the clock *expires*. Character `@` in a transition represents this event. If the clock of a transition expires, and the precondition is satisfied, the postcondition of the transition is applied. For instance, `[rc!] busy==0 @ recv->` $\cdots$ (line 6) tells that if clock `recv` expires, and `busy==0`, then the module will output action `rc` and proceed to execute the postcondition that follows the arrow `->`.

Postconditions. A postcondition is composed of one or more *options*, each weighed with a discrete probability value. Each option, chosen probabilistically, is a sequence of *effects* concatenated by `&`. The left-hand side of `=` in an effect is a variable name with a `'` suffix. If the variable is a clock, the right-hand side is a distribution: e.g. `recv'=`μ in line 6 samples a new clock value. Else, the right-hand side is an arithmetic expression: e.g. in line 7 the value `1` is assigned to variable `comm`, and `busy+1` is assigned as new value to variable `busy`.

5.3 Demonstration

Finally, we show the command-line interface (CLI) and capabilities of FIG to study rare-event properties in two small examples from its test suite.

FIG offers many options to simulate on IOSA models, for the estimation of rare properties specified in subsets of continuous-time stochastic logic (CSL, for steady-state properties) or probabilistic computation tree logic (PCTL, for transient properties). A full description of this CLI is out of scope, but users can get it by invoking the `--help` option of FIG, after downloading it from https://git.cs.famaf.unc.edu.ar/dsg/fig and following the installation instructions.

The first example that we will showcase is a triple tandem queue with Erlang service times: the IOSA model file is publicly available in the official website of FIG in the following path: tests/models/3tandem_queue.sa.

We compare crude Monte Carlo (CMC) and two RES strategies with the monolithic importance function, i.e. $f^\star$ built on the composition of all IOSA modules. The first strategy uses all of FIG default parameters, and the second one requests Expected Success to build thresholds, and the RESTART engine with level-2 prolongations. The corresponding commands are:

```
fig --stop-time 5m 3tandem_queue.sa --cmc
fig --stop-time 5m 3tandem_queue.sa --amono
fig --stop-time 5m 3tandem_queue.sa --amono -t es -e restart2
```

We estimated the CSL-like property $\varphi =$ `S(q3>=7)`, which asks the proportion of time that the third queue contains more than 7 elements. Comparisons were done for a fixed simulation budged, namely a wall-clock time of 5 min. When the time is due, simulations stop and CIs are reported: the estimation that achieves the narrowest CI for a fixed confidence level is the most efficient one.

Running these experiments in an Intel(R) Xeon(R) E-2124G CPU @ 3.40GHz (Linux kernel 5.14.8-arch1-1) resulted in the following 95% CIs: [3.81E-6, 4.52E-6] for CMC, [4.15E-6, 4.36E-6] for FIG defaults, and [4.25E-6, 4.40E-6] for the custom command. The widths of these intervals are 7.13E-7, 2.12E-7, and 1.53E-7 resp.

All CIs overlap and contain the expected value 4.25E-6. However and as expected, RES can achieve tighter estimates for the same simulation budget. We highlight that the default FIG command is as bare as crude Monte Carlo, yet it produced an estimate more than three times more precise.

Finally we experiment with a second model: a small repairable Fault Tree with non-Markovian failure and repair times (`FT.sa`), also available in the website of FIG as tests/models/resampling_tiny_FT.sa. The distribution families include exponential, Erlang, normal, and lognormal.

The case is quite interesting since ISPLIT has limited applications in FT analysis. Importance functions such as $f^\star$, that only observe failures and repairs of components, result in efficient RES applications iff the dominant failure can be layered, e.g. as the result of the conjunctive failure of many subcomponents. To exploit this, we have developed heuristics that automatically derive a composition strategy from the FT structure. *A similar approach is envisioned for cybersecurity studies, using the closely related theory of attack tree analysis.*

For this case, we estimated the time-bounded probability of observing a system failure before 150 time units. Again we compare CMC and two RES strategies: FIG with the `--ft` switch, Expected Success thresholds, Fixed Effort simulation engine, and (a) the default compositional importance function, and (b) the heuristic FT-structure importance function. The commands are:

```
fig --stop-time 5m FT.sa --cmc
fig --stop-time 5m FT.sa --ft -t es -e sfe --acomp +
fig --stop-time 5m FT.sa --ft -t es -e sfe --acomp \
    'BE_0+max(BE_1,BE_2)+BE_4'
```

These experiments resulted in the 95% CIs: [1.93E-4, 3.02E-4], [2.28E-4, 3.12E-4], and [2.39E-4, 2.70E-4], whose widths are 1.09E-4, 8.41E-5, and 3.12E-5. As before, all CIs contain the expected value (2.65E-4), and RES achieved the tightest intervals for the same simulation budget. In this case, however, the difference between CMC and the default compositional strategy of FIG is much less pronounced than in the previous example. This is expected given the low redundancy required to cause a system failure (three components must be simultaneously failed).

Yet in spite of this, the heuristic composition strategy performed significantly better, producing a CI almost an order of magnitude narrower than CMC. Perhaps the most appealing feature of this strategy is that it is automatic: it is computed from the FT structure, from which also the IOSA modules were created. In other words, this is effectively a fully-automatic deployment of RES. In subsequent research we intend to apply analogous approaches to study properties of models that encode cybersecurity problems.

6 Conclusions

This work discussed the use of Statistical Model Checking to study problems relevant for cybersecurity practices. SMC is a formal approach to model analysis via Monte Carlo simulation. Input/Output Stochastic Automata semantics are proposed as underlying formalism: they combine continuous time and probabilities, as required to estimate the likelihood and time of occurrence of future attacks. The need for rare event simulation is identified to achieve efficient computations, and the academic tool FIG is presented, which can deploy it automatically.

References

1. Akram, J., Luo, P.: SQVDT: a scalable quantitative vulnerability detection technique for source code security assessment. Softw. Practice Exp. **51**(2), 294–318 (2021). https://doi.org/10.1002/spe.2905
2. Alohaly, M., Takabi, H.: When do changes induce software vulnerabilities? In: CIC, pp. 59–66. IEEE (2017). https://doi.org/10.1109/CIC.2017.00020
3. Alves, H., Fonseca, B., Antunes, N.: Software metrics and security vulnerabilities: dataset and exploratory study. In: EDCC, pp. 37–44. IEEE (2016). https://doi.org/10.1109/EDCC.2016.34

4. Aumasson, J.P.: Serious Cryptography: A Practical Introduction to Modern Encryption. No Starch Press (2017)
5. Baier, C., Katoen, J.P.: Principles of Model Checking. MIT Press (2008)
6. Barbot, B., Haddad, S., Picaronny, C.: Coupling and importance sampling for statistical model checking. In: Flanagan, C., König, B. (eds.) TACAS 2012. LNCS, vol. 7214, pp. 331–346. Springer, Heidelberg (2012). https://doi.org/10.1007/978-3-642-28756-5_23
7. Bilgin, Z., Ersoy, M.A., Soykan, E.U., Tomur, E., Çomak, P., Karaçay, L.: Vulnerability prediction from source code using machine learning. IEEE Access **8**, 150672–150684 (2020). https://doi.org/10.1109/ACCESS.2020.3016774
8. Budde, C.E.: Automation of Importance Splitting Techniques for Rare Event Simulation. Ph.D. thesis, Universidad Nacional de Córdoba, Córdoba, Argentina (2017)
9. Budde, C.E.: FIG: The Finite Improbability Generator v1.3. SIGMETRICS Perform. Eval. Rev. **49**(4), 59–64 (2022). https://doi.org/10.1145/3543146.3543160
10. Budde, C.E., D'Argenio, P.R., Hartmanns, A.: Automated compositional importance splitting. Sci. Comput. Program. **174**, 90–108 (2019). https://doi.org/10.1016/j.scico.2019.01.006
11. Budde, C.E., D'Argenio, P.R., Monti, R.E., Stoelinga, M.: Analysis of non-Markovian repairable fault trees through rare event simulation. Int. J. Softw. Tools Technol. Transfer (to appear) (2022). https://doi.org/10.1007/s10009-022-00675-x
12. Chakraborty, S., Krishna, R., Ding, Y., Ray, B.: Deep learning based vulnerability detection: are we there yet. IEEE Trans. Softw. Eng. **48**(9), 3280–3296 (2021). https://doi.org/10.1109/TSE.2021.3087402
13. Chowdhury, I., Zulkernine, M.: Using complexity, coupling, and cohesion metrics as early indicators of vulnerabilities. J. Syst. Architect. **57**(3), 294–313 (2011). https://doi.org/10.1016/j.sysarc.2010.06.003
14. D'Argenio, P.R., Katoen, J.P.: A theory of stochastic systems part I: Stochastic automata. Inf. Comput. **203**(1), 1–38 (2005). https://doi.org/10.1016/j.ic.2005.07.001
15. D'Argenio, P.R., Monti, R.E.: Input/output stochastic automata with urgency: confluence and weak determinism. In: Fischer, B., Uustalu, T. (eds.) ICTAC 2018. LNCS, vol. 11187, pp. 132–152. Springer, Cham (2018). https://doi.org/10.1007/978-3-030-02508-3_8
16. Dragoni, N., Lafuente, A.L., Massacci, F., Schlichtkrull, A.: Are we preparing students to build security in? A survey of European cybersecurity in higher education programs [education]. IEEE Secur. Privacy **19**(01), 81–88 (2021). https://doi.org/10.1109/MSEC.2020.3037446
17. Fang, Z., Fu, H., Gu, T., Qian, Z., Jaeger, T., Hu, P., Mohapatra, P.: A model checking-based security analysis framework for IoT systems. High-Confidence Comput. **1**(1) (2021). https://doi.org/10.1016/j.hcc.2021.100004
18. Faqeh, R., Fetzer, C., Hermanns, H., Hoffmann, J., Klauck, M., Köhl, M.A., Steinmetz, M., Weidenbach, C.: Towards dynamic dependable systems through evidence-based continuous certification. In: Margaria, T., Steffen, B. (eds.) ISoLA 2020. LNCS, vol. 12477, pp. 416–439. Springer, Cham (2020). https://doi.org/10.1007/978-3-030-61470-6_25
19. Furnell, S., Clarke, N.: Power to the people? the evolving recognition of human aspects of security. Comput. Secur. **31**(8), 983–988 (2012). https://doi.org/10.1016/j.cose.2012.08.004

20. Ganesh, S., Ohlsson, T., Palma, F.: Predicting security vulnerabilities using source code metrics. In: SweDS, pp. 1–7. IEEE (2021). https://doi.org/10.1109/SweDS53855.2021.9638301
21. Ghaffarian, S.M., Shahriari, H.R.: Software vulnerability analysis and discovery using machine-learning and data-mining techniques: a survey. ACM Comput. Surv. **50**(4) (2017). https://doi.org/10.1145/3092566
22. Hartmanns, A.: On the analysis of stochastic timed systems. Ph.D. thesis, Saarland University (2015). https://doi.org/10.22028/D291-26597
23. Hole, K.J.: Anti-fragile ICT Systems. Springer (2016). https://doi.org/10.1007/978-3-319-30070-2
24. Khan, S., Katoen, J.P.: Synergising reliability modelling languages: BDMPs and repairable DFTs. In: PRDC, pp. 113–122. IEEE (2021). https://doi.org/10.1109/PRDC53464.2021.00023
25. L'Ecuyer, P., Le Gland, F., Lezaud, P., Tuffin, B.: Splitting techniques. In: Rubino and Tuffin [41], pp. 39–61. https://doi.org/10.1002/9780470745403.ch3
26. Li, H., Kwon, H., Kwon, J., Lee, H.: A scalable approach for vulnerability discovery based on security patches. In: Batten, L., Li, G., Niu, W., Warren, M. (eds.) ATIS 2014. CCIS, vol. 490, pp. 109–122. Springer, Heidelberg (2014). https://doi.org/10.1007/978-3-662-45670-5_11
27. Li, Q., Song, J., Tan, D., Wang, H., Liu, J.: PDGraph: a large-scale empirical study on project dependency of security vulnerabilities. In: DSN, pp. 161–173. IEEE (2021). https://doi.org/10.1109/DSN48987.2021.00031
28. Massacci, F., Pashchenko, I.: Technical leverage in a software ecosystem: development opportunities and security risks. In: ICSE, pp. 1386–1397. IEEE (2021). https://doi.org/10.1109/ICSE43902.2021.00125
29. Meneely, A., Williams, L.: Secure open source collaboration: an empirical study of linus' law. In: CCS, pp. 453–462. ACM (2009). https://doi.org/10.1145/1653662.1653717
30. Meneely, A., Williams, L.: Strengthening the empirical analysis of the relationship between Linus' law and software security. In: ESEM. ACM (2010). https://doi.org/10.1145/1852786.1852798
31. Parsons, K., Calic, D., Pattinson, M., Butavicius, M., McCormac, A., Zwaans, T.: The human aspects of information security questionnaire (HAIS-Q): two further validation studies. Comput. Secur. **66**, 40–51 (2017). https://doi.org/10.1016/j.cose.2017.01.004
32. Pashchenko, I., Plate, H., Ponta, S.E., Sabetta, A., Massacci, F.: Vulnerable open source dependencies: counting those that matter. In: ESEM, pp. 42:1–42:10. ACM (2018). https://doi.org/10.1145/3239235.3268920
33. Pashchenko, I., Plate, H., Ponta, S.E., Sabetta, A., Massacci, F.: Vuln4Real: a methodology for counting actually vulnerable dependencies. IEEE Trans. Software Eng. **48**(5), 1592–1609 (2022). https://doi.org/10.1109/TSE.2020.3025443
34. Post, G.V., Kagan, A.: Evaluating information security tradeoffs: restricting access can interfere with user tasks. Comput. Secur. **26**(3), 229–237 (2007). https://doi.org/10.1016/j.cose.2006.10.004
35. Prana, G.A.A., et al.: Out of sight, out of mind? how vulnerable dependencies affect open-source projects. Empir. Softw. Eng. **26**(4), 1–34 (2021). https://doi.org/10.1007/s10664-021-09959-3
36. Rindell, K., Ruohonen, J., Holvitie, J., Hyrynsalmi, S., Leppänen, V.: Security in agile software development: a practitioner survey. Inf. Softw. Technol. **131** (2021). https://doi.org/10.1016/j.infsof.2020.106488

37. Roberts, R., Lewis, B., Hartmanns, A., Basu, P., Roy, S., Chakraborty, K., Zhang, Z.: Probabilistic verification for reliability of a two-by-two network-on-chip system. In: Lluch Lafuente, A., Mavridou, A. (eds.) FMICS 2021. LNCS, vol. 12863, pp. 232–248. Springer, Cham (2021). https://doi.org/10.1007/978-3-030-85248-1_16
38. Rose, A.Z., Miller, N.: Measurement of Cyber Resilience from an Economic Perspective, chap. 10, pp. 253–274. John Wiley & Sons, Ltd (2021). https://doi.org/10.1002/9781119287490.ch10
39. Roumani, Y., Nwankpa, J.K., Roumani, Y.F.: Time series modeling of vulnerabilities. Comput. Secur. **51**, 32–40 (2015). https://doi.org/10.1016/j.cose.2015.03.003
40. Rubino, G., Tuffin, B.: Introduction to rare event simulation. In: Rubino and Tuffin [41], pp. 1–13. https://doi.org/10.1002/9780470745403.ch1
41. Rubino, G., Tuffin, B. (eds.): Rare Event Simulation Using Monte Carlo Methods. Wiley (2009). https://doi.org/10.1002/9780470745403
42. Stoelinga, M., Kolb, C., Nicoletti, S.M., Budde, C.E., Hahn, E.M.: The marriage between safety and cybersecurity: still practicing. In: Laarman, A., Sokolova, A. (eds.) SPIN 2021. LNCS, vol. 12864, pp. 3–21. Springer, Cham (2021). https://doi.org/10.1007/978-3-030-84629-9_1
43. Sultana, K.Z., Deo, A., Williams, B.J.: Correlation analysis among Java nano-patterns and software vulnerabilities. In: HASE, pp. 69–76. IEEE (2017). https://doi.org/10.1109/HASE.2017.18
44. Walden, J., Stuckman, J., Scandariato, R.: Predicting vulnerable components: software metrics vs text mining. In: ISSRE, pp. 23–33. IEEE (2014). https://doi.org/10.1109/ISSRE.2014.32
45. Weiss, J.: A system security engineering process. In: Proceedings of the 14th National Computer Security Conference. Information System Security: Requirements & Practices, vol. 249, pp. 572–581 (1991)
46. Yasasin, E., Prester, J., Wagner, G., Schryen, G.: Forecasting IT security vulnerabilities - an empirical analysis. Comput. Secur. **88** (2020). https://doi.org/10.1016/j.cose.2019.101610
47. Younes, H.L.S., Simmons, R.G.: Probabilistic verification of discrete event systems using acceptance sampling. In: Brinksma, E., Larsen, K.G. (eds.) CAV 2002. LNCS, vol. 2404, pp. 223–235. Springer, Heidelberg (2002). https://doi.org/10.1007/3-540-45657-0_17

Network Security and Privacy

A Need for Privacy-Assistive Technology in Notice and Consent Paradigm in IoT

Shukun Tokas(✉) and Gencer Erdogan

Sustainable Communications Technologies, SINTEF Digital, Oslo, Norway
{shukun.tokas,gencer.erdogan}@sintef.no

Abstract. A privacy notice is a document/notification that is addressed to consumers, describing how their personal information will be handled. While browsing the Internet, installing an app on smartphone, setting up a smart sensor or IoT devices in personal spaces, consumers are often asked to consent to privacy notices. Ideally, the consumer is expected to read and understand the notice and give an informed consent. These notices are often lengthy and complicated, containing legal-technical jargons and ambiguous statements describing commercial use of personal data. Most people reflexively choose "I consent", unknowingly agreeing to unfair-deceptive practices. Given the ubiquity of IoT and thus ubiquity of (personal) data collection, the reliance on notice and consent is inappropriate. In this article, we present the challenges of the *notice and consent* paradigm, and explore the idea of privacy-assistive solutions to enhance consumer privacy awareness and control in IoT.

Keywords: Privacy · automated notice processing · informed consent · consumer control · privacy-assistive technology · privacy-enhancing technology

1 Introduction

The Internet of Things (IoT) describes the network of physical objects embedded with sensors, software, and other technologies to exchange data with other devices and systems over the Internet. These objects deployed in public and private spaces enable use cases that enhance productivity and quality of life. There is a trend where companies offer cheap IoT devices in exchange for the data they collect from consumers using these devices. This trend is popularly known as *surveillance capitalism*, "it is an economic order that claims human experience as free raw material for hidden commercial practices of extraction, prediction, and sales" [46]. The data is used to "anticipate what you will do now, soon, and later " [46]. It raises privacy concerns as an enormous amount of personal data is collected through IoT devices such as fitness trackers, home sensors, and connected vehicles. Several research studies and surveys reveal that privacy concerns are at an all-time high, as the collection and use of data in IoT are happening with very little or no control, and organizations collecting data are most of the time unknown to data subjects. For example, a Norwegian population survey [26] reveals that two out of three respondents feel uncomfortable

A. Skarmeta et al. (Eds.): CyberSec4Europe 2022, CCIS 1807, pp. 35–49, 2023.
https://doi.org/10.1007/978-3-031-36096-1_3

about commercial actors collecting information about them. Cisco's value/trust paradox report [8] reveals the divide between IoT value and trust: 53% of participants feel IoT makes their life more convenient, while only 9% trust that their data collected and shared through IoT is secure. Despite the trust deficit and perceived risk, 42% say IoT is too integrated into their lives to disconnect from IoT services. This growing trend of lack of transparency and absence of support for data subjects to control the collection and processing of their data in IoT may heavily affect many areas of our lives and even constitute a long-term danger for democracy and voting [34]. In particular, the sensor data can be used in specific kind of marketing, i.e., election politics, where personalized marketing is used to target voters [34] by means of behavioral modification at scale [46]. It is evident that analysis of personal data had played a prominent role in Brexit campaign, and election campaigns in both the USA and France [27]. In response to the emerging privacy concerns, the European Parliament has approved the General Data Protection Regulation (GDPR) [14] to strengthen and impose data protection across the European Union (EU) and the European Economic Area (EEA). Several studies have investigated the impact of GDPR on consumers. For instance, a survey carried out by Cisco [9] confirms that 55% of respondents view GDPR very favorably, 84% respondents indicated that they care about privacy, and Of this group, 80% respondents said they are willing to act to protect it. Furthermore, an analysis from Godinho and Adjerid [19] found that only 6.2% of participants gave opt-in consent to the personal data collection (e.g., location data), in particular consumers to make deliberative choices and permit uses of data that directly benefit them and pose less risk. Overall, there is a positive view of GDPR among consumers, but there is a negative side to it, e.g., as per Cisco survey [9] 47% respondents expressed notification fatigue and said they receive far too many privacy notices as a result of GDPR. Moreover, Visa's Consumer Empowerment Study found that 76% of people desire greater control or the choice to have more control over their personal information [6].

In this article, we focus on a crucial privacy concept, *consent.* According to the GDPR there are six lawful basis of processing personal data: contractual necessity, consent, legal obligation, vital interests, public interests and legitimate interests. The service providers of data-enabled technologies or smart infrastructure must carry out the processing of personal data within the limit of the applicable processing grounds. Consent is one of the most discussed basis of processing, and is also a core principle of data protection as "it relates to the exercise of fundamental rights of autonomy and self-determination" [29]. Consent is the lawful ground that reflects a data subject's agreement and provides the data controller with permission to process a subject's personal data for specific purposes. Arguably, consent is often the most exploited legal ground for processing personal data.

Most of us have had these experiences of giving consent in different situations where stakes can be low, e.g., small financial transactions, browsing news on Internet, or even where stakes can be high, e.g., medical procedures, legal transactions, continuous monitoring through wearable technology. Consumers accept all the risks detailed in privacy notices, without even reading them. For example, an increasing number of consumers are using sophisticated fitness trackers, capable of sensing bodily states with precision, with very little awareness of privacy risks of collection and processing of fine-grained data. It appears that privacy notices primarily serve as a means of avoiding legal action for data controllers, rather than fulfilling their intended purpose of informing consumers about their data practices.

The paradigm of notice and consent, widely known as 'notice and choice', is based on a presupposition that consumers will adequately manage their privacy, if provided sufficient information about data collection and processing [31]. In fact, the GDPR resulted in more detailed and longer privacy notices. It is our experience since GDPR came into effect, we routinely encounter long and detailed notices.

Research [18,24] has shown that comprehending privacy notices imposes a high cognitive and time burden on data subjects [15]. In order to address this widespread issue of uninformed consent, research efforts are needed to advance the state-of-the-art in automatic processing of privacy notices (to extract relevant information) and use the extracted information to present the notices more intuitively to consumers so that these notices are more likely to be read and understood.

2 Background

Mark Weiser introduced the term ubiquitous computing in 1991 as "The most profound technologies are those that disappear. They weave themselves into the fabric of everyday life until they are indistinguishable from it" [42]. Internet of Things (IoT) [4] is meant to support this ubiquitous computing wave. The term IoT was coined by the British technology pioneer Kevin Ashton [3], who described it as a system of physical objects embedded with sensors and software, which are connected to the Internet. IoT devices are now ubiquitous in the very spaces (personal or public) the consumers move through, e.g., cars, wearables, healthcare devices, and electric systems. These connected devices create new types of unprecedented quantities of massive and nuanced datasets about consumer behavior [28]. All this information undoubtedly enhances productivity and quality of life. For example, a Fitbit activity tracker [38] allows consumers to track their daily physical activity, including the number of steps, amount of sleep, calories burned, heart rate, etc. Muse headband [22] can measure brain activity, brain health and performance, in real world environments to track the user's ability to focus. Information from these connected devices can in combination measure consumers' driving habits, behavioral patterns, and/or work productivity [28]. All these devices such as activity trackers, headbands, home sensors, baby monitors, and so on, continually generate personal data about the consumer. The GDPR is a intricate regulation that primarily focuses on data privacy, and regulates collection and processing of the personal data about EU citizens. Subsequently, we provide a foundational understanding of privacy and data protection, and then give a concise overview of the privacy principles outlined in the GDPR.

2.1 Privacy and Data Protection

Privacy is considered a fundamental human right [13], giving the right to a private life and associated freedoms to its citizens. The significance of privacy is reflected by the fact that the documents that define human rights, such as the Universal Declaration of Human Rights (UDHR, Article 12), the European Convention on Human Rights (UCHR, Article 8), incorporate references to privacy and related concepts. Interpreted broadly, privacy has a rich history in law and philosophy, and many definitions attempt to define privacy considering one or more distinct perspectives on privacy [7]. There are several interpretations of privacy, encompassing different perspectives such as privacy of person, privacy of personal communication, informational privacy, privacy of association etc. In [36], Sieghart describes privacy in terms of ensuring that "the right data are used by the right people for the right purposes". The *right data* requires the information to be accurate, complete, relevant and timely. The *right purpose* requires that the purposes are explicitly or implicitly agreed to by the data subject or are permitted by the law. The *right people* are the entities that will use the data for only the right purposes. Absence of these conditions may jeopardize critical rights, interests, and services [36]. To a great extent, this definition of privacy is still valid in current times, at least in the context of the GDPR.

The privacy literature introduced a term, namely *data protection*. Data protection can be defined as the law designed to protect personal data, and is recognized as a fundamental aspect of the right to privacy [30]. Data protection has been included as a standalone right under the Charter of Fundamental Rights [30] of the European Union (2012/C 326/02) under Article 8 [13], with emphasis on concepts such as lawfulness, fairness, and transparency, which are in line with GDPR's privacy principles. Note that the literature uses the terms individual/user/consumer/data subject interchangeably. In order to understand the privacy principles, it is necessary to be familiar with the following GDPR specific terminology:

- *Personal data:* the concept of personal data is central to data protection and its definition in the GDPR is kept intensionally broad. Article 4(1) of the GDPR defines personal data as "any information relating to an identified or identifiable natural person" [14]. Example of personal data include date of birth, gender, marital status, citizenship, association with organizations, address, phone number, and identity verification information. This also includes information such as dynamic IP addresses and cookies, as this information can be used to track online activities and generate a user profile which can be linked to devices and in most cases, an individual [40].
- *Data subject:* it is defined parenthetically within the definition of personal data, as an identified or identifiable natural person as being a data subject. In particular, the data subject is the individual about whom or from whom the information is being collected and processed.

- *Data controller and processor:* a data controller is a natural person, organization, public authority, or agency, which collects information about data subjects, determines the purposes of processing personal information, and processes the information (including its storage, disclosure). A data processor is a natural person, organization, public authority, or agency, that processes personal data on behalf of the data controller, which essentially means that a data processor is simply a service provider for a data processor [40]. The data controllers are the ones that exercise the decisions about collection, disclosure, processing, retention and destruction of personal data. As a result, a data controller is responsible for most of the compliance requirements (Article 5(1)). Through Article 24 and Article 25 of the GDPR, the requirements of integrating necessary safeguards into processing of personal information are imposed on the data controller.

2.2 Privacy Principles (GDPR)

The privacy profession offers established principles to guide information technology professionals in different stages of system engineering, for better and privacy-aware systems. The GDPR's processing principles [14] are set out in Article 5(1) and required to be followed by entities responsible for processing personal data. Data controllers are prescribed with the duty to demonstrate compliance (in Article 5(2)) with the privacy principles. The following points describe these principles.

1. *Lawfulness, fairness and transparency:* under the regulation, personal data shall be processed lawfully, fairly, and in a transparent manner. Fairness of the processing is linked to the idea that individuals must be aware of the fact that their personal data will be processed, including how the data will be collected, kept and used, to allow them to make an informed decision about whether they agree with such processing and enable them to exercise their data protection rights. Transparency is directly linked to fairness, and it means that the data controller must be open and clear towards data subjects when processing personal data. In summary, this principle requires honest usage and communication with the data subject about their personal data.
2. *Purpose limitation:* purpose limitation restricts the collection and processing of personal data for specific, explicit and legitimate purposes only, and requires that the data is not processed beyond such purposes. Secondary use of data, i.e., processing which does not fall within the boundaries of the purpose for which the personal data was collected, will be considered as incompatible and a separate legal ground will be required (such as consent) for processing secondary purposes. To determine if the personal data could be used for secondary purposes, the GDPR provides guidelines to assess the compatibility of the secondary purpose with the original purpose.
3. *Data minimization:* data minimization means that the data controllers must only collect and process personal data that is relevant, necessary, and adequate to accomplish the purposes for which it is processed. In other words, it

means the data controllers should collect only the personal data they really need. If a goal can be reached using anonymous data or methods that are less intrusive to privacy, those methods should be used instead of a strategy that involves collection and processing of all personal information without discrimination.

4. *Accuracy:* accuracy means that the data controllers must take reasonable measures to prevent inaccuracies and ensure that the data is accurate and up to date. It also includes taking necessary measures to respond to data subjects' request to correct inaccurate or incomplete information. For example, in a healthcare setting, the organization must ensure that the personal data it holds about each patient is accurate and up-to-date. This could include verifying the accuracy of the patient's name, address, medical history, and other relevant information. If the organization becomes aware that any of this information is incorrect, it must take steps to correct it as soon as possible.
5. *Storage limitation:* storage limitation means that personal data must not be kept for longer than necessary for the purposes for which it was collected for. Once the personal data is no longer needed, it must be securely deleted. However, there is a provision for data controllers to keep the personal data for unlimited period only when the data is irreversibly anonymized. In addition, data can be stored for longer periods for archiving purposes in public interest.
6. *Confidentiality and integrity:* confidentiality and integrity means that the controllers must take appropriate security measures to protect the data against unauthorized and unlawful processing, accidental loss, and so on. The regulation prompts the use of techniques such as pseudonymization and encryption, implementing information security framework, in order to protect the personal data throughout its lifecycle.
7. *Accountability:* the GDPR strengthens the six privacy principles by explicitly adding the accountability requirement (in Article 5(2)). It means that the data controller is responsible for complying with the aforementioned six principles, and they must be able to evidence their compliance. The principles are broadly interpreted, but their violators may incur large administrative fines (e.g., a financial penalty of 50 Million Euros against Google LLC [10]).

3 Notice and Consent

The *notice and consent* is a widely used regulatory approach for protecting privacy rights. It also encourages innovation and it appeals to individual choice [39]. It requires that individuals be informed and give their approval (informed consent) before any data regarding them is collected and processed. The aim of the notice and consent paradigm is to give individuals control over their personal information and to ensure that they are aware of how it will be used. In [44], OECD concludes that "consumer engagement - namely checking privacy policies and establishing one's own privacy preferences - are crucial elements without which privacy-enhancing technologies are largely ineffective".

3.1 Privacy Policy and Privacy Notice

In general, there are two types of documents that communicate privacy practices: a privacy policy and a privacy notice. A *privacy policy* is an internal document addressed to employees accessing personal information, clearly stating how the personal information will be collected, stored and disclosed to meet the organizational/regulatory privacy needs. A *privacy notice* is an external document and a transparent notification that is addressed to consumers that describes how their personal information is being handled, including information on the legal basis of processing and specific legitimate interests pursued by the data controller. In particular, a privacy notice is a legally mandated document for the collection and processing of personal data. As per GDPR, the privacy policy must be formulated by taking into account the privacy principles. The privacy notices should be consistent with the privacy policies. A data controller is required to provide relevant data practices, such as basis of processing, purpose of processing, legitimate interests etc., in the privacy notice. In summary, aligning a controller's internal privacy policy with its external privacy notice is important to ensure that the controller is meeting its obligations under privacy regulations, and consumer data is being used in a responsible manner. However, it is debatable whether consumers really benefit from lengthy and technical privacy notices loaded with legal jargon. Some argue that notices are insufficient instruments for providing individual users with a deep enough understanding of the data practices [24,39].

3.2 Consent

Consent is frequently an essential instrument in data protection and privacy laws, which puts individuals in control of their personal data. GDPR strengthens 'consent' in relation to use of personal data as compared with the 1995 Data Protection Directive. It is mentioned in the earlier section that the GDPR requires the data controllers to process personal data in a *lawful, fair and transparent* manner, meaning that there must be honest usage and communication with the data subject about their personal data. The three components here are linked with one another, and requires that the controllers are open and clear towards data subjects. The requirement of lawfulness means that personal data can only be processed if there is a legal basis for doing so. Article 6 of the GDPR outlines the legal bases of processing personal data:

1. *Consent:* the data subject has given consent to the processing of his or her personal data for one or more specific purposes. Consent requires a very clear and specific statement of consent. If the data subject's consent is to be given following a request by electronic means, the request must be clear, concise and not unnecessarily disruptive to the use of the service for which it is provided.
2. *Contract necessity:* it is a commonly used option and it is applicable when processing is necessary for the performance of a contract to which the datasubject

is party or in order to take steps at the request of the data subject prior to entering into a contract. For example, processing the address of the individual to deliver the products when a data subject makes online purchases.

3. *Legal obligation:* it is applicable when processing is necessary for compliance with a legal obligation to which the controller is subject. For example, disclosure of personal data to public authorities for the exercise of their official mission, such as tax and customs authorities, financial investigation units etc.
4. *Individual's vital interest:* it is applicable when processing is necessary in order to protect the vital interests of the data subject or of another natural person. It is applicable in scenarios such as, emergency medical care, monitoring epidemics etc.
5. *Public interest:* it is applicable when processing is necessary for the performance of a task carried out in the public interest or in the exercise of official authority vested in the controller. For example, processing data for archiving purposes in the public interest, historical research or statistical purposes, etc.
6. *Legitimate interest:* it is applicable when processing is necessary for the purposes of the legitimate interests pursued by the controller or by a third party, except where such interests are overridden by the interests or fundamental rights and freedoms of the data subject which require protection of personal data, in particular where the data subject is a child. In this case, processing is not required by law or for contract performance, but processing is of clear benefit to data subjects, for example, in fraud detection or for information security.

Legal bases such as performance of contract and legitimate interest often do not offer consumers with the same level of choice and control over their data, as offered by consent. For example, in the case of performance of contract, the processing of personal data is necessary in order to perform the contract, i.e., provide the necessary service or product. In the case legitimate interest, the data controller must balance their own interests in processing the personal data against the interests of the consumer. If the data controller's interests are deemed to outweigh consumer's interests, they may still process the personal data, as long as there is a clear justification for the impact on the consumer. Similarly, consumers do not have much choice and control over processing based on legal obligation, vital interest and public interest. Processing personal data under these legal bases is either required by law or necessary to protect the vital and public interests of the individual. Therefore, consent is the most suitable legal basis for processing personal data when the goal is to offer consumers choice and control over their data.

3.3 Discussion: Notice and Consent

While browsing the Internet, installing an app on our phone, or setting up a new IoT device, individuals are often asked to consent to privacy notices. This is intended to provide individuals with a clear understanding of how their personal data will be used and enable them to make informed decisions. The paradigm of *notice and consent* is grounded on the assumption that consumers will take appropriate measures to safeguard their privacy if they receive adequate information about data collection and processing [31].

Such explicit notifications are necessary towards achieving the ideal scenario (Fig. 1), where the individual recognize-read-understand the privacy notice, and once understood, gives informed consent. Actually, the GDPR led to the creation of lengthier and more detailed notices that contain a great deal of technical and legal terminology. Individuals do recognize the privacy notice, but due to longer, layered and complicated text it is hard to read and understand. Contrary to expectation, most people reflexively choose "I consent" or "I agree" [18]. They agree to unfair-deceptive practices with uninformed consent. Choosing "I consent" or "I agree" without reading and understanding the notices becomes increasingly problematic when it is about electronic devices used in everyday life in personal spaces, such as a fitness tracker constantly sensing our bodies, a voice assistant listening in. These devices collect a significant amount of data, including personal and sensitive data, and organizations use this data to understand user behavior and preferences. These insights are then used in marketing, (micro)targeted advertising, and creation of new products and services. However, some argue that the notice-and-consent may be exploited by commercial entities to extract more personal data from consumers than necessary, and that consumers may not fully understand what they are consenting to [18,26,39].

As computing becomes ubiquitous, the continued reliance on consumers to read several dozen such privacy notices and make informed decision is a practical problem. Comprehending privacy notices imposes a high cognitive and time burden on users [20]. Surveillance capitalism is the business model of the Internet [35] and Internet of Things. Surveillance capitalism's core idea is that the data generated by the users of digital platforms is a valuable asset that can be extracted, analyzed, and traded with third parties in the data market. This business model has given rise to a variety of malpractices. For example, "dark patterns" to manipulate users into agreeing to intrusive terms and conditions, and "notification overload" to create confusion and ultimately undermine informed consent. Combined effect of surveillance capitalism and connected malpractices is that privacy notices fails its very purpose of protecting privacy. This leads to provocation of *paradoxical behavior* [5], i.e., despite being very concerned about their privacy, consumers do not take necessary actions to protect their personal data, and *privacy resignation* [16], i.e., data subjects give up managing their privacy settings. Acquisti et al. [1], in their analysis of surveys, field studies and experiments in privacy literature conclude that privacy management that rely purely on consumer responsibilization have failed.

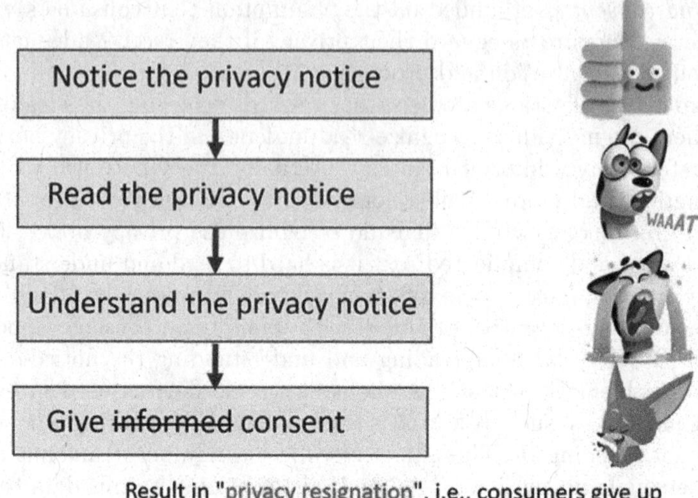

Fig. 1. GDPR's consent: expectation vs reality

4 Privacy-Assistive Technology

The notice-and-choice paradigm has been criticized in scientific literature [32, 37,39], seeking to move beyond the current consent model. The World Economic Forum (WEF) has published a white paper [18] that discusses the current state of the notice and consent paradigm, and the paper concludes that the existing mechanisms for notice and consent fail to account for the complex nature of human psychology. "Existing approaches do not scale for either traditional digital user interfaces or the emergent world of screenless internet of things (IoT) devices, smart cities or other connected environments" [18]. In another white paper [6], the WEF highlights the need to empower individuals, and thoughtful consent mechanisms to strengthen trust and maximize data sharing for common good. Clearly, there is a need to reconceptualize notice and consent mechanism, that shifts the burden of protecting privacy to business entities processing personal data, rather than placing it squarely on consumers.

One way to solve the challenges outlined in Sect. 3 is by utilizing privacy-assistive technology. In this context, privacy-assistive technology (PAT) means software-based solutions that could assist consumers in comprehending privacy notices, making meaningful privacy decisions, and managing their privacy settings. PAT includes tools such as interactive interfaces, visualizations, and summary explanations that aim to enhance the accessibility comprehension of notices. In this section, we present existing research in the field of privacy assistive technologies for IoT.

Morel et al. [25] provide a Personal Data Custodian, an edge-based tool that informs data subjects about privacy notices specified in a policy language endowed with formal semantics. Data practices (e.g., purpose, retention period, opt-out choice) are manually extracted from notices in this tool. Next in line are the research works which involves automation to process privacy notices. Amos et al. [2], analyzing the trend in privacy notices over the last 20 years, conclude that privacy notices show a disturbing lack of transparency: using third parties and tracking technologies is severely underreported. Sathyendra et al. [33] use a privacy corpus [43] to train models to automatically detect the provision of 'opt-out choice' in notices. Harkous et al. [21] provide a deep learning-based notice analysis tool, Polisis, which can automatically identify 122 data practices. Zhang et al. [45] developed a predictive model using clustering techniques to assist users in consenting to allow or deny personal data processing in video analytics deployments.

According to Lipman [23], "Consumers have the power to change the way companies handle their data. They just need to know about it first". Awareness is the key to autonomy. When consumers have more awareness of ongoing data collection and data practices then they would prefer to exercise control (as is evident from findings in [11,19]). Now we briefly present the research works which enhances consumer' s privacy awareness and control. Wang et al. [41] present a privacy-aware IoT architecture comprising several components, including a software module privacy mediator. The mediator runs on an edge device and receives user privacy preferences through a smartphone app, i.e., IoT Assistant (IoTA). It applies the privacy preferences to a real-time video before the video is stored or made available for analytics. IoTA communicates the available notices and choices of registered IoT devices to users. Feng et al. [16] propose a design space for privacy choices based on a user-centered analysis of what makes privacy notices effective.

A newer version of the IoTA app leverages this design space to implement meaningful privacy choices. Fernandez et al. [17] provide a novel augmented reality privacy management interface, i.e., Privacy Augmented Reality Assistant (PARA), for smart home devices. When a smartphone points to a smart IoT device, the PARA interface shows the data collected and allows users to switch on or off data collection, offering real-time privacy control. The evaluation results show that PARA users become more aware of IoT devices and their disclosed data, improving their privacy perception and control. IoTA and PARA offer simple interfaces enhancing the user awareness of deployed IoT systems and their data practices, but they do not directly work with privacy notices. IoTA requires IoTA owners to register privacy settings in a predefined template, and PARA uses hypothetical privacy settings. Habib et al. [20] leverage icons and their descriptions to effectively communicate privacy choices to consumers. Their assessment reveals that it is hard to communicate privacy choices without text.

As digital technologies evolve, various privacy-assistive technologies will be developed. Based on an analysis of existing privacy-assistive solutions in IoT domain, it can be inferred that the solutions will more likely be based on *(i)* sophisticated machine learning based automatic processing of privacy notices, to automatically extract precise and nuanced information, and *(ii)* present the extracted information intuitively in ways that enhance consumers' privacy awareness, understandability, and control without overburdening them with notice comprehension and privacy configurations. In particular, the success of privacy-assistive technology depends on two crucial elements, i.e., consumer awareness and participation in establishing their own privacy preferences.

Further research is needed for rethinking and redesigning the notice and consent paradigm in a way that better empowers individual and provides a level of regulatory certainty to businesses so that they can invest in innovation. Existing research may be utilized (e.g., [2,12,16,20,25,31,33]) to advance the state-of-the-art. According to WEF's white paper [18], the aim is to have technology serve people, rather than the reverse. Our assessment of existing research also converge to a similar note that privacy-assistive technology has potential to address the challenges of notice and consent paradigm, and enhance consumers' privacy awareness and control over personal data collected and processed by IoT systems.

5 Conclusion

In this article we looked at the notice and consent paradigm, from two sides: the regulatory (GDPR) expectation and the reality. We briefly discussed regulatory text and its interpretation. The notice and choice paradigm has been a cornerstone of personal data processing for many years. It is clear the objectives of the Notice and Consent paradigm are worthy. Nonetheless, it is apparent that the implementation of this paradigm is obsolete and falls short in obtaining meaningful consent. Its execution needs to be reassessed to empower consumers, and balance the information asymmetry between organizations and consumers.

With the growth in awareness of privacy concerns, privacy assistive technology is emerging as a critical tool to assist individuals. We suggest that one way to solve the challenges is by developing software-based privacy-assistive technology, which could assist consumers in comprehending privacy notices, making meaningful privacy decisions, and managing their privacy settings. Designing effective privacy assistive technology is not without its challenges. It requires a deep understanding of various fields, such as privacy risks, multi-stakeholder exchange of personal data, consumers' privacy sensitivity and their cost-benefit assessment, user-friendly interfaces, human-technology interaction. We presented state-of-the-art in the field of privacy assistive technologies for IoT.

Overall, the design and development of privacy assistive technology relies on a diverse range of technologies. According to our assessment of existing research, it is probable that the solutions will rely on (i) advanced machine learning algorithms to automatically analyze privacy notices and accurately extract detailed information, and (ii) presentation of the extracted information in an intuitive manner that enhances consumers' privacy awareness, understanding, and control without overwhelming them with complex privacy notices or configurations.

Funding

This work has been carried out as part of the CyberSec4Europe project (830929) and CyberKit4SME project (883188) funded by the European Union's Horizon 2020 Research and Innovation Programme, as well as the CINELDI project (257626/E20) funded by the Research Council of Norway.

References

1. Acquisti, A., Brandimarte, L., Loewenstein, G.: Secrets and likes: the drive for privacy and the difficulty of achieving it in the digital age. J. Consum. Psychol. **30**(4), 736–758 (2020)
2. Amos, R., Acar, G., Lucherini, E., Kshirsagar, M., Narayanan, A., Mayer, J.: Privacy policies over time: curation and analysis of a million-document dataset. In: Proceedings of the Web Conference 2021, pp. 2165–2176 (2021)
3. Ashton, K.: That 'Internet of Things' thing. RFiD J. **22**(7) (2011)
4. Atzori, L., Iera, A., Morabito, G.: The internet of things: a survey. Comput. Netw. **54**(15), 2787–2805 (2010)
5. Barth, S., De Jong, M.D.T.: The privacy paradox-investigating discrepancies between expressed privacy concerns and actual online behavior-a systematic literature review. Telematics Inform. **34**(7), 1038–1058 (2017)
6. Bella, K., Carugati, C., Mulligan, C., Piekarska-Geater, M.: Data for common purpose:leveraging consent to build trust. https://www.weforum.org/whitepapers/data-for-common-purpose-leveraging-consent-to-build-trust/ (2021)
7. Breaux, T., et al.: An Introduction to privacy for technology professionals. IAPP Publication (2020)
8. Cisco. The iot value/trust paradox: Building trust and value in the data exchange between people, things and providers (2017). https://newsroom.cisco.com/c/r/newsroom/en/us/a/y2017/m12/cisco-survey-reveals-divide-between-iot-value-and-trust.html. Accessed: 2021-12-21
9. Cisco. Consumer privacy survey: The growing imperative of getting data privacy right (2019). https://www.cisco.com/c/dam/global/en_uk/products/collateral/security/cybersecurity-series-2019-cps.pdf. Accessed: 2022-01-06
10. CNIL. The CNIL's restricted committee imposes a financial penalty of 50 million euros against google llc (2019). https://www.cnil.fr/en/cnils-restricted-committee-imposes-financial-penalty-50-million-euros-against-google-llc
11. Emami-Naeini, P., et al.: Privacy expectations and preferences in an iot world. In: Thirteenth Symposium on Usable Privacy and Security ({SOUPS} 2017), pp. 399–412 (2017)
12. Emami-Naeini, P., Dheenadhayalan, J., Agarwal, Y., Cranor, L.F.: Which privacy and security attributes most impact consumers' risk perception and willingness to purchase IoT devices? In: 2021 IEEE Symposium on Security and Privacy (SP), pp. 1937–1954 (2021)
13. EP and CEU. Charter of Fundamental Rights of the European Union (2012). https://eur-lex.europa.eu/legal-content/EN/TXT/PDF/?uri=CELEX:12012P/TXT&from=EN. Accessed: 2020-04-29
14. EP and CEU. The General Data Protection Regulation (GDPR) (2016). https://eur-lex.europa.eu/eli/reg/2016/679/oj. Accessed: 2019-11-24

15. Fabian, B., Ermakova, T., Lentz, T.: Large-scale readability analysis of privacy policies. In: Proceedings of the International Conference on Web Intelligence, pp. 18–25 (2017)
16. Feng, Y., Yao, Y., Sadeh, N.: A design space for privacy choices: towards meaningful privacy control in the internet of things. In: Proceedings of the 2021 CHI Conference on Human Factors in Computing Systems, pp. 1–16 (2021)
17. Fernandez, C.B., Lee, L.H., Nurmi, P., Hui, P.: Para: privacy management and control in emerging iot ecosystems using augmented reality. In: ACM International Conference on Multimodal Interaction. Association for Computing Machinery (ACM) (2021)
18. Flanagan, A.J., King, J., Warren, S.: Redesigning data privacy: reimagining notice & consent for human-technology interaction (2020). https://www3.weforum.org/docs/WEF_Redesigning_Data_Privacy_Report_2020.pdf
19. Godinho de Matos, M., Adjerid, I.: Consumer consent and firm targeting after gdpr: The case of a large telecom provider. Management Science (2021)
20. Habib, H., et al.: Toggles, dollar signs, and triangles: how to (in) effectively convey privacy choices with icons and link texts. In: Proceedings of the 2021 CHI Conference on Human Factors in Computing Systems, pp. 1–25 (2021)
21. Harkous, H., Fawaz, K., Lebret, R., Schaub, F., Shin, K.G., Aberer, K.: Polisis: automated analysis and presentation of privacy policies using deep learning. In: 27th USENIX Security Symposium (USENIX Security 18), pp. 531–548 (2018)
22. Krigolson, O.E., et al.: Using muse: Rapid mobile assessment of brain performance. Frontiers Neurosci. **15** (2021)
23. Lipman, R.: Online privacy and the invisible market for our data. Penn St. L. Rev. **120**, 777 (2015)
24. McDonald, A.M., Cranor, L.F.: The cost of reading privacy policies. Isjlp **4**, 543 (2008)
25. Morel, V., Cunche, M., Le Métayer, D.: A generic information and consent framework for the iot. In: 2019 18th IEEE International Conference on Trust, Security And Privacy In Computing And Communications/13th IEEE International Conference on Big Data Science and Engineering (TrustCom/BigDataSE), pp. 366–373. IEEE (2019)
26. Norwegian Consumer Council. Surveillance-based advertising: Consumer attitudes to surveillance-based advertising (2021). https://fil.forbrukerradet.no/wp-content/uploads/2021/06/consumer-attitudes-to-surveillance-based-advertising.pdf. Accessed: 2021-12-21
27. O'Brian, C.: How nationbuilder's platform steered macron's en marche, trump, and brexit campaigns to victory (2017). https://venturebeat.com/business/how-nationbuilder-helped-emmanuel-macron-secure-a-landslide-in-frances-legislative-elections/https://venturebeat.com/business/how-nationbuilder-helped-emmanuel-macron-secure-a-landslide-in-frances-legislative-elections/
28. Peppet, S.R.: Regulating the internet of things: first steps toward managing discrimination, privacy, security and consent. Tex. L. Rev. **93**, 85 (2014)
29. Privacy International. Grounds for processing of personal data (2018). https://privacyinternational.org/sites/default/files/2018-09/Part%205%20-%20Grounds%20for%20Processing%20of%20Personal%20Data_0.pdf. Accessed: 2022-03-17
30. Privacy International. A guide for policy engagement on data protection : Part 1 Data protection, explained (2018). https://privacyinternational.org/sites/default/files/2018-09/Data%20Protection%20COMPLETE.pdf. Accessed: 2021-12-22

31. Ravichander, A., Black, A.W., Norton, T., Wilson, S., Sadeh, N.: Breaking down walls of text: how can nlp benefit consumer privacy? In: Proceedings of the 59th Annual Meeting of the Association for Computational Linguistics and the 11th International Joint Conference on Natural Language Processing (Volume 1: Long Papers), pp. 4125–4140 (2021)
32. Richards, N., Hartzog, W.: The pathologies of digital consent. Washington University Law Review **96**, 1461 (2018)
33. Sathyendra, K.M., Wilson, S., Schaub, F., Zimmeck, S., Sadeh, N.: Identifying the provision of choices in privacy policy text. In: Proceedings of the 2017 Conference on Empirical Methods in Natural Language Processing, pp. 2774–2779 (2017)
34. Schneier, B.: Data and Goliath: The hidden battles to collect your data and control your world. WW Norton & Company (2015)
35. Schneier, B.: New Data Privacy Regulations (2018). https://www.schneier.com/blog/archives/2018/06/new_data_privac.html. Accessed: 2022-12-18
36. Sieghart, P.: Privacy and computers (1976)
37. Solove, D.J.: Murky consent: an approach to the fictions of consent in privacy law. Social Science Research Network (SSRN) (2023)
38. St Fleur, R.G., St George, S.M., Leite, R., Kobayashi, M., Agosto, Y., Jake-Schoffman, D.E.: Use of fitbit devices in physical activity intervention studies across the life course: narrative review. JMIR mHealth and uHealth **9**(5), e23411 (2021)
39. Susser, D.: Notice after notice-and-consent: why privacy disclosures are valuable even if consent frameworks aren't. J. Inf. Policy **9**, 148–173 (2019)
40. Ustaran, E.: European Data Protection: Law and Practice. an IAPP Publication, International Association of Privacy Professionals (2018)
41. Wang, J., Amos, B., Das, A., Pillai, P., Sadeh, N., Satyanarayanan, M.: A scalable and privacy-aware iot service for live video analytics. In: Proceedings of the 8th ACM on Multimedia Systems Conference, pp. 38–49 (2017)
42. Weiser, M.: The computer for the 21st century. Sci. Am. **265**(3), 94–104 (1991)
43. Wilson, S., et al.: The creation and analysis of a website privacy policy corpus. In: Proceedings of the 54th Annual Meeting of the Association for Computational Linguistics (Volume 1: Long Papers), pp. 1330–1340 (2016)
44. Working Party on Information Security and Privacy. Inventory of privacy-enhancing technologies (pets) (2002). https://www.oecd.org/officialdocuments/publicdisplaydocumentpdf/?doclanguage=en&cote=dsti/iccp/reg%282001%291/final
45. Zhang, S., Feng, Y., Das, A., Bauer, L., Cranor, L.F., Sadeh, N.: Understanding people's privacy attitudes towards video analytics technologies. In: Proceedings of the FTC PrivacyCon, pp. 1–18 (2020)
46. Zuboff, S.: The age of surveillance capitalism: The fight for a human future at the new frontier of power: Barack Obama's books of 2019. Profile books (2019)

Privacy-Preserving Cyber Threat Information Sharing Leveraging FL-Based Intrusion Detection in the Financial Sector

Pablo Fernández Saura(✉), Juan Francisco Martínez Gil, Jorge Bernal Bernabé, and Antonio Skarmeta

University of Murcia, Murcia, Spain
{pablofs,juanfrancisco.martinezg,jorgebernal,skarmeta}@um.es

Abstract. This paper presents an architectural proposal for enhancing anomaly detection in the CyberSec4Europe project use case Open Banking. It proposes a trusted privacy-preserving ecosystem of threat intelligence platforms, based on MISP, to automatically exchange and process cyber threat information in an auditable and privacy-preserving manner. Additionally, a Federated Learning scheme is deployed to share machine learning models trained on a synthetic fraud transactions dataset, and the impact of data anonymization on model accuracy is measured and analyzed. This proposal provides a valuable contribution to the development of robust and efficient threat detection systems to enhance the resilience of organizations in the financial sector.

Keywords: Cyber Threat Information Sharing · Financial · Federated Learning · Intrusion Detection Systems · Machine Learning · Deep Learning

1 Introduction

Over the last few years, financial entities are improving the digitalization of their critical processes, thus amplifying the attack surface being exposed. Meanwhile, cyberattacks against the financial sector are evolving quickly and becoming more refined. In the current state, attackers may hurt several entities without even changing the attack vector, due to the lack of resources to provide fast reaction and response actions. In this context, Threat Intelligence Platforms (TIPs) enable organizations to exchange critical threat information in order to prevent further similar attacks to those that have already occurred. However, the sensitive nature of data managed in the financial sector may cause entities to refuse to share certain information mainly because of privacy concerns.

A. Skarmeta et al. (Eds.): CyberSec4Europe 2022, CCIS 1807, pp. 50–64, 2023.
https://doi.org/10.1007/978-3-031-36096-1_4

Given these premises, the main contributions of this paper are listed below:

- Analysis of existing works on Cyber Threat Information (CTI) sharing in the financial sector.
- Design and implementation of a privacy-preserving and trust-minimized architecture that enables financial organizations to share critical information related to specific attacks or fraud events they may encounter in real-time.
- Combination of well-known privacy-preserving mechanisms, Distributed Ledger Technology (DLT) and Federated Learning (FL) to protect sensitive attributes, assess the provenance, integrity and immutability of shared information, and to provide an alternative mechanism in which Machine or Deep Learning (ML/DL) models are exchanged instead of raw data.
- Quantitative analysis of the impact of obfuscated data in the accuracy of models trained using FL, to demonstrate the feasibility of using FL along with privacy-preserving techniques applied to data instead of model parameters.

2 Background

2.1 Cyber Threat Information Sharing

Cyber Threat Intelligence (CTI) is any information that can help an entity identify, assess, monitor, or respond to cyber threats. However, CTI is not simply collected information, it is considered information that has been previously analyzed and actionable, i.e., with automation capability.

Sharing CTI efficiently is an important part of the cyber threat detection and prevention core since it allows building multiple layers of automation and effective defense that continuously analyze the large heterogeneous amounts of data related to attackers, tactics-techniques-procedures (TTP), active incident indicators, and so on. Some examples of CTI could be indicators of compromise or observations about an attack, security alerts triggered by devices such as IDS, incident reports, vulnerabilities in tools or even recommended configurations.

Given the different ecosystems, architectures, and devices used as sources for the collection of these types of data, it is necessary to standardize their representation to enable interoperability between the different organizations involved in this process [10]. The concept of interoperability refers to the ease of dissemination and the need to establish standard formats that define how CTI-related information is structured.

As shown in a study by the European Union Agency for Network and Information Security (ENISA) in 2014 [1], there are about 53 CTI formats that had been adopted by the community. The adaptation of information to these formats sometimes forces entities to lose valuable time in the transformation of data received in a different structure than expected, and unnecessary transformations of data to use them in a specific format can affect the ease and immediacy of their dissemination, which damages the sharing model that is to be achieved.

Other studies, such as [22], explain the development paths in the field of cyberintelligence, its usefulness and use cases, the main standards that have been adopted in the industry, the most used platforms, and a comparison between them. It shows that the most widespread CTI sharing standards are Structured Threat Information Expression (STIX) and Trusted Automated Exchange of Indicator Information (TAXII). Nevertheless, it is also important to mention other standards also used today, such as OpenTPX, MAEC, IODEF or VERIS.

All these standards are usually based on *json* and *xml* formats, aiming for a lightweight state of data representation. STIX and TAXII are the standards recommended by the ENISA for implementation as CTI standards in the member states of the European Union.

2.2 Federated Learning

Federated Learning was proposed in 2017 by McMahan *et al.* [16] as a collaborative decentralized learning paradigm designed to address the limitations of the traditional centralized learning approaches. In such centralized schemes, clients in the scenario are required to share their local data with a third-party, typically centralized on the cloud, where a final ML/DL model is trained based on data from all clients. This scheme could involve a threat to users' privacy since local data could be sensitive in some cases.

This new approach allows the training of a final model while keeping data private for each client. To do this, every client, instead of chunks of data, shares only model parameters with an entity called an aggregator, coordinator, or server. This information exchanged from clients to the aggregator is usually called *model update*. The aggregator is in charge of mixing all clients' updates and obtaining a single model as a result of this procedure. More in detail, a typical FL process is composed of the following steps:

1. Clients register against the aggregator.
2. The aggregator selects a subset of registered clients to participate in the training process by considering a certain *client selection* approach. For instance, in the context of IoT, operational conditions of the device (e.g., battery consumption) could be considered.
3. The aggregator creates a new general model and shares its parameters with the selected clients.
4. Each client takes the shared model, and trains it with its local data, generating a particular model whose parameters are fed back to the aggregator (model update).
5. Aggregator combines all the received updates from all clients and generates a new aggregated model. To do so, it employs an aggregation algorithm such as *FedAvg*.

6. Another subset of registered clients is selected to perform the next FL round.
7. The aggregated model is sent to the new clients, and the process repeats from step 4 until some completion criterion is met, such as reaching a specific number of rounds, a target accuracy, etc.

The critical point of this procedure is the fusion of all model updates that take place in the aggregator for a certain training round. To perform this task, several aggregation algorithms have been proposed in recent years [7,23–25]. However, there is one fusion algorithm, named *FedAvg* and proposed by McMahan *et al.* in [16], that is widely used in the state-of-the-art since it was the first proposed algorithm to address this model fusion task, and also since it has proven to be effective with several ML and DL models. This algorithm is based on averaging models' parameters, i.e., model updates, coming from clients in the FL scenario. Once the aggregator receives all the updates for a certain FL round, it generates the new model by averaging, equally or weighted, all the parameters, e.g., weights and biases from a neural network, contained in each model update. Nevertheless, this algorithm cannot be applied to all scenarios. For instance, when a clustering model such as K-means is employed, other fusion algorithms such as *SPAHM* [24] should be used.

In Fig. 1, a comparison between the traditional centralized, distributed, and FL scenarios can be consulted. In the first one, clients send their data to the central server, where training will be done and the final model will be generated. In the distributed one, also named on-device scheme, clients keep their local data, and train a particular model with it. With this approach, although data privacy is preserved since data never leaves the device in which it was generated, clients cannot improve their learning capacity based on the information contained in other clients [19]. By last, the FL approach mixes the benefits from the previous two, allowing to train a global model using data from several clients without the need of sharing this data with a third-party, thus preserving its privacy.

The application of Federated Learning techniques enables financial organizations to have a more complete view of the threat landscape, allowing them to identify and mitigate new attacks faster and more precisely. Additionally, the overall accuracy of the trained models could be enhanced since data privacy preservation allow entities to access larger datasets, although they contain sensitive information. On the other hand, a privacy-preserving component which implements several anonymization mechanisms, such as the one proposed in this work, could be used to either protect sensitive attributes in case raw CTI information is exhanged, and model updates, for instance using differential-privacy mechanisms, to avoid membership inference attacks, that represent an important threat in many FL scenarios.

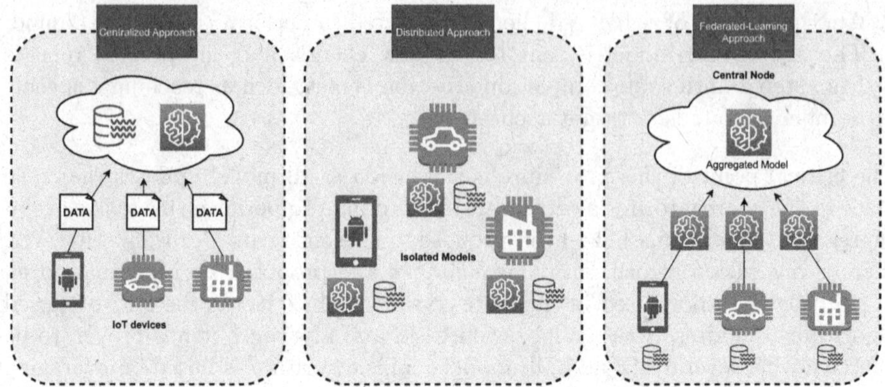

Fig. 1. Comparison between centralized, distributed and FL approaches [9].

2.3 Related Work

According to [22], CTI in many use cases can contain information that should only be transmitted to trusted stakeholders or not at all, such as Personally Identifiable Information (PII) which is irrelevant to create situation awareness. In wrong hands, this information could enable a successful attack, severely damaging the reputation of the stakeholder. Therefore, a trust mechanism, as well as a way to protect sensitive data before sharing has to be implemented in almost any CTI environment.

In recent years, several works have proposed solutions to solve this problem. For instance, [3] proposed a combination of Hyperledger Fabric and InterPlanetary File System (IPFS), along with real-world use cases extracted from the MITRE ATT&CK framework. The result is an ecosystem that can share and store threat files in a secure and trusted way. However, the work does not cover the application of anonymization techniques to sensitive attributes, so the receiver of the data, although trusted, still can access to sensitive data, such as the identification number of a bank account in a financial environment.

Also in this line, [5] presented a privacy-preserving protocol for threat intelligence sharing, based on the collaborative training of a decision tree classifier, and exchanging training data between organizations in a private way using homomorphic encryption. Anyhow, this approach can be replaced by Federated Learning [16], that preserves the privacy of data used for training by default. Moreover, this approach does only provide a final model, but there may be scenarios where it is necessary to access the original data for provenance and inspection purposes, e.g., in the event of a cybercrime.

In [4], authors propose a framework for privacy-preserving collaborative data analysis, that allows different providers to share their information according to privacy requirements contained in a Data Sharing Agreement (DSA), and apply data mining techniques to extract additional knowledge from it. Their framework computes the best trade-off between privacy and accuracy using a model that is trained over decentralized data, that needs to be distributed. However, it does not cover the case of an entity refusing to share data, although it is being anonymized, but that still wants to participate in the learning process. In addition, it does not provide an access control mechanism for prosumers, which can be fixed by using some Identity and Access Management (IAM) Software.

The system proposed in this paper covers the exchange of CTI information in a privacy-preserving manner by the use of several well-known anonymization techniques, and the training and sharing of a global detection model based on Federated Learning. With this approach, entities participating in the network can receive raw CTI information or a final model that can be imported to a local intrusion detection system, updated with the threat status of all entities involved. In addition, to the best of our knowledge, this is the first proposal that covers a solution of this kind applied to a financial environment.

3 Proposal

The proposed system is designed on the basis of Malware Information Sharing Platform (MISP), an open-source Threat Intelligence Platform, enhanced with the following modules:

1. Permissioned Blockchain platform for auditing purposes.
2. Access control mechanisms based on a distributed Identity Management (IdM) system.
3. Privacy-Enhancing Technologies (PETs), based on the use of well-known anonymization algorithms such as K-anonymity, L-diversity or T-closeness, to protect sensitive data that needs to be shared, along with noise addition using differential privacy.
4. Federated Learning (FL) environment to enhance the accuracy of local intrusion detection mechanisms, making possible the use of private data of external parties to train a global threat-detection ML/DL model without sharing any data, thus ensuring its privacy. Once the final model is obtained, it will be shared through the proposed CTI sharing network so involved entities that did not participate in the FL training process (they might not have the infrastructure to do so) will be also able to download it and update their detection models accordingly.

In Fig. 2, the architecture of the proposal is shown. The architecture leverages our previous work in [18], including Federated learning capabilities as well as PET techniques for privacy-preserving CTI sharing. The scenario depicts the overall mode of operation of the whole ecosystem. As it should be noted, firstly, the MISP platform has been leveraged as Threat Intelligence Platform (TIP) to collect, store, distribute and share the CTI information. In this proposed

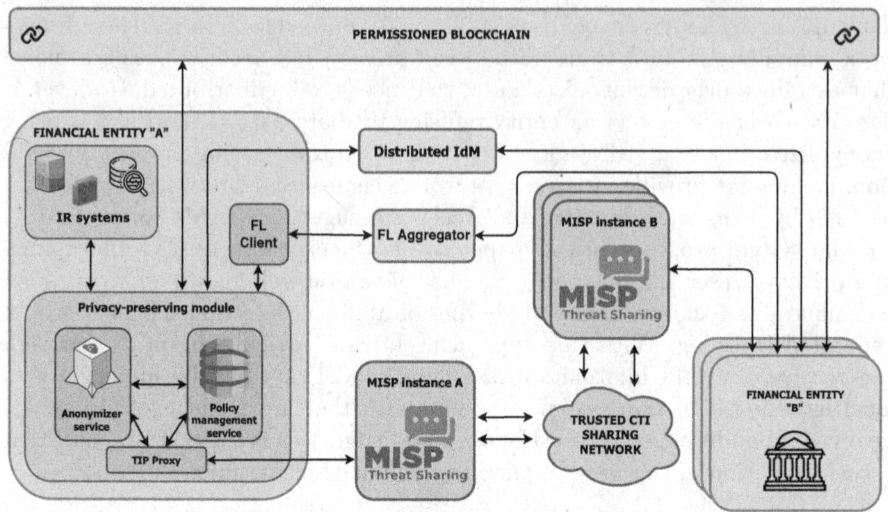

Fig. 2. Architecture of the proposal

scenario, each entity implements its own MISP instance and all entities form a trusted CTI sharing network, through the synchronisation process of their MISP instances, which allows an event published in a local instance to appear in the other synchronized instances. Consequently, this ensures trust in the ecosystem, since the synchronisation process requires a prior configuration that needs the coordination of the entities involved, therefore not trusted entities could not send or receive any information as they do not belong to the network.

Alongside the local MISP instance, there is a privacy-preserving module composed by an anonymizer service that is able to obfuscate specific sensitive attributes of an event also based on policies specified by the user and managed by a policy management service. This module supports several anonymization algorithms, such as data suppression, data generalization, K-anonymity [21], L-diversity [15] and T-closeness [13], that are previously selected by the user based on the specified policies. These policies are defined through extensible and interoperable models that follow a specific design, that in turn, allows determining adaptively which technique should be applied for each type of object and for each specific attribute of each object. In the end, it enables the anonymization of events with several different kind of objects. This module is also endowed with a TIP proxy, that is responsible for communicating with the MISP instance and the IdM for user credentials verification.

The permissioned blockchain, located at the top of the figure, is used to securely and traceably store some important metadata related to the provenance of a shared event such as the publisher, user, the anonymization technique used, hashes of the event and hashes of the privacy policies applied for each protected attribute. Thus, entitled users will be able to query and verify in real-time not only a published event and associated privacy policies and techniques applied, but also, in case an inspection is needed, to request a comparison of the original event with the anonymized one. This would help, for instance, to uncover an attacker who is delivering malicious obfuscated events.

Moreover, an FL scenario is set up with a single aggregator and multiple FL clients, ideally one per entity or domain, receiving training data, i.e., CTI events, from the local MISP instance in real-time. It may be the case that some entities do not implement this functionality, but nevertheless, they could still receive the final model as it will be uploaded and broadcasted to the MISP network once the federated training has finished, based on [17].

Furthermore, the scenario will be also endowed with a distributed identity management system (IdM), in order to ensure that users are authenticated and have permissions to share or receive events, thus ensuring access control.

In Figs. 3 and 4, the steps followed in order to publish and consume events are shown, respectively. This depicts the workflow of the whole system. As can be seen firstly, the communication between the event producer/consumer and the privacy-preserving module is done over HTTPs. This is because it is implemented as a service and offers a REST API. The communication with MISP is also performed using its REST API.

In case of event publication, before event anonymization, the user is authenticated against the IdM, and before event publication in the local MISP instance, the protected event metadata is published in the blockchain. In the event retrieval process, the user is authenticated as well before retrieving the events from the MISP instance, and the provenance of each event is checked against the blockchain before sending them back to the consumer.

On the other hand, in Fig. 5, the FL agent workflow is depicted. As can be noted, there are two fixed parameters, R and T. The first one is the time interval used by the agent to retrieve last events from MISP. For instance, if R is equal to 60, it polls the local MISP instance for new events every minute. Besides, T is the instance threshold to trigger the FL process. The agent collects events until this threshold is reached. When this happens, it registers against the aggregator and the federated training is performed along with other agents, representing further financial entities, that had previously registered from their domains.

Once the final model is obtained at the end of the final round, it is published to the local MISP instance as an event with an attachment. This attachment is a file containing the model serialized in a specific format, for example HDF5. This would allow an entity that did not participate in the training process but that belongs to the trusted CTI sharing network to access the model.

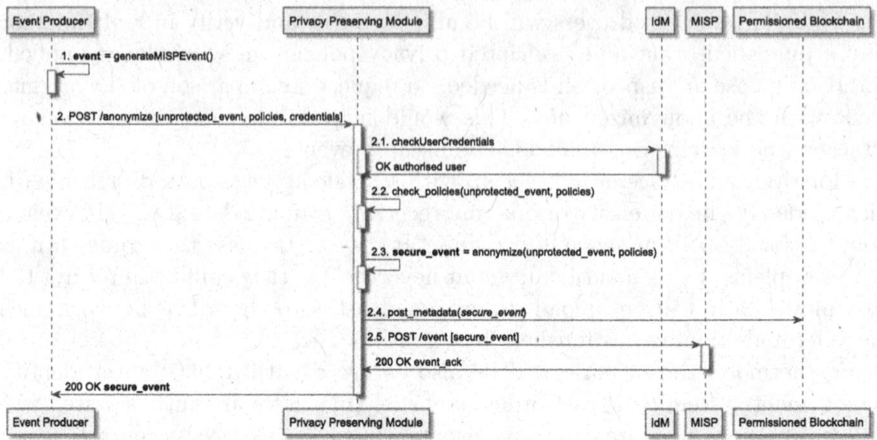

Fig. 3. Event publishing workflow

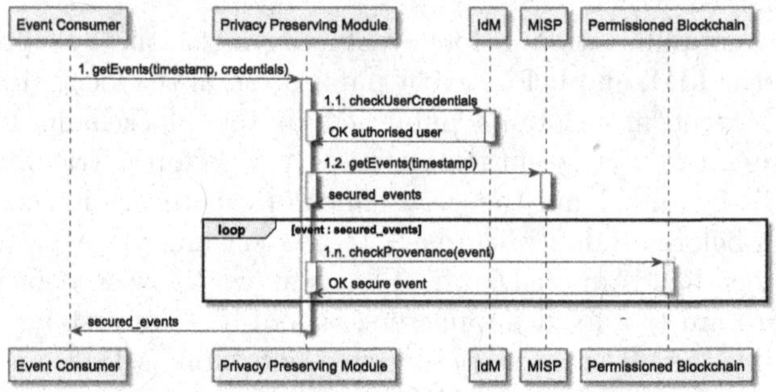

Fig. 4. Event retrieval workflow

4 Experimentation

In this section, we analyze how partial data anonymization influences the performance of a model trained by federated learning. To conduct the experiments, first, the privacy-preserving component is leveraged to obfuscate the sensitive attributes of the original data based on different algorithms. Then, the federated learning subsystem consumes the anonymized data to perform training and obtaining the final aggregated model at the end of the final round. Although local data will never leave the domain where it has been generated, we will anonymize sensitive attributes to emulate threat information coming from an entity that will not participate in the training process.

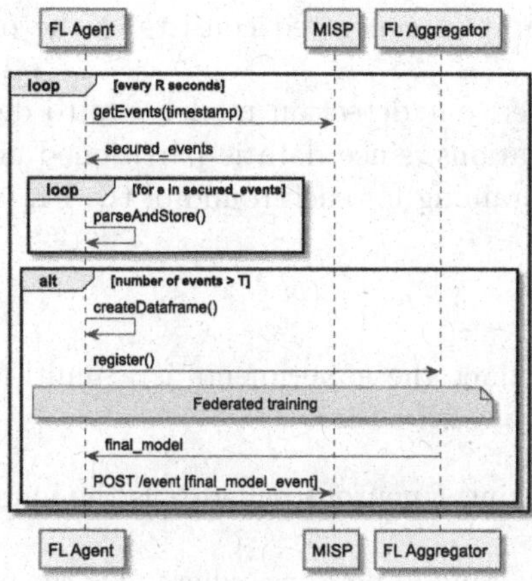

Fig. 5. FL Agent workflow

In the following subsections, each step of the procedure will be detailed, i.e., description of the dataset, setup of the model used for training, setup of the parameters for FL, how data is splitted and distributed among clients, as well as how it is preprocessed by each one of them, definition of sensitive attributes and how they are anonymized, and analysis of metrics of the federated training process.

4.1 Dataset

As data, a synthetic financial dataset for fraud detection is leveraged. This dataset has been generated using PaySim [14], a tool that simulates mobile money transations based on an original dataset. By the use of some techniques such as Agent-Based simulation and the application of mathematical statistics, the result is a synthetic dataset similar to the original one. Each row in the dataset represents a transaction that is defined by 9 features except for the last one, which is the label. Concretely, these features are the source and destination accounts numbers, the type and the amount of the transaction, the initial and final balances of each account, and the step of the simulation to which the transaction belongs, that represent 1 h of real-world time.

For our experiments, we downloaded a version which is scaled down to one-fourth of the original dataset presented in the previously cited work. Moreover, we have balanced the dataset, i.e., equalized the number of normal and fraud samples, to maximize the performance of the model. To do this, we applied the ADASYN oversampling technique [11], and generated a total of 6,346,164 synthetic samples of the minority class, which in this case indicates that the transaction represents a fraud. In total, the final dataset after oversampling is composed of 12,708,785 samples, of which 6,354,407 are normal and 6,354,377 are fraud. The difference between the total number of fraud samples and the total number of synthetic samples generated consists of the original fraud samples present in the dataset.

By using this dataset, our detection models are to detect fraud happening across multiple organizations, since data is partitioned and distributed among them to perform local training for each round of the FL training.

4.2 Model Setup

The model used to conduct the experiments is a multi-layer Artificial Neural Network with the following structure:

- **Input layer:** containing I neurons, where I is the number of columns of the dataset.
- **Output layer:** containing O neurons, where O is the number of labels of the dataset. For this case, since there are only instances from two classes, normal and fraud, O will be equal to two. This converts the model into a binary classifier.
- **Hidden layer:** containing H neurons, where H is the arithmetic mean of I and O.

Regarding the activation functions used for each layer, ReLU [2] is employed for the hidden layer while SoftMax [8] is employed for the output layer. The input layer does not need an activation function. Below, the mathematical expressions of the previously cited activation functions can be consulted:

$$ReLU(z) = max(0, z) \tag{1}$$

$$SoftMax(z_i) = \frac{e^{z_i}}{\sum_{j=1}^{K} e^{z_j}} \quad for\ i = 1, 2, \ldots, K \tag{2}$$

The algorithm is also configured to work with the Adam optimizer [12], which is an evolution of the classical Stochastic Gradient Descent (SGD) that fixes some of its weaknesses and improves slightly memory consumption and overall training times. By last, the Sparse Categorical Cross Entropy is used to calculate the loss function.

4.3 FL Setup

As for the FL details, *FedAvg* [16] has been leveraged as the aggregation function, and further parameters such as the number of rounds, local epochs to be executed for every round or batch size have been left for the user to be configured before the execution. For this experiment, we set 500 rounds, 1 local epoch, 32 as batch size, and 1 step per epoch.

The scenario is comprised of an aggregator and two clients. To implement these, the Flower FL research framework [6] has been employed.

4.4 Data Preparation

From the final dataset created and described in Sect. 4.1, two subsets are generated, one for each client in the scenario. To do this, we selected a random portion of 100,000 samples for each client. Then, each client splits its portion into training and testing sets, being the testing set one third of the portion.

Since data contains some categorical features such as source and destination accounts identifiers, a label encoding technique is applied to transform each unique categorical value to a unique numerical identifier, starting from 0. In addition, values are scaled to unit variance so that the mean is 0 and the standard deviation is 1, resulting in a Standard Normal Distribution (SND) of the data.

4.5 Anonymization of Sensitive Attributes

In order to study the influence of these privacy-preserving techniques on the usability of the data, suppression was applied on attribute values that would identify a particular individual. All the mechanisms supported by our solution, enumerated previously in Sect. 3, have been evaluated with respect to their applicability on this dataset. In this case, there are two attributes that completely identify an individual: source and destination accounts identifiers. Therefore, at least these two attributes are considered sensitive and need to be protected.

Among the anonymization techniques that our module implements, L-Diversity and T-Closeness have no applicability since the dataset does not include non-identifying attributes that describe characteristics that can be related to a specific entity. Apart from the source and destination accounts of the transaction, the rest of the attributes are informative about the type of transaction or numeric such as the amount transferred or the balance of the source and destination accounts. For this case, we consider that suppression is the mechanism that fits the best, so this will be the technique used for this experiment.

To test the impact of anonymizing data in the model accuracy, we generated three anonymized versions for each of the dataset portions assigned to each client, with an incremental number of obfuscated last digits i.e., 2,4,6 in the destination and source accounts.

4.6 Training Results

In Fig. 6, the accuracy throughout training rounds over local testing data for each client and for each configuration described in previous section is shown. As can be seen, there is no big difference between the performance obtained using clear data, i.e., with the account identifiers in clear, and using anonymized data in any of its versions. In fact, we observe that anonymized versions of the dataset allow the model to learn at a higher pace, i.e., reaching accuracy levels of around 75% faster than the clear data configuration. However, all accuracy trends could be considered very similar. Conversely, if account identifiers are removed completely, which would be the most aggressive anonymization, the accuracy drop is more noticeable.

It can be said, then, that the last digits of source and destination accounts identifiers are not decisive for AI-based anomaly detection, at least using this dataset, as they do not impact negatively the accuracy of the model, and therefore they can be fully anonymized. In addition, the accuracy obtained (around 80%) is competitive compared to other existing works, such as [20], that obtains values around 88% on binary classification using a Probabilistic Neural Network (PNN). However, the model is trained in a centralized way, the training dataset is considerably smaller (around 10.000 samples), and no oversampling or undersampling technique has been applied to balance the data. These conditions, as well as the fact that a centralized approach usually achieves greater accuracy since there is no need to merge models in any step of the process, would explain the difference between their work and ours.

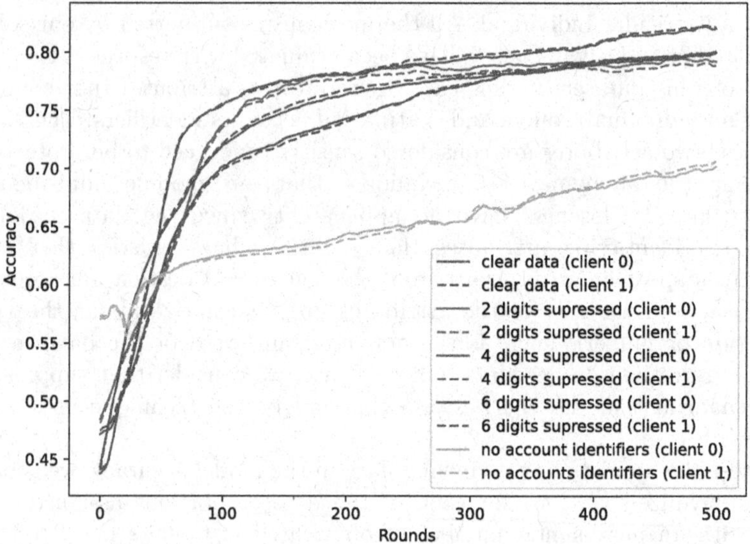

Fig. 6. Local accuracy evolution throughout rounds with different supression configurations

5 Conclusion and Future Work

This paper presented an ecosystem capable of preserving the privacy of financial entities through a trusted CTI-sharing network based on MISP, endowed with a privacy-preserving and a FL subsystem, making possible the exchange of sensitive threat information in an anonymized way based on several well-known anonymization techniques, as well as a DL model which is trained in a federated manner from local and private data. It is also shown, using a synthetic fraudulent transactions dataset publicly available, that protecting a subset of attributes, considered sensitive, do not have a significant impact on the accuracy of the trained model using FL, and therefore the system can operate normally while fully preserving the data flowing through the whole architecture. In addition, this paper presented an alternative solution to obfuscate model gradients in the FL process, based on privatizing the original data, that could be useful to prevent inference attacks during the FL training process.

As future work, it could be interesting to test the whole environment with real-time data and attack situations, to show how components and functionalities that were not covered in our experimentation, such as the DLT, IdM or the policy generation and management. Additional future work could involve adapting the system to work in other scenarios, testing with different machine learning/deep learning algorithms and anonymization techniques, and assessing the performance of the proposed architecture in a real-world setting.

Acknowledgments. This work has received funding from the Grant PID 2020-112675RB-C44 funded by MCIN/AEI/10.13039/501100011033. It has been also partially funded by the European Commission through the H2020 project CyberSec4Europe (g.a. 830929).

References

1. Standards and tools for exchange and processing of actionable information (Nov 2014), https://www.enisa.europa.eu/publications/standards-and-tools-for-exchange-and-processing-of-actionable-information
2. Agarap, A.F.: Deep learning using rectified linear units (relu). arXiv preprint arXiv:1803.08375 (2018)
3. Ali, H., Papadopoulos, P., Ahmad, J., Pitropakis, N., Jaroucheh, Z., Buchanan, W.: Privacy-preserving and trusted threat intelligence sharing using distributed ledgers (12 2021)
4. Alishahi, M., Saracino, A., Martinelli, F., Marra, Á.: Privacy preserving data sharing and analysis for edge-based architectures. Int. J. Inf. Secur. **21**, 1–23 (02 2022). https://doi.org/10.1007/s10207-021-00542-x
5. Badsha, S., Vakilinia, I., Sengupta, S.: Privacy preserving cyber threat information sharing and learning for cyber defense. In: 2019 IEEE 9th Annual Computing and Communication Workshop and Conference (CCWC), pp. 0708–0714 (2019). https://doi.org/10.1109/CCWC.2019.8666477
6. Beutel, D.J., et al.: Flower: a friendly federated learning research framework (2020). https://arxiv.org/abs/2007.14390
7. Blanchard, P., El Mhamdi, E.M., Guerraoui, R., Stainer, J.: Machine learning with adversaries: Byzantine tolerant gradient descent. In: Guyon, I., et al. (eds.) Advances in Neural Information Processing Systems. vol. 30. Curran Associates, Inc. (2017). https://proceedings.neurips.cc/paper/2017/file/f4b9ec30ad9f68f89b29639786cb62ef-Paper.pdf
8. Bridle, J.S.: Training stochastic model recognition algorithms as networks can lead to maximum mutual information estimation of parameters. In: Proceedings of the 2nd International Conference on Neural Information Processing Systems, pp. 211–217. NIPS'89, MIT Press, Cambridge, MA, USA (1989)

9. Campos, E.M., et al.: Evaluating federated learning for intrusion detection in internet of things: review and challenges. Comput. Netw. **203**, 108661 (2022). https://doi.org/10.1016/j.comnet.2021.108661, https://www.sciencedirect.com/science/article/pii/S1389128621005405
10. van Haastrecht, M., et al.: A shared cyber threat intelligence solution for SMEs. Electronics **10**(23) (2021). https://doi.org/10.3390/electronics10232913, https://www.mdpi.com/2079-9292/10/23/2913
11. He, H., Bai, Y., Garcia, E.A., Li, S.: Adasyn: adaptive synthetic sampling approach for imbalanced learning. In: 2008 IEEE International Joint Conference on Neural Networks (IEEE World Congress on Computational Intelligence), pp. 1322–1328 (2008). https://doi.org/10.1109/IJCNN.2008.4633969
12. Kingma, D.P., Ba, J.: Adam: a method for stochastic optimization (2014). https://arxiv.org/abs/1412.6980
13. Li, N., Li, T., Venkatasubramanian, S.: t-closeness: privacy beyond k-anonymity and l-diversity. In: 2007 IEEE 23rd International Conference on Data Engineering, pp. 106–115 (2007). https://doi.org/10.1109/ICDE.2007.367856
14. Lopez-Rojas, E.A., Elmir, A., Axelsson, S.: Paysim: a financial mobile money simulator for fraud detection (09 2016)
15. Machanavajjhala, A., Kifer, D., Gehrke, J., Venkitasubramaniam, M.: L-diversity: privacy beyond k-anonymity. ACM Trans. Knowl. Discov. Data 1(1), 3-es (Mar 2007). https://doi.org/10.1145/1217299.1217302
16. McMahan, B., Moore, E., Ramage, D., Hampson, S., y Arcas, B.A.: Communication-efficient learning of deep networks from decentralized data. In: Artificial Intelligence and Statistics, pp. 1273–1282. PMLR (2017)
17. Preuveneers, D., Joosen, W.: Sharing machine learning models as indicators of compromise for cyber threat intelligence. J. Cybersecur. Privacy, 140–163 (04 2021). https://doi.org/10.3390/jcp1010008
18. Preuveneers, D., Joosen, W., Bernal Bernabe, J., Skarmeta, A.: Distributed security framework for reliable threat intelligence sharing. Security and Communication Networks 2020 (2020)
19. Rahman, S.A., Tout, H., Talhi, C., Mourad, A.: Internet of things intrusion detection: centralized, on-device, or federated learning? IEEE Netw. **34**(6), 310–317 (2020). https://doi.org/10.1109/MNET.011.2000286
20. Sa'adah, S., Pratiwi, M.S.: Classification of customer actions on digital money transactions on Paysim mobile money simulator using probabilistic neural network (PNN) algorithm. In: 2020 3rd International Seminar on Research of Information Technology and Intelligent Systems (ISRITI), pp. 677–681 (2020). https://doi.org/10.1109/ISRITI51436.2020.9315344
21. Sweeney, L.: K-anonymity: a model for protecting privacy. Int. J. Uncertain. Fuzziness Knowl.-Based Syst. **10**(5), 557–570 (oct 2002). https://doi.org/10.1142/S0218488502001648
22. Wagner, T.D., Mahbub, K., Palomar, E., Abdallah, A.E.: Cyber threat intelligence sharing: survey and research directions. Comput. Secur. **87**, 101589 (2019). https://doi.org/10.1016/j.cose.2019.101589, https://www.sciencedirect.com/science/article/pii/S016740481830467X
23. Yu, P., Kundu, A., Wynter, L., Lim, S.H.: Fed+: a unified approach to robust personalized federated learning (2021)
24. Yurochkin, M., Agarwal, M., Ghosh, S., Greenewald, K., Hoang, T.N.: Statistical model aggregation via parameter matching (2019)
25. Yurochkin, M., Agarwal, M., Ghosh, S., Greenewald, K., Hoang, T.N., Khazaeni, Y.: Bayesian nonparametric federated learning of neural networks (2019)

Generative Methods for Out-of-distribution Prediction and Applications for Threat Detection and Analysis: A Short Review

Erica Coppolillo[1,3], Angelica Liguori[2,3](✉), Massimo Guarascio[3], Francesco Sergio Pisani[3], and Giuseppe Manco[3]

[1] Department of Mathematics and Computer Science, University of Calabria, Rende, Italy
erica.coppolillo@unical.it

[2] Department of Computer Engineering, Modeling, Electronics and Systems, University of Calabria, Rende, Italy

[3] Institute for High Performance Computing and Networking of Italian National Research Council, Rende, Italy
angelica.liguori@dimes.unical.it,
{massimo.guarascio,francesco.pisani,giuseppe.manco}@icar.cnr.it

Abstract. In recent times, Machine Learning has played an important role in developing novel advanced tools for threat detection and mitigation. Intrusion Detection, Misinformation, Malware, and Fraud Detection are just some examples of cybersecurity fields in which Machine Learning techniques are used to reveal the presence of malicious behaviors. However, *Out-of-Distribution*, i.e., the potential distribution gap between training and test set, can heavily affect the performances of the traditional Machine Learning based methods. Indeed, they could fail in identifying out-of-samples as possible threats, therefore devising robust approaches to cope with this issue is a crucial and relevant challenge to mitigate the risk of undetected attacks. Moreover, a recent emerging line proposes to use generative models to yield synthetic likely examples to feed the learning algorithms. In this work, we first survey recent Machine Learning and Deep Learning based solutions to face both the problems, i.e., outlier detection and generation; then we illustrate the main cybersecurity application scenarios in which these approaches have been adopted successfully.

Keywords: Threat Detection · Outlier Generation · Deep Learning · Ensemble Learning · Generative Model · Autoencoder

E. Coppolillo, A. Liguori, M. Guarascio, and F. Sergio Pisani—Equally contributed to the paper and are all considered first authors.

A. Skarmeta et al. (Eds.): CyberSec4Europe 2022, CCIS 1807, pp. 65–79, 2023.
https://doi.org/10.1007/978-3-031-36096-1_5

1 Introduction

In the last few years, we have experienced exponential growth in the number of attacks performed against companies and organizations. Often, these attacks remain undetected for months or more before being identified. This is mainly due to the fact that the detection models have been trained against data exhibiting a different distribution from the real ones. Indeed, anomalous data and shifts in the data distribution can greatly affect the performances of Machine Learning (ML) models. It mainly depends on how these models are learned: in real application scenarios, the *closed-world assumption*, i.e., training data are a representative sample of the test ones, is not realistic.

From a cybersecurity perspective, the perturbations on data we are interested in handling can concern both adversarial and defense strategies. Therefore, learning robust models against these changes represents a challenging and relevant research topic for mitigating the risk due to malicious behaviors. Outlier detection and generation techniques represent a precious tool for identifying malicious behaviors and strengthening Artificial Intelligence (AI) based security systems. While outlier detection is a well-known research area in ML research [41] and has been widely adopted for identifying anomalies in several cybersecurity scenarios (e.g., Network and Host Intrusion Detection Systems, Malware Detection, Fraud Detection, etc.), outlier generation is a relatively new research line and focuses on devising algorithms for generating realistic examples so to enrich the ground truth for model learning. Recently, with the rise of deep generative models, there has been a growing interest in these solutions [16,28,49] since they represent an effective method for generating realistic cyberattacks. Indeed, the adoption of the Deep Learning (DL) paradigm [30] represents a natural solution for the application scenarios mentioned above, as DL techniques permit the learning of accurate detection models also from raw data (e.g., traffic flows, processes, manipulated images, etc.) without the necessity of heavy intervention by domain experts [19]. Basically, these DL models are structured according to a hierarchical architecture (consisting of several layers of base computational units, i.e., the artificial neurons are stacked one upon each other), allowing for learning features at different abstraction levels to represent raw data. Differently from traditional algorithms based on shallow hierarchies that fail to explore and learn highly complex patterns, DL-based approaches allow for intrinsically exploit of the large amounts of data yielded in cybersecurity domain, can analyze raw data provided in different formats and by different types of source, and can leverage GPUs to parallelize the computation and to reducing the learning times.

In this chapter, we survey some recent Deep Learning-based methods and techniques for outlier detection and generation, and we provide an overview of the main application scenarios in the cybersecurity domain in which these approaches can be effectively adopted. The rest of the work is organized as follows: in Sect. 2, we provide a detailed overview of the main generative approaches for outlier detection and generation; Sect. 3 describes some relevant application scenarios in cybersecurity in which Deep Learning techniques are used to mitigate the out-of-distribution problem; Sect. 4 introduces open challenges and emerging research lines; finally, Sect. 5 concludes the work and suggest some new interesting research lines.

2 State-of-the-Art Approaches for Outlier Detection and Generation in Cyber-Security Scenarios

This section is devoted to illustrating recent approaches proposed in the literature to cope with the out-of-distribution problem. Specifically, first, we survey Machine and Deep Learning methods for anomaly detection, then we illustrate recent generative approaches for realistic anomaly generation.

2.1 Deep Learning Models for Outlier Detection

Class imbalance, i.e., the overwhelming of a class w.r.t. the other ones, represents a main issue in devising outlier detection techniques. In many cyber-security scenarios, a large part of the available data contains information on normal/expected behaviors. Therefore, unsupervised and semi-supervised approaches are the most frequently used methods for addressing this problem. In particular, one-class classification, e.g., One-Class Support Vector Machines (OC-SVM) [45], distance-metrics, e.g., Isolation Forest (IF) [33] or nearest neighbor algorithms [38] are considered state-of-the-art techniques in this research field. In the last years, with the rise of Deep Learning, there has been a growing interest in anomaly detection models exploiting Deep Neural Networks (DNNs) [37]. This is mainly due to the capability of DNNs to learn directly from raw data in an incremental fashion without the need for a manual feature engineering phase. In this context, solutions based on the usage of autoencoders (AE) [6] have gained increasing attention among researchers and practitioners [4,5,11,23,55].

An autoencoder is a neural architecture trained to reproduce as output a duplicate of its input. It is composed of two components, as shown in Fig. 1: (*i*) the encoder Θ, a neural network whose goal is to map the input x to a low-dimensional latent space $z = \Theta(x)$, (*ii*) the decoder Φ, a further neural network that, given the latent representation z, aims to produce an output $y = \Phi(z)$ that is as close as possible to the original input. The autoencoder structure is optimized by minimizing the error between the original data and the reconstructed ones, as shown in Eq. 1.

$$\mathcal{L}(\Theta, \Phi; x) = ||x - y||_p \tag{1}$$

The main capability of the AE is to yield an encoding that ignores the noise. Therefore, the adoption of these architectures for anomaly detection tasks represents a natural choice since high reconstruction errors on new data are likely related to anomalies (e.g., cyberattacks). Basically, the reconstruction error estimates the outlierness score associated with a given instance. In more detail, AEs are trained only against normal samples; therefore, they learn to model normal behaviors. Hence, when a deviant example is provided as input, the output will diverge from the expected one, and an alarm is raised. However, the threshold τ, required to establish if a score is anomalous, plays a crucial role in this framework since it greatly affects the performance of the model. Some preliminary studies tried to address this issue, e.g., [48] introduce a (weakly) supervised anomaly detection model able to discover anomalies without setting τ. Basically, the proposed AE integrates two decoders, named inlier decoder (D_{in}) and outlier decoder (D_{out}), respectively. These sub-networks are trained in a competitive fashion and allow for modeling inliers and outliers' data distributions. Unlabeled data are provided as input to both the sub-networks, which are responsible for labeling them as outliers or inliers based on the reconstruction errors. Specifically, the strategy relies on comparing the scores yielded by two decoders: if the inlier reconstruction error is smaller than the outlier reconstruction error, the former label is assigned to the instance, the latter one otherwise.

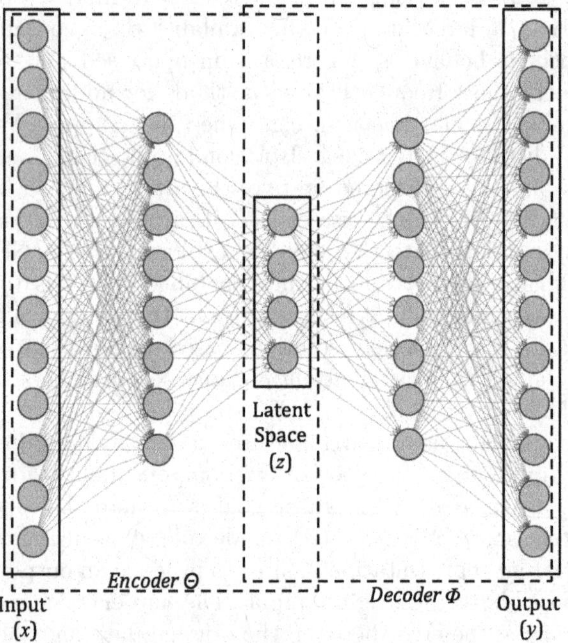

Fig. 1. Architecture of an Autoencoder.

A further emerging research line in outlier detection focuses on the use of Generative Adversarial Networks (GANs) [34]. The main idea is to define a single comprehensive generative framework in which the detection process is directly embedded. Basically, two components, respectively generator G and discriminator D, are trained through an adversarial process [16], as shown in Fig. 2. The generator attempts to yield examples able to fool the discriminator and undermine its predictive performances, whereas the discriminator acts in the role of estimating the probability that a given example belongs to the training data or has been generated by G. The generative distribution over the data is estimated by learning the mapping from an initial noise distribution (used as prior) to the data space. The discriminator D is trained to correctly classify the input data as either real or fake, i.e., maximize the probability that any real data is classified as belonging to the training data while minimizing the probability that any fake (generated) data is classified as belonging to the original data. Since the generator attempts to fool the discriminator, its objective is to maximize the probability that any fake image is classified as belonging to the real data. Thus, D and G are simultaneously optimized through the following two-player minimax game with value function $V(D, G)$:

$$\min_G \max_D V(D,G) = \mathbf{E}_{x \sim p_{data}(x)}[\log D(x)] + \mathbf{E}_{z \sim p_z(z)}[log(1 - D(G(z)))] \quad (2)$$

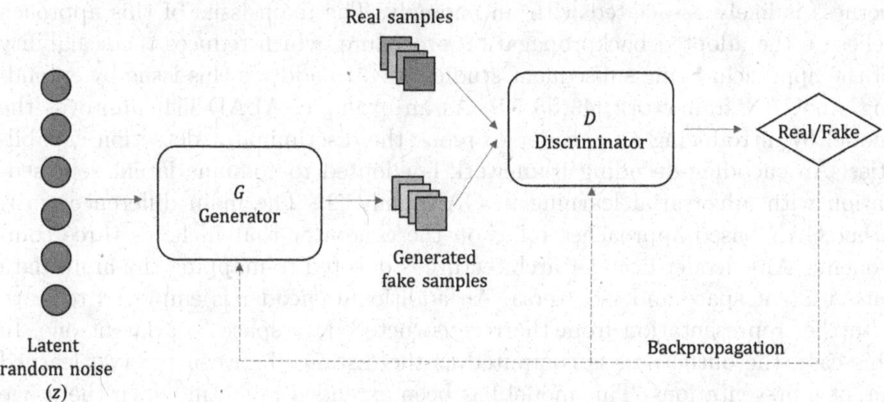

Fig. 2. GAN Learning Scheme.

where $D(x)$ represents the probability that x came from the data rather than p_g (i.e., the probability that x to be a real instance); $\mathbf{E}_{x \sim p_{data}(x)}$ is the expected value over all real data instances $p_{data}(x)$; G is a differentiable function that maps the latent random noise z to the data space; $D(G(z))$ is the discriminator's estimate of the probability that a fake instance is real, and $\mathbf{E}_{z \sim p_z(z)}$ is the expected value over all random inputs to the generator.

As mentioned above, due to the ability to perform distribution fitting, generative models are considered among the best solutions in the anomaly detection field [52], and in particular, VAE and GAN are the most representative methods. However, in different application scenarios, GAN exhibited superior ability in generating real examples. GAN architectures (trained against normal instances) allow for effectively detecting abnormal examples since they will be poorly reconstructed by the model. Therefore, one of the main benefits of these approaches is their capability to alleviate the data scarcity problem. Moreover, they can effectively and efficiently process complex datasets and handle high-dimensional data distributions. This is particularly important in the cybersecurity domain where data scarcity, unbalanced class distributions, and high dimensional and complex data are typically issues to cope with (see, for example, attacks in traffic flows, malware, frauds, and image manipulations). In the following, we surveyed some recent works exploiting GAN to detect anomalies without the necessity of a labeled training set.

AnoGAN [44] represents a first attempt to adopt GAN framework for outlier detection. The main idea consists in using an iterative process for learning the mapping from latent space to realistic normal examples. The final result of this process is a point z in the latent space such that the generated sample is as similar as possible to the input one. The similarity between generated and input data is used as an anomaly score and calculated as a combination of residual and matching loss [42]. Low values of anomaly scores are associated with examples seen in the training phase (i.e., the normal data), while a high outlierness is likely associated with an anomaly. The main issue of this approach relies on the adopted backpropagation procedure, which reduces the scalability of the approach. Some subsequent studies tried to address this issue by extending AnoGAN framework [43,53,54]. As an example, ALAD [54] improves the model by introducing an encoder to refine the discriminator detection capabilities. An encoding-decoding framework is adopted to combine latent representation with adversarial learning in GANomaly [2]. The main difference w.r.t. other GAN-based approaches relies on the generator that includes three components. An encoder-decoder architecture is devoted to mapping the input data into a latent space and vice versa. An additional encoder is employed to learn a further representation from the reconstructed data space to a latent one. In this case, the outlierness is computed as the distance between the two learned latent representations. This model has been extended in [3], in which the usage of skip connections improves the convergence of the model and the detection performances.

In [31], the authors propose an unsupervised multivariate anomaly detection method based on Generative Adversarial Networks (GANs) that adopts LSTM (Long Short Term Memory) [24] as generator and Recurrent Neural Network (RNN) [17] as discriminator in a GAN framework to learn the temporal correlation of time series distributions. The Multivariate Anomaly Detection with GAN (MAD-GAN) framework leverages the whole variable set concurrently to capture the latent interactions among the variables.

In ADAE [50], an autoencoder architecture is used to model both discriminator and generator. Here, the idea is to use the reconstruction error of the discriminator autoencoder to estimate the anomaly score. Finally, recent approaches propose to combine ensemble learning with autoencoders [10] or GANs [21]. Ensembles are well-known ML methods where the output of several models

Table 1. Deep Learning models for outlier detection

Solution Approach	Dataset(s)	Data Type	Learning Scheme	Neural Model	Evaluation Metrics
CoRA [48]	KDDCUP99, MNIST, Fashion MNIST, CIFAR10, ImageNet-20, Caltech-101, Caltech-256	Flat, Image	Semi-Supervised	AE	AUROC, F1
AnoGAN [44]	Clinical Dataset	Image	Unsupervised	GAN	Precision, Recall, Sensitivity, Specificity, AUROC
ALAD [54]	KDDCUP99, Arrhythmia, SVHN, MNIST	Flat, Image	Unsupervised	BiGAN	Precision, Recall, F1, AUROC
GANomlay [2]	MNIST, CIFAR10, University Baggage Anomaly Dataset (UBA), Full Firearm vs. Operational Benign (FFOB)	Image	Unsupervised	Combining GAN and AE	AUROC
MAD-GAN [31]	SWaT, WADI, KDDCUP99	Time-Series	Unsupervised	GAN	Precision, Recall, F1
ADAE [50]	MNIST, CIFAR10, HCP, BRATS 2017	Image	Unsupervised	Combining GAN and AE	AUROC

trained against different data samples or using different algorithms is then combined according to a given strategy for classifying new unseen instances. In the GAN framework, they are typically used by exploiting combinations of different generators and discriminators.

2.2 Anomaly Generation via Deep Learning

Artificial outlier generation represents an effective solution for addressing the class unbalance problem and can be exploited for both evaluating the prediction quality of the outlier detection models and improving their performances by feeding them with these data. The DL-based architectures discussed in the following exploit a general approach that consists in adapting probabilistic generative models so as to yield anomalous examples by sampling from low-density regions. For example, a VAE-based approach for generating synthetic time series including also outliers is proposed in [29]. Basically, the solution consists in sampling anomalies from the outlier region of the latent space. The main issue in using this approach depends on the training data distribution, i.e., complex manifolds in original data can lead to learning overgeneralized models exhibiting weak performances. WALDO - Wasserstein Autoencoder for Learning the Distribution of Outliers - defined in [40] is a (weakly) supervised framework integrating detection and generation capabilities in a single solution. In more detail, it integrates the Wasserstein autoencoders [49] with the technique proposed in [48]. WALDO architecture is composed of two decoders, respectively, for inliers and outliers, stacked on a common encoder that is trained by using the Wasserstein distance. The objective is learning to generate distributions by minimizing the Wasserstein Distance among inliers and outliers. A different approach is used to learn FenceGAN [36]. The standard GAN framework is extended based on the following observation, i.e., adversarial samples tend to overlap the true distribution. Then, the main idea consists in devising a generator able to yield samples distributed on the boundaries of the data distribution. As a result, the learned discriminator is robust against difficult outliers, i.e., able to correctly classify these challenging examples. ARN (Adversarial Reconstruction Network) [32] combines Variational Autoencoders (VAE) and Generative Adversarial Networks for the generation and identification of outliers. The main goal is to generate realistic outliers for the learning phase of an outlier detector. Specifically, ARN exploits normal data to generate their abnormal counterpart, i.e., a synthetic but realistic outlier that is similar to the normal data but differs from it for minimal but substantial differences. The generation of realistic outliers enables the learning of an outlier detector that is able to identify real outliers without the need to be fed with explicit information about them.

Table 2. Deep Learning models for outlier generation

Solution Approach	Dataset(s)	Data Type	Learning Scheme	Neural Model	Evaluation Metrics
AnoGen [29]	Synthetic	Time-Series	Unsupervised	VAE	Precision, Recall
WALDO [40]	MNIST, FMNIST, CIFAR10, KDDCUP99	Image, Flat	Semi-Supervised	Combining WGAN and AE	AUROC, AUPRC
FenceGAN [36]	MNIST, CIFAR10, KDDCUP99	Image, Flat	Unsupervised	GAN	AUPRC, AUROC, Precision, Recall, F1
ARN [32]	KDDCUP99, NSL-KDD, DoH, CoverType, CreditCard, Bank, MNIST	Flat, Image	Unsupervised	Combining GAN and VAE	AUROC, AUPRC

3 Applications in Cyber-security Domain

Since the main aim of cybersecurity is to protect systems, organizations, and users against attacks (in many cases, anomalous and rare events) perpetrated by black hats, the usage of outlier detection techniques in cybersecurity domain has become more popular in recent years. As highlighted in the previous sections, many different types of malicious behaviors can be considered as attacks, e.g., network intrusions, insurance, and credit card frauds, diffusion of fake information, and image manipulation. In principle, all these deviant behaviors can be discovered by exploiting anomaly detection techniques which are able to process large amounts of data efficiently and also identify slight changes w.r.t. an expected behavior. In the following, we illustrate some of the most relevant cybersecurity scenarios where these techniques can be adopted.

Intrusion Detection. Intrusion Detection Systems (IDSs) are hardware and software systems able to identify malicious behaviors and are widely reckoned as an important tool for timely recognizing security breaches and attacks. The problem of detecting malicious activities in a host or network environment [35] is currently being studied, and many approaches have been proposed in the literature. In particular, since the intrusions are typically rare events exhibiting slight differences in terms of traffic flow statistics, outlier detection techniques based on GANs can represent an effective solution to discover these anomalies as shown in [8]. A BiGAN-inspired model combined with a custom loss function is adopted for identifying intrusions in computer networks. In [14], the authors propose a supervised incremental Deep Learning scheme to cope with concept drifts and data shifts: a number of Residual Neural Networks (ResNet) are trained against disjoint data chunks gathered in different time windows. Then, the single models are combined in an ensemble model, which is further fine-tuned on a subset of data extracted by each data chunk. As shown in [20], the performances of different ML-based detection methods (including also [14]) can be further improved by embedding them in an Active Learning scheme. A different solution to deal with the problem proposes the usage of the Federated Learning framework: the underlying idea of this approach is to distribute the computation of the model among different nodes, which are the owner of data. A coordinator iteratively will get the models yielded by each node and will combine them on the basis of a suitable strategy for further fine-tuning. As an example, in [12], the authors propose a federated learning approach embedding a GAN model to detect malicious activity possibly related to attacks.

Fraud Detection. Fraud detection represents a challenging issue in several application scenarios, and the automatic discovery of these fraudulent behaviors represents a very important task with great impact in many real-life situations. The main goal consists in detecting criminal activities and preventing unauthorized operations. In this domain, outlier detection techniques can be leveraged to detect *(i)* fraudulent credit card applications or usage, *(ii)* illicit usage of a mobile phone account, or *(iii)* insurance fraud claims in which an attacker manipulates the claim processing system for unauthorized and illegal claims [7]. As an example, [9] propose a DL-based model to address the fraud detection problem. The framework exploits a combination of Sparse Autoencoder (SAE) and GAN to detect whether a transaction is fraudulent or not. Again, in [13], the authors propose the usage of a GAN architecture to yield synthetic examples belonging to the minority class. Hence, training data are enriched with these artificial examples to improve the effectiveness of the classifier acting in the role of fraud detector.

Malware Detection. Malware Detection refers to the process of detecting anomalous flows (possibly related to malicious code) through the monitoring of computer systems' activity. Velocity, volume, and complexity of these threats represent some relevant challenges to overcome for developing effective solutions. In particular, some recent works proposed the adoption of ML and DL techniques [39] to effectively cope with these issues. As an example, random feature nullification [51], stacked autoencoders [22], and adversarial architectures [18,26,47] have been successfully used to devise accurate detection methods. However, an emerging research line focused on the usage of generative approaches. For example, in [15], the authors embed a deep generative model in a semi-supervised malware detection system to reveal the presence of anomalous behaviors. A stochastic gradient optimization technique is exploited to improve the efficiency of the learning method and process large datasets. Moreover, in [27], a hybrid deep generative model is trained against global and local features: the main idea consists in modeling the malware as an image (which represents the global features), while local features are extracted as binary code sequences. These features are concatenated and used to feed the malware detector in order to improve its quality.

Image Manipulation. The main aim of Image Manipulation Detection is to discover any unauthorized modification in an image. *Splicing*, *copy-move*, and *removal* are some of the most common techniques used in this field to manipulate the content of an image. Manipulated images may seem normal to the human eye, but typically they can exhibit artifacts that make them anomalous. A different type of manipulation relies on the usage of *information hiding* technique. As an example, by using steganography techniques, malware or sensitive data can be embedded into an image and sent/exfiltrated. Once again, the human eye is not able to perceive the differences w.r.t. the original image (i.e., the image without the hidden information), therefore AI-based tools can represent an effective solution for analyzing the image and discovering tampering, in particular when they are synthetically generated via advanced manipulation tools. For example, [25] propose a deep forgery discriminator (DeepFD) based on the usage of contrastive loss to detect computer-generated images.

Misinformation. Timely detection of fake news spreading over well-known social networks (SN) represents a relevant research topic since fake/errata news can grow in popularity, becoming a real fact for entities belonging to such SN communities. Fake news can be regarded as low-quality news with intentionally false information [46]. With the aim of fighting the rise and spread of fake news, different automatic detection methods based on AI and ML have been proposed in the literature. In particular, the recent results obtained by DL techniques in complex natural language processing tasks make them a promising solution for effectively detecting fake news. From this perspective, although Deep Learning approaches have already been adopted in literature to detect fake news, the usage of GAN-based models is still unexplored. In particular, GAN-based models have mainly been employed to address similar tasks, such as fake review detection. As an example, [1] demonstrated that FakeGAN, an architecture based on the simultaneous usage of two discriminators, can be effectively used to detect deceptive reviews in a real scenario.

4 Challenges and Opportunities

Although cybersecurity tools can greatly benefit from the integration of ML/DL techniques, several issues are still open. First, the boundary between the normal and anomalous regions is very difficult to define. Different strategies have been proposed in the literature, but there is no consensus on a specific solution. Moreover, the lack of (labeled) data (e.g., due to privacy issues, limited computation resources, etc.) can affect the performances of the detection models; therefore, it is important to yield reliable models also when training data are scarce. In this respect, some recent approaches based on Federated Learning represent an emerging and relevant research line to cope with this issue. The class imbalance problem requires defining specific approaches in order to be handled since they can conduct to learn models with poor predictive performances. As mentioned above, there exist outliers with different natures, such as novelty, deviations, and concept drifts. The diversity of the different forms of anomaly makes the evaluation of OOD detectors a difficult problem. Therefore, a current issue is to define a suitable protocol to effectively evaluate the detection model performances. Neural networks are typically considered *black box* models; therefore, in several contexts, it is difficult to interpret the reasons for a prediction yielded by the detector. Explainable AI (XAI) can play a crucial role in the recently proposed deep network architectures, in particular when they are leveraged in critical applications (such as the cybersecurity domain). Indeed, XAI-Based techniques can be used to justify an alert generated by the detection system or possibly understand/correct a false alarm. Fairness and bias in the data represent another relevant issue to address in the development of effective anomaly detection systems in OOD scenarios. It has been highlighted that spurious correlations in the training data affect OOD detection. Indeed, the OOD detection performance degrades when the correlation between spurious features and labels is increased in the training set. For example, the presence of non-relevant recurrent patterns in the training set (e.g., criminal acts performed by a specific gender or race) can yield detection models based on spurious features with good performance on the training set but poor ones at testing time. Finally, the capability of adversarial examples to disguise as normal instances represents a challenging issue that needs further studies. Indeed, it has been shown that the performances of the detection models can be affected by adversarial attacks, which are able to reduce the detection capabilities of the models. Therefore, in OOD detection, robustness against adversarial attacks is crucial to yield reliable models.

5 Conclusions

The usage of Machine Learning techniques for automating and improving the detection of cyberattacks is rapidly gaining importance. Unfortunately, AI-Based tools may exhibit poor performances when deployed in real environments since the training data used in the learning phase could greatly differ from the test ones. The development of new methods and techniques for learning models robust against out-of-distribution represents an emerging and challenging research line. In this chapter, we described some approaches based on innovative Deep Learning architectures moving a step in this direction and analyzed their application in different cybersecurity scenarios. Specifically, we provided a detailed overview of the main generative approaches used to address two challenging tasks: *(i)* detecting anomalous behaviors (possibly related to threats); *(ii)* generating artificial instances/examples to enrich the training set and make more robust traditional learning scheme. We concluded our study by introducing some relevant cybersecurity application scenarios, describing some preliminary work based on the generative methods used in these cases, highlighting some open challenges, and suggesting some emerging research topics.

Acknowledgements. This work was partially supported by EU H2020-SU-ICT-03-2018 Project No. 830929 CyberSec4Europe (cybersec4europe.eu) and by project SERICS (PE00000014) under the MUR National Recovery and Resilience Plan funded by the European Union - NextGenerationEU.

References

1. Aghakhani, H., Machiry, A., Nilizadeh, S., Kruegel, C., Vigna, G.: Detecting deceptive reviews using generative adversarial networks. CoRR abs/1805.10364 (2018)
2. Akcay, S., Atapour-Abarghouei, A., Breckon, T.P.: GANomaly: semi-supervised anomaly detection via adversarial training. In: ACCV (2018)
3. Akçay, S., Atapour-Abarghouei, A., Breckon, T.P.: Skip-GANomaly: skip connected and adversarially trained encoder-decoder anomaly detection. In: IJCNN (2019)
4. Alfeo, A.L., Cimino, M.G., Manco, G., Ritacco, E., Vaglini, G.: Using an autoencoder in the design of an anomaly detector for smart manufacturing. Pattern Recogn. Lett. **136**, 272–278 (2020)
5. An, J., Cho, S.: Variational autoencoder based anomaly detection using reconstruction probability (2015). http://dm.snu.ac.kr/static/docs/TR/SNUDM-TR-2015-03.pdf
6. Bank, D., Koenigstein, N., Giryes, R.: Autoencoders. CoRR (2020)
7. Chandola, V., Banerjee, A., Kumar, V.: Anomaly detection: a survey. ACM Computing Surveys (CSUR) **41**, 1–72 (2009)
8. Chen, H., Jiang, L.: Gan-based method for cyber-intrusion detection. CoRR abs/1904.02426 (2019)
9. Chen, J., Shen, Y., Ali, R.: Credit card fraud detection using sparse autoencoder and generative adversarial network. 2018 IEEE 9th Annual Information Technology, Electronics and Mobile Communication Conference (IEMCON), pp. 1054–1059 (2018)

10. Chen, J., Sathe, S., Aggarwal, C., Turaga, D.: Outlier detection with autoencoder ensembles. In: SDM (2017)
11. Chen, Z., Yeo, C.K., Lee, B.S., Lau, C.T.: Autoencoder-based network anomaly detection. In: WTS (2018)
12. Das, S.: FGAN: federated generative adversarial networks for anomaly detection in network traffic (2022). https://doi.org/10.48550/ARXIV.2203.11106. https://arxiv.org/abs/2203.11106
13. Fiore, U., De Santis, A., Perla, F., Zanetti, P., Palmieri, F.: Using generative adversarial networks for improving classification effectiveness in credit card fraud detection. Inf. Sci. **479**, 448–455 (2019). https://doi.org/10.1016/j.ins.2017.12.030. https://www.sciencedirect.com/science/article/pii/S0020025517311519
14. Folino, F., Folino, G., Guarascio, M., Pisani, F., Pontieri, L.: On learning effective ensembles of deep neural networks for intrusion detection. Inf. Fusion **72**, 48–69 (2021). https://doi.org/10.1016/j.inffus.2021.02.007. https://www.sciencedirect.com/science/article/pii/S1566253521000245
15. Fu, Y., Lan, Q.: Deep generative model for malware detection. In: 2020 Chinese Control And Decision Conference (CCDC), pp. 2072–2077 (2020). https://doi.org/10.1109/CCDC49329.2020.9164231
16. Goodfellow, I.J., et al.: Generative adversarial nets. In: NIPS, pp. 2672–2680 (2014)
17. Graves, A.: Supervised Sequence Labelling with Recurrent Neural Networks. Studies in Computational Intelligence. Springer, Heidelberg (2012). https://doi.org/10.1007/978-3-642-24797-2
18. Grosse, K., Papernot, N., Manoharan, P., Backes, M., McDaniel, P.: Adversarial examples for malware detection. In: Foley, S.N., Gollmann, D., Snekkenes, E. (eds.) ESORICS 2017. LNCS, vol. 10493, pp. 62–79. Springer, Cham (2017). https://doi.org/10.1007/978-3-319-66399-9_4
19. Guarascio, M., Manco, G., Ritacco, E.: Deep learning. Encycl. Bioinform. Comput. Biol. ABC Bioinf. **1–3**, 634–647 (2018)
20. Guarascio, M., Cassavia, N., Pisani, F.S., Manco, G.: Boosting cyber-threat intelligence via collaborative intrusion detection. Future Gener. Comput. Syst. **135**, 30–43 (2022). https://doi.org/10.1016/j.future.2022.04.028. https://www.sciencedirect.com/science/article/pii/S0167739X22001571
21. Han, X., Chen, X., Liu, L.P.: Gan ensemble for anomaly detection. In: AAAI (2020)
22. Hardy, W., Chen, L., Hou, S., Ye, Y., Li, X.: DL 4 MD : a deep learning framework for intelligent malware detection (2016)
23. Hawkins, S., He, H., Williams, G.J., Baxter, R.A.: Outlier detection using replicator neural networks. In: DaWaK (2002)
24. Hochreiter, S., Schmidhuber, J.: Long short-term memory. Neural Comput. **9**(8), 1735–1780 (1997)
25. Hsu, C., Lee, C., Zhuang, Y.: Learning to detect fake face images in the wild. CoRR abs/1809.08754 (2018)
26. Kim, J.Y., Bu, S.J., Cho, S.B.: Zero-day malware detection using transferred generative adversarial networks based on deep autoencoders. Inf. Sci. **460–461**, 83–102 (2018). https://doi.org/10.1016/j.ins.2018.04.092. https://www.sciencedirect.com/science/article/pii/S0020025518303475
27. Kim, J.Y., Cho, S.B.: Obfuscated malware detection using deep generative model based on global/local features. Comput. Secur. **112**, 102501 (2022). https://doi.org/10.1016/j.cose.2021.102501
28. Kingma, D.P., Welling, M.: Auto-encoding variational bayes. In: ICLR (2014)
29. Laptev, N.: Anogen: Deep anomaly generator (2018). https://tinyurl.com/fbanogen

30. Le Cun, Y., Bengio, Y., Hinton, G.: Deep learning. Nature **521**(7553), 436–444 (2015)
31. Li, D., Chen, D., Jin, B., Shi, L., Goh, J., Ng, S.-K.: MAD-GAN: multivariate anomaly detection for time series data with generative adversarial networks. In: Tetko, I.V., Kůrková, V., Karpov, P., Theis, F. (eds.) ICANN 2019. LNCS, vol. 11730, pp. 703–716. Springer, Cham (2019). https://doi.org/10.1007/978-3-030-30490-4_56
32. Liguori, A., Manco, G., Pisani, F.S., Ritacco, E.: Adversarial regularized reconstruction for anomaly detection and generation. In: 2021 IEEE International Conference on Data Mining (ICDM), pp. 1204–1209 (2021). https://doi.org/10.1109/ICDM51629.2021.00145
33. Liu, F.T., Ting, K.M., Zhou, Z.H.: Isolation forest. In: ICDM (2008)
34. Mattia, F.D., Galeone, P., Simoni, M.D., Ghelfi, E.: A survey on GANs for anomaly detection. CoRR (2019)
35. Milenkoski, A., Vieira, M., Kounev, S., Avritzer, A., Payne, B.D.: Evaluating computer intrusion detection systems: a survey of common practices. ACM Comput. Surv. **48**(1), 2808691 (2015). https://doi.org/10.1145/2808691
36. Ngo, C.P., Winarto, A.A., Li, C.K.K., Park, S., Akram, F., Lee, H.K.: Fence GAN: towards better anomaly detection. In: ICTAI (2019)
37. Pang, G., Shen, C., Cao, L., Hengel, A.V.D.: Deep learning for anomaly detection: a review. ACM Comput. Surv. **54**(1), 1–38 (2021)
38. Ramaswamy, S., Rastogi, R., Shim, K.: Efficient algorithms for mining outliers from large data sets. In: SIGMOID (2000)
39. Rathore, H., Agarwal, S., Sahay, S.K., Sewak, M.: Malware detection using machine learning and deep learning. In: Mondal, A., Gupta, H., Srivastava, J., Reddy, P.K., Somayajulu, D.V.L.N. (eds.) BDA 2018. LNCS, vol. 11297, pp. 402–411. Springer, Cham (2018). https://doi.org/10.1007/978-3-030-04780-1_28
40. Rizzo, S.G., Pang, L., Chen, Y., Chawla, S.: Probabilistic outlier detection and generation. CoRR (2020)
41. Ruff, L., et al.: A unifying review of deep and shallow anomaly detection. Proceedings of the IEEE (2021)
42. Salimans, T., Goodfellow, I., Zaremba, W., Cheung, V., Radford, A., Chen, X.: Improved techniques for training GANs. In: NIPS (2016)
43. Schlegl, T., Seeböck, P., Waldstein, S.M., Langs, G., Schmidt-Erfurth, U.: f-AnoGAN: fast unsupervised anomaly detection with generative adversarial networks. Medical Image Analysis **54**, 30–44 (2019)
44. Schlegl, T., Seeböck, P., Waldstein, S.M., Schmidt-Erfurth, U., Langs, G.: Unsupervised anomaly detection with generative adversarial networks to guide marker discovery. In: IPMI (2017)
45. Schölkopf, B., Williamson, R.C., Smola, A.J., Shawe-Taylor, J., Platt, J.C., et al.: Support vector method for novelty detection. In: NIPS (1999)
46. Shu, K., Sliva, A., Wang, S., Tang, J., Liu, H.: Fake news detection on social media: a data mining perspective. CoRR abs/1708.01967 (2017)
47. Suciu, O., Coull, S., Johns, J.: Exploring adversarial examples in malware detection, pp. 8–14 (2019). https://doi.org/10.1109/SPW.2019.00015
48. Tian, K., Zhou, S., Fan, J., Guan, J.: Learning competitive and discriminative reconstructions for anomaly detection. In: AAAI 33 (2019)
49. Tolstikhin, I., Bousquet, O., Gelly, S., Schoelkopf, B.: Wasserstein auto-encoders. In: ICLR (2019)
50. Vu, H.S., Ueta, D., Hashimoto, K., Maeno, K., Pranata, S., Shen, S.M.: Anomaly detection with adversarial dual autoencoders. CoRR (2019)

51. Wang, Q., Guo, W., Zhang, K., Xing, X., Giles, C., Liu, X.: Random feature nullification for adversary resistant deep architecture (2016)
52. Xia, X., et al.: GAN-based anomaly detection: a review. Neurocomputing **493**, 497–535 (2022). https://doi.org/10.1016/j.neucom.2021.12.093. https://www.sciencedirect.com/science/article/pii/S0925231221019482
53. Zenati, H., Foo, C.S., Lecouat, B., Manek, G., Chandrasekhar, V.R.: Efficient GAN-based anomaly detection. CoRR (2019)
54. Zenati, H., Romain, M., Foo, C.S., Lecouat, B., Chandrasekhar, V.R.: Adversarially learned anomaly detection. In: ICDM (2018)
55. Zhou, C., Paffenroth, R.C.: Anomaly detection with robust deep autoencoders. In: KDD (2017)

Distributed Filtering in Industrial Networks

Manuel Cheminod[(✉)] and Luca Durante

National Research Council of Italy - Institute of Electronics, Information and Telecommunications Engineering (CNR-IEIIT), Torino, Italy
{manuel.cheminod,luca.durante}@cnr.it

Abstract. The security of large interconnected systems is a major concern and a priority to address. This concern is especially pronounced for industrial systems and critical infrastructures, where the cyber aspects are closely interwoven with the physical reality. Although the architectural and technological advancements in such systems have provided greater flexibility and more efficient management, they have also increased the attack surface. One key aspect to consider is the security of the communication network, which can be vulnerable to attacks involving anomalous spikes of traffic that can lead to a denial-of-service on the network itself. In this paper, we focus on recent techniques that take advantage of multiple firewalls in the system to distribute the allocated filtering rules, thus reducing the overall device load.

Keywords: Industrial cybersecurity · firewalls · distributed filtering

1 Introduction

Modern society relies on large interconnected systems that are constantly facing numerous cyber security threats coming from heterogeneous sources. There is an ever-ending race between cyber attackers and cyber defenders. The former are constantly developing new skills and new attacks to compromise the systems while the latter continuously struggle to stay ahead developing new technologies and strategies to protect those same systems. This is more and more true and alarming in industrial networks and, in general, in critical infrastructures. Such systems are deeply intertwined with the physical world, and, in fact, are cyber-physical systems. In this scenario, security-related accidents can quickly escalate and cause physical damage and harm to persons, together with costly production stops.

Industrial systems have experienced a slow but steady evolution toward the modern principles of Industry 4.0 [12]. This evolution has increased dramatically in speed in recent times, with the wide adoption of recent communication technologies and architectures such as Industrial IoT, WiFi, 5G, and the cloud.

There is, in fact, a convergence in technologies and architectures between the OT (Operational Technology) and the standard IT (Information Technology)

A. Skarmeta et al. (Eds.): CyberSec4Europe 2022, CCIS 1807, pp. 80–93, 2023.
https://doi.org/10.1007/978-3-031-36096-1_6

worlds. This convergence is required to enable a more flexible and dynamic approach to production and also to optimize management and deployment costs. The widespread trend is to avoid a strict dependence on proprietary technologies for either devices or communications, as this does not facilitate high-level integrations among different parts of production systems. Instead, the convergence of technologies and communication protocols does encourage the creation of dynamic systems that can quickly adapt to market needs and high-level management decisions.

The structure of a typical industrial system is shown in Fig. 1, where it is possible to identify different layers in the production plants, related to different operations and functionalities provided by the included devices.

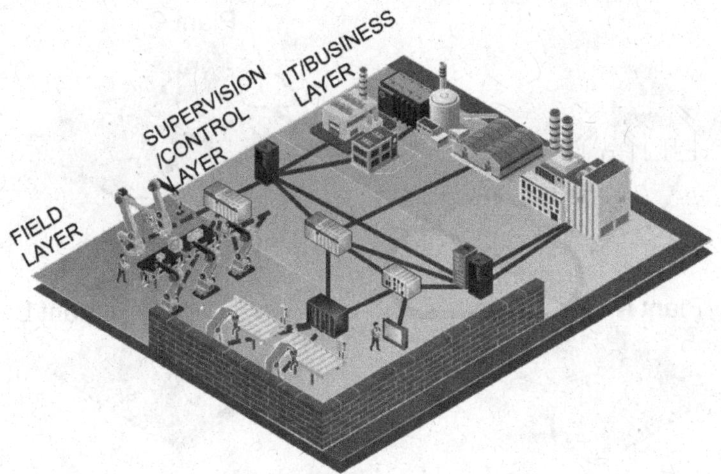

Fig. 1. An industrial network system

Starting from the left in Fig. 1, we identify the field layer where the actual manipulation of physical entities is performed. At this layer, sensors and actuators collect production data and apply commands coming from the higher level management. In fact, the next layer to consider is the supervision/control layer where process controllers are deployed and regulate the correct execution of the production process while providing also a bridge toward the high-level business layer of the plant. In this top layer, the plant strategy is decided, by taking into account the data coming from the lower level but also coming from the external world, regarding, for instance, the market needs. These layers are more and more interconnected and dependent upon each other, and often there is not a sharp separation between communication channels among the layers. In fact, stream of data related to the monitoring of the production could be directly forwarded to the upper layers to speed up the acquisition and interpretation of information. This scenario in which data is shared between different layers enables the creation of high-level services that can help in the decision-making process at the business level.

However, the other side of the coin is that modern industrial systems have an ever-increasing number of interconnections between different parts of the plants and with the external world. Moreover, many industrial plants are nowadays geographically distributed while belonging to the same communication network, which is possible through Internet-based channels. To add further complexity, we have to take into account the ever-increasing need for remote connections (eg. remote maintenance, smart working, and so on) that open further communication channels. Given this scenario, depicted in Fig. 2, there is a constantly rising awareness of the critical aspect of cyber security in these systems [15].

Fig. 2. Complexity of modern threat scenarios

In this described context, we have to consider the possible sources of threats that are no more limited to the "Internet" or the "external world". Internal threats are more and more critical in such scenarios, including accidental misuses by legitimate users (operators, employees), software threats (malware, compromised devices), and malicious users (disgruntled employees). In this context, a specific aspect to consider is the security of the communication network, and in particular the effective protection against unwanted or malicious traffic [10].

2 Security of Communication Network

One central element in any networked system is, in fact, the communication network infrastructure, which enables the exchange of messages between the different devices, effectively providing the mean for service provision. In a typical industrial network, we have several different types of communication flows between different parts of the plant. Communications flow both horizontally, between devices of the same production layer, but also vertically, connecting entities belonging to upper layers. These exchanges include the execution of the production processes at the lower layers, involving sensors, actuators and controllers. The high-level control of the production process, the monitoring, the supervision, instead, is executed at the higher layers, with a continuous exchange of updated data coming from the lower levels.

With respect to the past, it is worth noting that modern industrial systems are more and more dynamic in their nature and their configurations. The need for quick adaptability in the production objectives translates into flexible deployement of production processes in the plant. These aspects add to the complexity of the underlying communication network and, in particular, of its security requirements.

There are several possible approaches to the management of the security of communication networks. The more general approach, and reliable in a sense, is the "security by design" approach, where the configuration of all the element of the system is developed offline with some assurance about its correctness with respect to the security policies.

Recent work in [8] presented a solution able to provide this "security by design" objective. In particular, a formal model of the network and the related security policies has been developed and, with the support of a SAT solver, a formally correct configuration for the network elements is provided. This approach is also able to take into account the capabilities of the available nodes and leverages modern technologies such as SDN (software-defined networking) and NFV (network function virtualization).

A different approach has been proposed in [3], where the model of the system configuration, including the configuration of network devices, is formally checked against the model of the system security policies, and in particular, those related to the access control. The proposed formal verification investigates exhaustively all possible system state evolutions to verify that security properties are always satisfied.

Both approaches give the system administrator the assurance about the correctness of the system configuration with respect to the security policies. However, this correctness must be ensured even after the initial system deployement and, in particular, it is important to ensure compliance with security policies while also ensuring the continuous operation of the system. This is especially critical in the presence of anomalous network traffic. This can be caused by errors or attacks. In fact, devices could be affected by errors that force them to flood the network with unexpected network packets, or they could be compromised by an attacker and used to perform a denial-of-service (DoS) attack.

Such a scenario is particularly detrimental and dangerous in industrial networks. A successful DoS attack would break communications possibly interrupting the regular execution of production processes, causing damages on different levels. Monitoring could be interrupted and the overall management of the plant could be affected. This could happen if the DoS is targeting one or more devices involved in the process control but also if the attack is affecting the network devices filtering the communications. In fact, an overloaded firewall could lose packets breaking communication channels and blocking the interactions between devices. However, even before reaching the saturated point in which a firewall starts to lose packets, a surge in network traffic could stress the firewall such that the time required to process a packet increases considerably. The resulting delay introduced in the communication flow could break temporal constraints in critical control processes, even without losing packets.

To address this problem, a viable approach is to find a way to reduce the impact of anomalous traffic on network devices. The solution described here considers the overloaded firewall and provides an updated configuration to reduce its load, distributing part of it throughout different firewalls in the network.

3 State of the Art

In the considered scenario of large distributed systems, it is reasonable to expect the deployment of multiple firewalls, distributed throughout the network [14]. In industrial systems, this is very desirable to obtain the "defense in depth" suggested by many standards and best practices (e.g. IEC 62443 [4]), that is to protect the different logical and physical layers in which we can partition the system. However, two main problems arise when dealing with firewall deployment: the number and location of firewalls, and their configuration. The particular problem addressed here, about firewall performance, has been addressed from several points of view. For example [9] proposed a solution based on modifications of low-level components related to the Linux kernel. Other works in [6,7] proposed the manipulation of existing filtering rules so as to minimize their number or to adapt their order, to minimize their impact. Another work in [13], proposed an approach to distribute the set of rules among available firewalls, with the limitation of requiring to modify the managed packets thus affecting the firewall behaviour.

4 Distributed Firewall Configurations

To develop this solution, the first required ingredient is a model of the firewall in terms of functionality and behaviour. A first model is formalized in [5] where a firewall is described as a set of filtering rules that evaluate and make decisions upon network packets. A filtering rule is defined as by a (condition, action) pair, where the condition is a logical formula over the fields of the evaluated network packet, and an action is a decision over that matching packet. A decision can be of accepting and forwarding the packet or to block and discard it (respectively "allow" or "deny" action). These rules are evaluated in order, and the first rule that matches the packet is used and its action is applied. This behaviour belongs to the "first matching rule" model.

A third type of action is included in the model, namely the "goto" action. This action, if applied, modifies the order of rules to evaluate, by "jumping" to a specified rule in the set.

Given the behavioural model of a firewall, it is possible to build an analytical model of it, including the computational cost of rule evaluation against network packets. So, starting from this model of the firewall, and considering a network traffic with specific packet characteristics, it is possible to calculate the average time needed to evaluate a packet, and thus the average *delay* introduced by the firewall.

In order to fully address the problem of anomalous network traffic, we need to define a reference topology, describing the elements involved in the scenario and showing how they are connected.

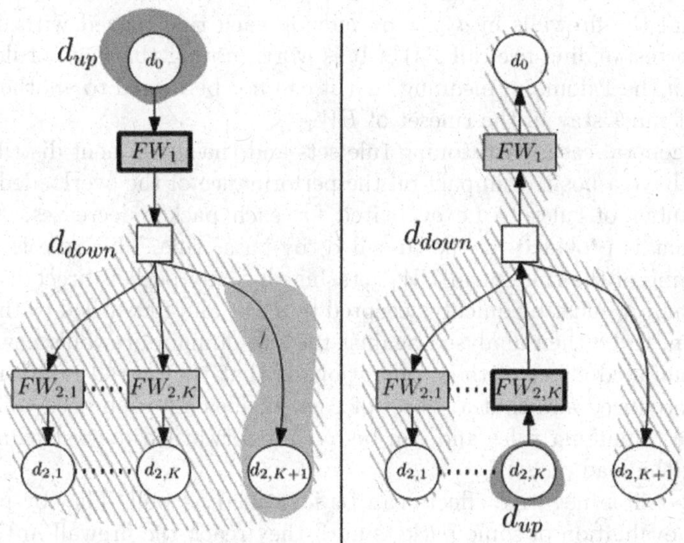

Fig. 3. Reference topology

This reference topology is depicted in Fig. 3, where circles represent devices or sub-domains and yellow squares represent firewalls. We identify the *overloaded firewall* FW_1. We also identify two network sub-domains, d_{up} and d_{down}, one for each side of the overloaded firewall. In particular, we consider the source of the anomalous traffic and its direction so as to identify, in Fig. 3, the d_{up} domain, highlighted in red as the source of anomalous traffic and d_{down}, which includes the nodes that are targets of the anomalous flows. In Fig. 3 it is worth noting that the same physical topology, used in both left and right images, identify different scenarios and different label assignment, depending on the location of the anomalous traffic and the location of the overloaded traffic. In particular, in Fig. 3 the overloaded firewall is the FW_1 in the left side, and, instead, is the

$FW_{2,K}$ node in the right side. The d_{up} and d_{down} are updated accordingly. This is particularly relevant to assess the generality of the considered topology.

In the reference topology the d_{down} domain is further divided into additional sub-domains ($d_{2,1}$, ..., $d_{2,K}$, $d_{2,K+1}$) which may be protected by specific firewalls ($FW_{2,1}$, ..., $FW_{2,K}$), as illustrated in Fig. 3. The partitioning of d_{down} in further sub-domains (usually representing sub-networks with a specific range of IP addresses) allows to identify partitions in the filtering rules deployed on FW_1. Each rule, in fact, may be classified depending on the condition expressed upon the destination address of the packet. If the destination address is strictly included in a specific sub-domain $d_{2,x}$, then the rule is flagged with the corresponding $(2, x)$ domain. If the considered destination is not clearly included in one of the protected sub-domains, then the rule is flagged as belonging to the domain 1. This procedure is applied for all the rules on FW_1 and, as a result, the entire set of rules is partitioned. It is now possible to modify the configuration of FW_1 and the firewalls in d_{down} by moving each rule tagged with domain x into the corresponding firewall FW_x. It is worth noting that some rule may be tagged with the 1 domain, meaning that it can not be moved to another firewall and that it must stay in the ruleset of FW_1.

In the general case, partitioning rule sets and the subsequent distribution of rules does have a positive impact on the performance of the overloaded firewall, as the number of rules to be evaluated for each packet decreases. A further improvement is provided by the so-called "by-pass" rule. This rule is added at the beginning of the rule set in FW_1, stating that any packet directed to a sub-domain in d_{down} must be quickly accepted by FW_1 and forwarded to the correct sub-domain, to be then analysed against the sub-domain firewall's new ruleset.

The combined effect of these operations is that the overall number of rules on FW_1 is reduced and that a subset of packets does not even need to be tested against the remaining rules and can be quickly forwarded downstream, further decreasing the load on FW_1.

Some possible negative effects can be identified as well. The "by-pass" rule delays the evaluation of some packets until they reach the firewall in the downstream domain. This means that packets that would have been rejected by FW_1 are now allowed to flow through the downstream sub-network. This may be dangerous, in case of malicious packets, or at least a waste of resources , as it consumes more network bandwidth. Additionally, while rule distribution reduces the load on FW_1, it increases the load on downstream firewalls. Depending on the capabilities of those firewalls, this may result in a negative performance impact.

To assess the efficacy of this rule distribution process in a variety of scenarios, a comprehensive testing and validation process was conducted in [5], using a simple topology and two cascading firewalls, one of which was overloaded. Tests were designed to assess the system's behavior with different network traffic characteristics, varying numbers of configured rules, and changing distribution ratios. All tests validated the approach as correct and reported a significant performance improvement.

To further assess the feasibility of the approach, a more complex firewall model has been considered. Specifically, the IPTables [1] software firewall has been selected as it is a widely used and stable, and well-known firewall. The filtering rules configured in this firewall are organized in tables that includes several chains that include ordered sets of rules. A packet entering the IPTables firewall is analyzed against a sequence of table/chain pairs depending on the source and destination of the packet. Packets directed towards the firewall itself, or coming from the firewall, are evaluated by a different set of tables and chains with respect to packets that simply flow through the firewall (i.e. with external source and destination).

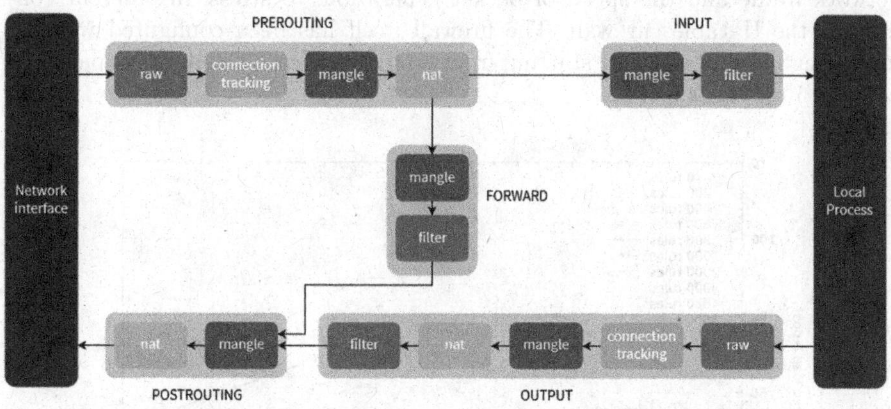

Fig. 4. Reference diagram for IPTables firewall [2]

The model of the IPTables firewall is deeply connected to the diagram shown in Fig. 4. Each node represents a table/chain pair that includes the filtering rules against which the packet is tested, while the edges select the flow to follow depending on the source and destination addresses of the packet. Each packet comes from a network interface (left in the figure), is processed through a sequence of filtering rules and, if accepted, reach its final state and is forwarded to the correct destination. Otherwise, the packet is dropped. It is worth noting in this model that each time a rule matches a packet with an "allow" action, that packet enters the next node in the diagram and is evaluated by its set of rules. Instead, a rule matching with a "deny" action, will instantly drop the packet, without any further step in the diagram. The precise meaning of the node labels is omitted here but the interested reader can find the full explanation in [2].

Besides the "allow" and "deny" actions, the IPTables firewall may specify a "goto" or "jump" action. Both actions affect the sequence of evaluated rules within a table and a chain. In particular, the "goto" operation moves the evaluation of current rules into a different chain. The "jump" action, instead, is similar to the "goto" one but in this case there is a memory of "from where we jumped", so that, if no rule matches the packet, the evaluation process can return to the previously considered chain.

The availability of the extended firewall model and the possibility to deploy an instance of such software into a general purpose PC, enabled the real performance evaluation of a real firewall and allowed to verify the rule distribution approach on a physical topology. In order to do so, an instance of IPTables has been installed and configured on a PC equipped with two hardware network interfaces, connected, respectively, to a client and a server node. This PC includes an Intel Q9550 dual-core CPU @2.83GHz with 8 GB RAM, running Ubuntu 20.04.2.0. The client and server nodes were used to generate several streams of packets with variable characteristics, changing the size of the used network frame and the speed of packet generation, to stress, in different conditions, the IPTables firewall. The firewall itself has been configured with an increasing number of rules, starting from 0 (the base case where every packet is accepted) up to 5000.

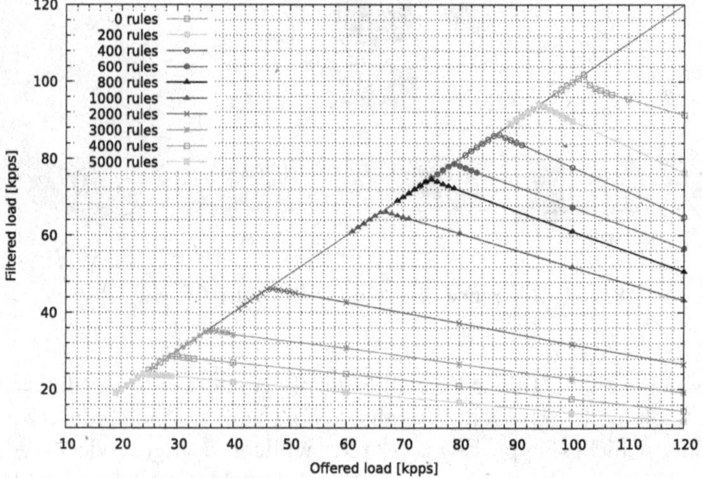

Fig. 5. Performance of IPTables with different input stream features

The results of this real world evaluation are depicted in Fig. 5. On the x-axis is reported the speed of packet generation, in terms of packets per second. On the y-axis, instead, it is represented the number of packets that are correctly managed (filtered) by the firewall. As long as the load of the firewall does not reach a specific "saturation" point, the filtered load follows the offered load, meaning that all the incoming packets have been correctly managed and are delivered to their destination. When the generation speed reaches the critical point, instead, the firewall starts to lose packets, and this is visible in Fig. 5 where the value of the filtered load "bends" and starts to drop.

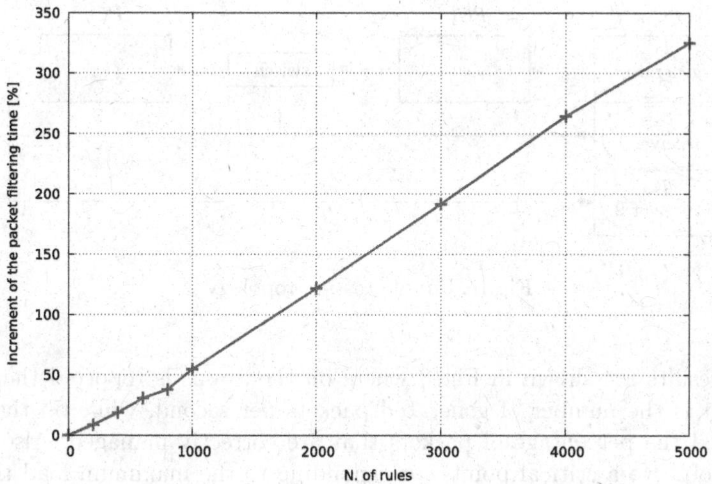

Fig. 6. Critical point vs number of deployed rules.

This critical point depends on the number of rules configured on the firewall. This value is directly related to the time needed to process a packet. In fact, the firewall starts to lose packets when the average processing time for each packet is higher than the packet generation time. With this consideration it is possible to analyse the increment of processing time depending on the number of rules. The results of this analysis are visible in Fig. 6. It is clear that there is a linear dependence between the number of rules and the time required to process each packet.

Having assessed the performance of a single software firewall, the next step is to evaluate the performance of a cascade of two firewalls deployed in a real topology, with two sub-domains, as depicted in Fig. 7, where, with respect to the reference topology of Fig. 3, we identify three domains (d_0, $d_{2,1}$, $d_{2,2}$) allocated on a single PC_{sr} machine, and two firewalls (fw_1 and $fw_{2,1}$) allocated to two different physical machines. The fist firewall protects both $d_{2,1}$ and $d_{2,2}$ domains while $fw_{2,1}$ only filter traffic toward $d_{2,1}$. This type of topology allows to perform several different tests varying the type of traffic used. Two flows are generated by d_0 with different destinations ($d_{2,1}$ or $d_{2,2}$). By varying the relative bandwidths between these two flows, it is possible to stress differently the two firewalls. In particular, by increasing the traffic going towards $d_{2,1}$ both firewalls are involved.

The testing process thus involves changing the speed of the generated stream ("offered load") and the ratio of traffic directed towards $d_{2,1}$. Regarding the firewall configuration, instead, we fix the total number of deployed rules to the value of 600 and then we perform the experiments by changing the number of rules that are distributed to $fw_{2,1}$, decreasing the load on fw_1. In order to assess the impact of this changes, we measure the "critical point" for fw_1 in the different configurations, remembering that its value is directly related to the processing time, and thus the load of the firewall.

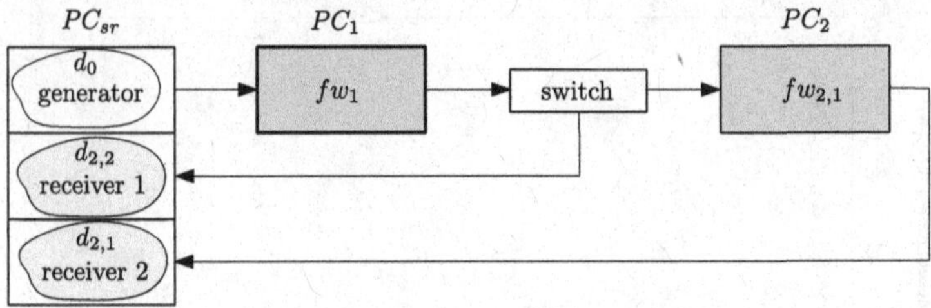

Fig. 7. Simple testing topology

The results are shown in Fig. 8 where on the x-axis is reported the offered load, that is the number of generated packets per second, while on the y-axis is reported the percentage of packets that are correctly managed. Also in this case, we observe a critical point, corresponding to the maximum load that can be managed before starting to lose packets.

This diagram helps us in understanding the impact of the distribution algorithm. We start considering the leftmost series of data in Fig. 8, where all the rules are allocated to fw_1 and which shows a critical point around an offered load of 80 kpps. We see that all the other three series, corresponding to different configurations, show an improvement in the critical value, as it is moved toward the right side, corresponding to an increased traffic load that is correctly managed. In all three cases, 200 rules have been moved from fw_1 to $fw_{2,1}$, while a different ratio of traffic towards $d_{2,1}$ has been used.

These results confirmed the soundness of the proposed approach, and provided some real-world evaluation of the performance gains.

A further evaluation has been proposed in [11] by considering a different software firewall. Specifically, the IPFire product has been used. IPFire is a distribution that includes an linux-based operating system and that uses the IPTables software to provide filtering capabilities. IPFire is relevant as it is used in commercial-products and is specifically tailored to provide an efficient and manageable software firewall. Even though IPFire uses IPTables, it forbids a direct access to the underlying IPTables configuration and forces the user to manage the firewall via a set of predefined graphical interfaces. This allows for a more robust management of the firewall, with many specific helpers that hide the full complexity of an IPTables configuration. For the experimental evaluation of this firewall, the IPFire distribution has been installed in the same general purpose PC used to test IPTables alone. This allows us to reason about the performance independently on the underlying hardware, which is the same in both cases. A summary of the results is shown in Fig. 9 where the critical point values, and related service time, for different number of configured rules, are drawn for both IPTables alone and IPFire. The overall behaviour is confirmed while a slight loss in performance is reported for IPFire.

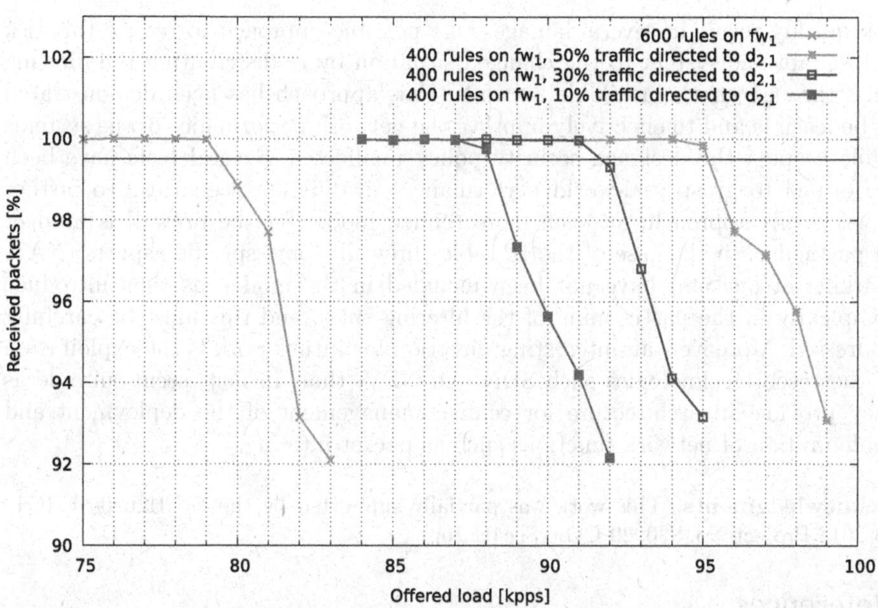

Fig. 8. Performance improvements on firewall fw_1 with different traffic distribution.

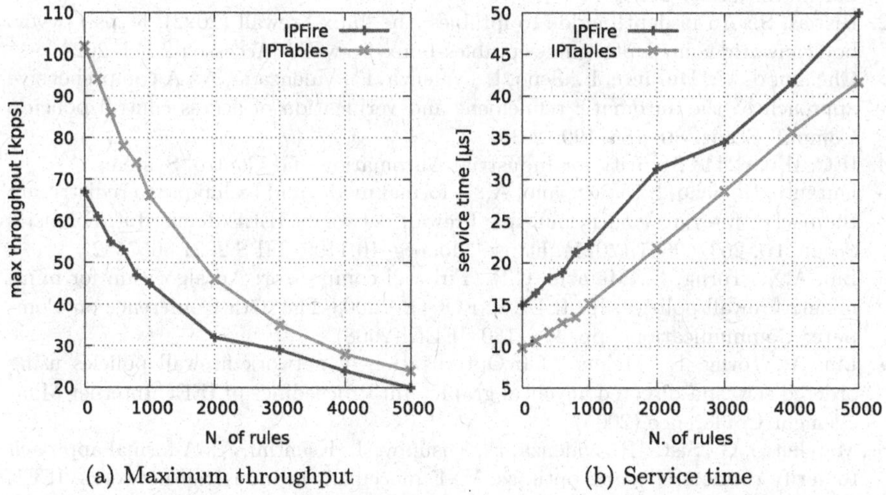

(a) Maximum throughput (b) Service time

Fig. 9. Comparison between IPTables and IPFire performances

5 Conclusion and Future Work

The security of industrial networks and critical infrastructures is a priority. One of the utmost important aspects to consider is the security and the availability of the underlying communication network. Surges in traffic loads in these systems can quickly result in severe damage. One possible approach to reduce this risk is to adapt the system to the changed situation by re-distributing the filtering rules throughout the available firewalls. This approach has been demonstrated to be feasible and to effectively improve the network performance of the systems while keeping the designed security policy unaffected. Several tests have been performed to grasp real-world performances in different scenarios. To further develop this approach, an even more refined model for the firewall is needed. In particular, in the case of the IPTables firewall, some specific aspects (NAT, marking of packets) have not been included in the model, as they introduce complexity in the partitioning of the filtering rules, and this must be carefully addressed. Moreover, an interesting direction for future work is the exploitation of the recent technologies such SDN and NFV, that, in fact, seem suitable as they provide an architecture for central management of the deployment and configuration of network functions such as packet filtering.

Acknowledgments. This work was partially supported by the EU H2020-SU-ICT-03-2018 Project No. 830929 CyberSec4Europe.

References

1. The netfilter.org “iptables” project. https://www.netfilter.org/projects/iptables/index.html (1999–2021)
2. Biswas, S.: An in-depth guide to iptables, the linux firewall (2022). https://www.booleanworld.com/depth-guide-iptables-linux-firewall/. Accessed 2 Feb 2023
3. Cheminod, M., Durante, L., Seno, L., Valenza, F., Valenzano, A.: A comprehensive approach to the automatic refinement and verification of access control policies. Comput. Secur. **80**, 186–199 (2019)
4. IEC: IEC 62443 Security for Industrial Automation and Control Systems
5. Durante, L., Seno, L., Valenzano, A.: A formal model and technique to redistribute the packet filtering load in multiple firewall networks. IEEE Trans. Inf. Forensics Secur. **16**, 2637–2651 (2021). https://doi.org/10.1109/TIFS.2021.3057552
6. Liu, A.X., Torng, E., Meiners, C.R.: Firewall compressor: An algorithm for minimizing firewall policies. In: IEEE INFOCOM 2008-The 27th Conference on Computer Communications, pp. 176–180. IEEE (2008)
7. Liu, A., Torng, E., Meiners, C.: Optimization of network firewall policies using ordered sets and directed acyclical graphs. In: Proceedings of IEEE Internet Management Conference (2005)
8. Marchetto, G., Sisto, R., Valenza, F., Yusupov, J., Ksentini, A.: A formal approach to verify connectivity and optimize VNF placement in industrial networks. IEEE Trans. Industr. Inf. **17**, 1515–1525 (2021)
9. Miano, S., Bertrone, M., Risso, F., Bernal, M.V., Lu, Y., Pi, J.: Securing linux with a faster and scalable iptables. ACM SIGCOMM Comput. Commun. Rev. **49**(3), 2–17 (2019)
10. Rubio, J.E., Alcaraz, C., Roman, R., Lopez, J.: Current cyber-defense trends in industrial control systems. Comput. Secur. **87**, 101561 (2019)
11. Seno, L., Cheminod, M., Bertolotti, I.C., Durante, L., Valenzano, A.: Improving performance and cyber-attack resilience in multi-firewall industrial networks. In: 2022 IEEE 18th International Conference on Factory Communication Systems (WFCS), pp. 1–8. IEEE (2022)

12. Wollschlaeger, M., Sauter, T., Jasperneite, J.: The future of industrial communication: automation networks in the era of the internet of things and industry 4.0. IEEE Indust. Electron. Mag. **11**(1), 17–27 (2017)
13. Yan, G., Chen, S., Eidenbenz, S.: Dynamic balancing of packet filtering workloads on distributed firewalls. In: 2008 16th Interntional Workshop on Quality of Service, pp. 209–218. IEEE (2008)
14. Yuhong, W., Xiangdong, H.: Industrial internet security protection based on an industrial firewall. In: IEEE International Conference on Artificial Intelligence and Computer Applications (ICAICA), pp. 239–247 (2021). https://doi.org/10.1109/ICAICA52286.2021.9497973
15. Zunino, C., Valenzano, A., Obermaisser, R., Petersen, S.: Factory communications at the dawn of the fourth industrial revolution. Comput. Stand. Interfaces **71**, 103433 (2020)

6G Technologies: Key Features, Challenges, Security and Privacy Issues

Narges Arastouei(✉)

Chair of Mobile Business & Multilateral Security, Goethe University Frankfurt Am Main, 60323 Frankfurt, Germany

aNarges.arastouei@m-chair.de

Abstract. This paper provides a comprehensive overview of the sixth-generation (6G) networks. 6G with cheap and fast internet technology, connectivity without distances between people, and incredible terabit transmission speed will complete a wireless network without limitations and maximize data throughput and IOPS. The wireless evolution from "connected things" to "connected intelligence" will be dramatically reshaped by the 6G. The objective of this paper is to provide an overview of the benefits of 6G in mobile and satellite communications, as well as the challenges and potential solutions arising from the new networks and their key technologies. One of the critical challenges is the provision of secure and intelligent 6G networks, but multidisciplinary challenges such as policy, technology and ethics should also be considered.

Keywords: 6G · AI/ML · DLT · Quantum computing · Safety/Privacy · Terahertz Communications

1 Introduction

By the end of 2025, it is estimated that more than half of the world's population will have access to 5G networks [1, 2]. While these networks are still being deployed around the world, research and development for 6G networks have already started, as the bandwidth of 5G networks is insufficient to accommodate new technologies such as holographic apps, and the increasing popularity of wearables and mobile video services is further straining bandwidth [3–7]. 6G, integrated with 5G and satellite networks for global coverage, is expected to radically depart from traditional wireless mobile communications [1] and will enable the synergy between AI and mobile networks to be maximized. In addition, the introduction of 6G will mark the transition to a radio-optical system that uses both electronic and phonetic technologies. It has high-speed broadband signals transmitted through the air via high-speed optical fiber to transfer the secured information from transmitters to destinations. Moreover, with cheap and fast internet technology, connectivity without distances between people, and incredible terabit transmission speed, 6G is expected to complete the wireless network without limitations and maximize data throughput and IOPS (Input-Output Operations per Second) [2, 6, 8]. The wireless evolution from "connected things" to "connected intelligence" will be dramatically reshaped by the 6G.

A. Skarmeta et al. (Eds.): CyberSec4Europe 2022, CCIS 1807, pp. 94–109, 2023.
https://doi.org/10.1007/978-3-031-36096-1_7

Since the beginning of 2020, there has been an increase in research on 6G. Large companies such as Facebook and Verizon, as well as political and academic institutions such as the Chinese Ministry of Science and Technology and the European Commission, are discussing how the mobile networks of the future can be realized. Not only new technologies such as Holographic-type Communication (HTC) and the tactile Internet with their higher bandwidth demands have to be accommodated in the new networks, but also the increasingly emerging cloud computing [2, 6]. Ethical issues such as privacy preservation must also be addressed, as the risk of misuse and loss of personal data increases as the physical and digital worlds become interconnected [9]. In addition, the development of 6G networks must aim at a smart, green, sustainable, and secure system [6].

Figure 1 shows the different communication generations (from 1G to 6G) from different aspects at a glance. In this paper, a broad overview of 6G networks is given. The aim is to discuss the benefits of 6G in mobile communications as well as the challenges and potential solutions arising from the new networks and their key technologies [1, 10, 11].

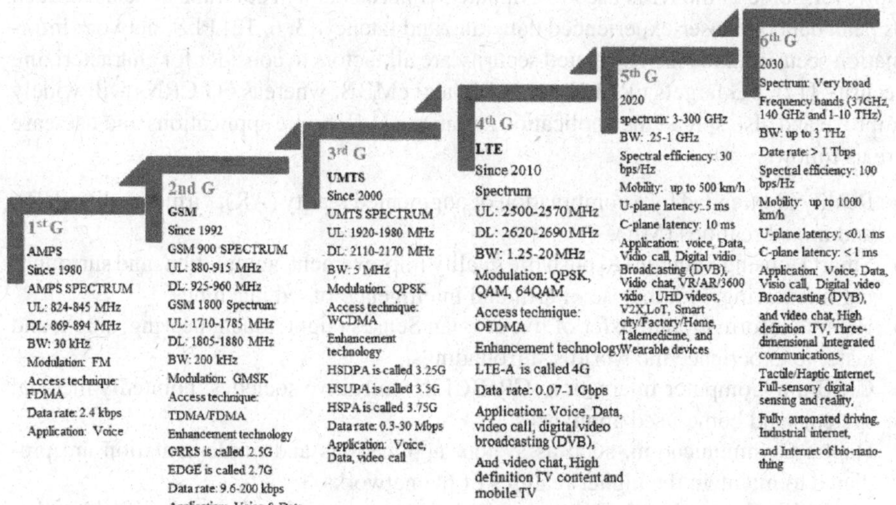

Fig. 1. Different generations of communications

2 Key Features and Use-Cases for Future 6G Networks

The first 6G network is expected to be deployed in 2030, possibly earlier. It will need to meet remarkably high demands in terms of latency [2], reliability, mobility [5], and security. The new 6G technology is characterized by a shift to a radio-optical system taking advantage of both electronic and photonic technologies, as well as maximized synergy between AI and mobile networks. Further characteristics that distinguish 6G from other network technologies are the ubiquitous 3D coverage of the surface of Earth, a smart compute-connect entity, as well as its higher intelligence and sustainability.

The advantages of 6G are as follows:

- Protect your mobile and tremendously secure your data
- Provide a real online gaming experience and reduce the lag while gaming
- The extremely fast data transmission
- Super-fast streaming with no buffering and highly efficient
- Record calls and forward them smartly to email also forward calls to other numbers
- Provide intelligent batteries and Improved storage capacity
- High mobile TV resolution
- Increase the availability of social network
- Control natural disaster quickly
- Satellite-to-satellite communication for the event of mankind
- Create smart homes, cities, and village

New KPIs measured in 6G network performance are reliability, signal bandwidth, positioning accuracy, coverage, timeliness, security and privacy, as well as capital and operational expenditure. For instance, the peak data rate of 6G is anticipated 1–10 Tbps with optical frequency band and THz assistance, whereas this data rate in 5G is 20 Gbps. However, some of the KPIs used to evaluate 5G networks will continue to be used, such as peak data rate, user-experienced data rate, and latency [3, 6, 12] PLS, network information security, and AI/ML-related security are all factors to consider for characterizing security [12]. 5G targets uRLLC, umMTC, and eMBB, whereas 6G CRNs will widely improve and also spread the application situations [14]. Some applications and use-case are as follows:

- Reality is extended by a combination of augmented reality (AR), virtual reality (VR), and mixed realities (MR).
- Smart Housing Societies to push life quality improvement, automation, and surrounding monitoring with the use of artificial intelligence-based machines.
- Remote Information transfer of five Human Senses (sight, touch, hearing, smell, and taste) to experience the world's surroundings.
- CR Brain-Computer Interaction (CR-BCI in innovative societies, pointedly medical systems and home-used appliances.
- Haptic Communication, such as system applications and implementation are predicted to maintain the higher features of 6G networks.
- Internet of Everything (IoE) stands for autonomous coordination and unified integration among many elements (computing elements); people, objects, devices or sensors, and the internet using data and processing.
- AI-based manufacturing and industrial intelligence automation [13].
- Digital Twin technology, involves the creation of comprehensive and detailed virtual copies of physical objects.
- Intelligent healthcare systems by innovation in VR, XR, MR, AR, mobile edge computing, telepresence, holographic, and artificial intelligence [3, 13].

2.1 Key Features for Future 6G

The future 6G networks will be defined by key technologies such as AI, terahertz (THz), Blockchain, three-dimensional networking, wireless optical communication, and other potential technology which we discuss in detail.

2.1.1 AI Technology

AI and ML play a key role in 6G networks [6, 15, 16]. AI technologies can be utilized to enable 6G wireless systems to be in Autonomy [16, 17]. Edge Intelligence (EI) is also partly based on AI technology and can be applied to use cases such as the automation of the management and orchestration tasks of the virtual resources in NG-RAN architecture [6, 18]. It is crucial to offer AI technology to end-users in an AI-as-a-service paradigm [6]. AI provides intelligence for wireless networks by simulating some pointing at specific human processes and intelligent behaviors. In addition, autonomous applications such as autonomous aerial vehicles and autonomous robots are used in 6G [7, 19]. AI Applications in 6G are capable of handling both the physical layer and network layers with unsupervised learning algorithms. These algorithms can be used in routing, traffic control, parameter prediction, resource allocations, etc. To put in a nutshell, we have

- Supervised learning to train the machine model using labeled training data.
- Unsupervised learning to be leveraged to look for invisible patterns without using labels.
- Model-driven approach to be used in Artificial Neural Networks (ANN) with prior information based on professional knowledge.
- Deep reinforcement learning (DRL) for Markov decision models to select the next action based on the state transition models
- Explainable AI to build trust between humans and machines [7].
- Federated Learning (FL) to develop a machine learning model with training data remaining distributed at clients to protect data owners' privacy [7, 16], and [20].

2.1.2 Terahertz Communications

The THz spectrum is expected to provide extra high bandwidth [2, 13, 21]. Not only do they work with smaller antenna sizes, but they also are not limited by atmospheric effects either. Applications of Terahertz limit the use of THz for short-distance transmission such as indoor communications [7].

2.1.3 Blockchain-Based Networks

Blockchain technologies have rapidly grown both in the industry and academic institutions, because of decentralized transparency, security, and privacy. Blockchain can provide a more flexible, secure, and efficient information infrastructure in 6G networks. New types of wireless communication such as Visible Light Communications (VLC) [7], which implement transceivers with the help of illumination sources, and Optical wireless communications (OWC), with advantages in deployment scenarios such as smart transportation systems and airplane passenger lighting, also show considerable potential for future networks [6, 16].

2.1.4 Satellite Communication

By integrating with satellite communication (i.e. earth stations communicate with each other via satellites), 6G can provide localization services, broadcast, Internet connectivity, and weather information to cellular users [2, 6]. Therefore, enablers with new spectrum technologies will play a crucial role in supporting 6G key; such as mmWave [1], THz communications, and also softwarization and virtualization. Other enablers are new air interfaces technologies such as massive MIMO, IRS, and CoMP, as well as new architecture like 3D coverage using integrating large-scale satellite constellations and new technologies [6].

2.1.5 Index Modulation

Index Modulation (IM) has high spectral- and power efficiency due to its idea of sending extra information through the indexed resource entities. IM used in 6G Networks are as follows:

- Time Division Duplex (TDD)
- The Orthogonal Frequency Division Multiplexing (OFDM) due to its high spectral efficiency
- SD-IM Technique or Spatial Modulation (SM), without inter-antenna synchronization and interference, and with low complexity in the receiver. The spare information bits can trigger the transmit antennas.
- CD-IM Technique, by changing the property of the radio frequency (RF) environment due to employing RF mirrors or electronic switches [7].

2.1.6 Full-Duplex and In-Band Full-Duplex (IBFD)

As a full-duplex and in-band full-duplex (IBFD) technologies improve communication efficiency by considering Frequency-(FDD) and Time-Division-Duplex (TDD) in scheduling algorithms. Therefore, devices can transmit and receive a signal in the same frequency band.

2.1.7 Holographic Radio

To develop holographic radio, one of the most promising interference-exploiting technologies, unwanted signals can be useful.

2.1.8 The NIB Technique or Network in Box

The NIB technique or Network in-box needs to be taken care of due to a device that can provide seamless connectivity between different services [7].

3 Top Challenges of 6G Network

The 6G, the next-generation advanced mobile communications system, is expected to integrate mobile and AI networks and to work as a huge supercomputer. Different aspects such as distributed communication, computing, and storage will be combined in this system [6]. Since the networks will need to meet higher demands than their predecessors, particularly in terms of bandwidth, privacy preservation, and sustainability, questions on factors such as safety and energy efficiency need to be solved [22].

3.1 Security and Privacy

In the Evolution of the mobile security landscape from 4G towards 6G, LTE, LTE advanced technology used in 4G makes MAC layer threats and attacks. Similarly, in 5G with NR, SDN, NFV, and NS technologies, we can see critical infrastructure threats, SDN/NFV threats, and cloud computing-related threats. In 2030 at 6G networks with new technologies (i.e. AI/ML, Blockchain, VLC, THz, quantum computing), there would be AI/Ml-based intelligent attacks, zero-day attacks, quantum attacks, PHR layer attacks for VLC, THz, etc. The privacy types in 6G networks (like Data, image, personal behavior, communication, location, and actions) have to be protected as described in Fig. 2. We will discuss security in different dimensions; Platform and architecture, applications, and technologies. Ensuring the confidentiality, integrity, and availability of data through security design can serve as a basis for privacy preserving.

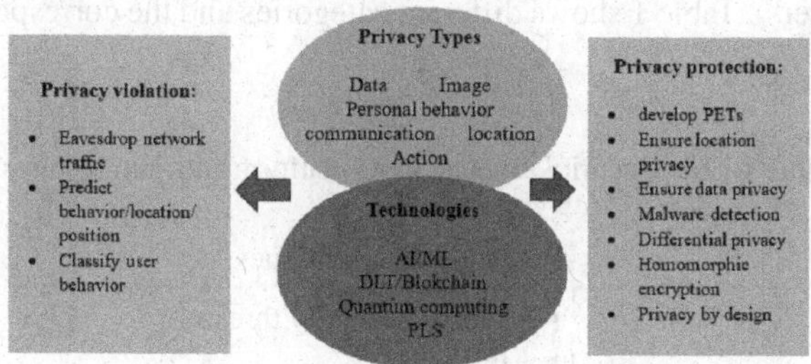

Fig. 2. Summary of 6G privacy [12]

3.1.1 Security Impact on 6G Platforms and Architectures

Due to the interlink of physical and digital worlds in 6G, it is necessary to address safety and security issues, especially in platforms and architectures. Since it is expected to be linked to mobile technology (stronger mobile than now), not only private security but also national security play a key role in insufficient trust models, clear practices and rules.

3.1.1.1 Connection and Network Layer

The increasingly widespread use of IoT technology, in particular, raises the demand for more network access points, network capacity and service capabilities, which in turn creates a need for reliable trust models [2]. This need is amplified by the rise of cloud and edge computing. Also, a new routing solution must be developed because Border Gateway Protocol (BDP) more efficient than currently used [9].

In order to achieve user trust, it is mandatory to aim for a holistic security approach. Classic cryptographic methods must be enhanced and end-to-end security must be provided. Physical layer security is one method that can complement classic cryptographic methods [9, 23]. Another promising approach is using AI for end-to-end security. Other ways to achieve this include the combination and harmonization of technologies such as SDN and NFV [9, 15].

A new alternative for trust verification is Distributed Ledgers (DL). Current DL-related research challenges include improvement of DL privacy, trust management for the wide area across multiple domains, and a specific DL for the 6G mobile network [9, 23]. Execution offloading is another promising method for enhancing privacy preservation. However, it might increase the risk of data abuse and data loss. In order to counter this, the following methods could be used: authentication of remote endpoints, certification of the platforms, support of remote attestation, and support of secure properties in spite of insecure execution platforms [9]. As far as ML is concerned, Federated Learning technology can be used in order to pre-process the data before distribution, thus omitting any information that cannot be distributed legally [6].

To summarize, the development of huge connections in 6G architecture and platforms raises security and privacy issues. These issues are defined in different categories; orchestration, intelligence network management, edge intelligence, cloudification, specialized 6G networks, intelligence radio [12], RAN-core convergence, and end-users (terminals and users). Table 1 shows different categories and the corresponding security issues.

Table 1. Key security aspects of 6G platform and architectures

6G Architecture	Potential Security Issues
Orchestration Intelligence network management	• Open API security threats • AI/Ml attacks • Security threats with closed loop network automation
Edge intelligence Cloudification	• Data privacy threats • AI/ML attacks • Security threat on cloud • Security threat edge
Specialized subnetworks	• Trust violations • AI/ML attacks • PHY security threats
Intelligence radio RAN core convergence	• AI/ML attacks • PHY layer security threats
Devices Consumer or End user	• DDoS attack on devices • User privacy threats

3.1.1.2 Physical Layer Security (PLS)

PLS techniques have a very important role in 6G architecture and are defined in four techniques. PLS techniques to improve confidentiality and conduct lightweight authentication and key exchange depend on the unique physical features of the random and noisy wireless channels,

- Terahertz Technology: Data transmission exposure, eavesdropping, and access control assaults are all possible with THz communications. The potential solution for the

challenge is to characterise the channel's backscatter to discover some eavesdroppers, to improve information security. In order to investigate THz propagation multipath and path-loss, a device fingerprint in a THz time-domain spectroscopy setup may be developed.
- Visible Light Communication (VLC) technology: Eavesdropping attacks are common on VLC systems. Therefore designing PLS mechanisms play a key role, since VLC have fast data rates, a lot of available spectrum, and robustness against interference. Designing the linear precoding in terms of the reachable secrecy rate enriches the secrecy performance of a multiple-input multiple-output (MIMO) VLC system. The transmitted signal is subjected to a peak-power limit, and only discrete input signalling schemes are employed. To improve the secrecy of a VLC system, a jamming receiver with the spread spectrum watermarking scheme (a watermark-based blind PLS) were combined.
- Reconfigurable Intelligent Surface (RIS): RIS is a software-controlled meta-surface that can dynamically regulate their reflective coefficients, allowing them to control the amplitude and/or phase shift of reflected signals and thus improve wireless propagation performance. The reflected signals can be added coherently at the intended receiver to improve the quality of the received signal, or destructively at a non-desired receiver to improve security, by intelligently managing the phase shifts of RIS [13, 24].
- Molecular Communication (MC): Molecules in an aqueous environment or chemical signals are a communicating way in healthcare 6G-applications such as wearable body sensors and telemedicine. Security and privacy issues in the communication, authentication and encryption processes in sensitive data have to be addressed at the beginning of its actual development by calculating the secrecy capacity, i.e. the number of secure symbols that may be sent via a diffusion-based channel [13].

3.1.2 Security Impact on 6G Applications

The identified important applications and use-cases in 6G (summarized in Table 2) [12, 25] have varying security requirements and implementation issues in three levels of requirement/impact: low (L), medium (M), and high (H) (L) (see Table 3, L in orange color, M in yellow, H in red). Because of their essential nature and also the need for a high level of trust, the 6G applications and services have highly challenging performance requirements in addition to extremely rigorous security standards.

3.1.3 Security Impact on 6G Technologies

The new technologies used in 6G (such as distributed ledger technology (DLT), distributed and scalable AI/ML and quantum computing, and some PLS related topics (THz, VLC, RIS, MC)) mitigate security threats [12].

3.1.3.1 Distributed Ledger Technology (DLT)

DLT and 6G are expected to operate together. Blockchain technology, as the most attractive among DLTs, can integrate various advantages in 6G technology with privacy and security [13]; such as non-reputation, disintermediation, and proof of provenance, immutability, pseudonymity, and integrity. Blockchain can handle trust elements (e.g. immutable records for AI data integrity and distributed trust across different stakeholders

Table 2. Key security requirements of prominent 6G applications

<table>
<tr><th>6G Application</th><th>Requirements</th></tr>
<tr><td>Holographic Telepresence</td><td>• Reduce operational cost
• Diversity of devices
• High Bandwidth
• High Privacy</td></tr>
<tr><td>Digital Twin</td><td>• Secure Communication
• High scalability
• IoT data security
• AI security</td></tr>
<tr><td>Industry</td><td>• Reduced operational cost
• Interoperability
• Real-time Operation
• High Scalability
• IoT data security</td></tr>
<tr><td>Connected Autonomous Vehicle (CAV)</td><td rowspan="2">• Reduced operational cost
• Diversity of devices
• Interoperability
• Real-time Operation
• High Scalability</td></tr>
<tr><td>UAV based mobility</td></tr>
<tr><td>Intelligent Healthcare</td><td>• Ethical AI security
• Interoperability
• Real-time Operation
• High Privacy
• Scalable IoT data security</td></tr>
<tr><td>Smart Grid 2</td><td>• Grid attacks
• Scalable IoT security
• Physical Tampering
• Intermittent Connectivity</td></tr>
<tr><td>Extended Reality</td><td>• Reduced operational cost
• Diversity of devices
• Limited Resources
• High Privacy</td></tr>
</table>

[12, 15] and privacy by combining the communication process, access control, and verification. However, Blockchain may have unintended security impacts on 6G networks, as described in Table 4. As potential solutions for the security issues are:

- Assuring the smart contract's accuracy
- Testing functionality, before deploying a smart contract across thousands of Blockchain nodes
- Use suitable access control and authentication techniques to identify malicious bots and AI-agent-based Blockchain nodes

Table 3. 6G applications: security requirement and possible challenges

Potential 6G Applications (Security Requirement (SR) and Implementation Challenges(IC))		UAV based mobility	Holographic Telepresence	Extended Reality	Connected Autonomous Vehicles	Smart Grid 2.0	Industry 5.0	Hyper-Intelligent Healthcare	Digital Twin
SR	Ultra-lightweight security	L	M	H	M	H	M	H	M
	Zero-touch security	H	L	M	M	M	H	M	H
	High privacy	L	H	H	H	M	L	H	L
	Proactive security	M	L	L	H	H	H	M	L
	Security via Edge	H	M	H	H	L	H	H	M
	Domain specific security	M	L	M	H	H	H	H	M
IC	Limited resources	H	H	H	L	H	H	H	L
	Diversity of devices	M	M	M	M	L	H	H	M
	High Mobility	H	L	M	H	L	H	M	L
	Physical Tempering	M	M	H	M	H	M	M	L
	Grid Attacks	H	L	L	H	H	L	L	H
	Intermittent Connectivity	M	L	L	L	H	M	M	M
	Localized environment	L	M	L	M	L	L	H	L
	Lack of security standards	L	M	H	L	L	H	M	L
	E2E security orchestration	H	H	H	H	L	M	H	H
	Energy Efficiency	H	H	H	M	M	H	H	M

- incorporating additional privacy preservation mechanisms to mitigate privacy leakages (as privacy by design) and TEE can be into Blockchain-based 6G services
- selecting the appropriate Blockchain/DLT type for the 6G application and services to mitigate certain attacks' impact

3.1.3.2 Quantum Computing

Quantum computing is expected to be used in 6G communication networks for security vulnerability detection, mitigation, and prevention [1, 12, 26]. Post-quantum safe cryptography, quantum-resistant networking hardware, quantum key distribution (QKD), and quantum-based attacks will be the advantage of quantum computing in 6G, especially IoT networks and devices (as shown in Fig. 3). Incorporating post-quantum crypto solutions that are resistant to quantum-based attacks into IoT devices is a hot challenge, in which IoT needs lightweight cryptographic solutions. The Oblivious Transfer (OT) is incapable of retaining quantum information since any leakage might jeopardize the entire two-party communication system. Quantum computers feature a no-cloning characteristic that makes maintaining an exact copy of a quantum state difficult [15].

Quantum-resistant technologies and encryption solutions have previously been investigated by researchers. Lattice computational issues perform better in IoT devices in the current environment. They fit better in 32-bit architecture due to the smaller key length. However, due to performance and memory restrictions, as well as communication capabilities, these categories are still being developed and are suggested for IoT devices.

3.1.3.3 Distributed and Scalable AI/ML

The relation between security and AI is shown in Fig. 4. The security and data privacy issues in 6G will be more challenging when the number of smart devices is increasing and tracking every move of a person with a lack of transparency about what is exactly collected. Therefore, Zero-touch Network & Service Management (ZSM), defined as autonomous networks performing Self-X activities without the need for human

Table 4. Key security issues of Blockchain in 6G services

Potential security issue	Description
Majority attack	A group of malicious users could capture the 51% or more nodes and take over the control of the Blockchain
Double spending attack	A user spends a single token multiple time
Re-entrancy attack	A smart contract invokes another iteratively and the invocation of the second contract is malicious
Sybil attacks	An attacker attempts to take over the peer network by conceiving fake identities explicitly
Broken authentication and access control	potential vulnerabilities and issues in the implementation of authentication and access control mechanisms
Security misconfiguration	use of insecure security configurations or outdated configurations that make the system vulnerable to attack
Privacy leakages	vulnerable to leakage privacy of transaction data, smart contract logic, and user privacy
Other Vulnerabilities	Other security threats such as destroyable contracts, exception disorder, call stack vulnerability, bad randomness, underflow/overflow errors, and unbounded computational power-intensive operation

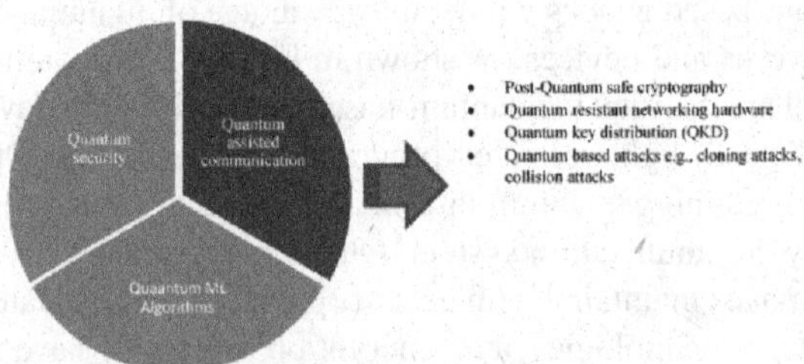

Fig. 3. Role of quantum computing in 6G [12]

involvement in 6G networks., are very important. On the one hand, Differential Privacy (DP), which considers privacy in the context of statistical and machine learning analysis, is another emerging privacy-preserving technology that will likely feature in future 6G wireless applications [12, 15]. On the other hand, the factors such as the ML-components trustworthiness, visibility, AI-Ethics and -Liability, scalability and feasibility, and model- and data resilience are the AI/ML challenges in 6G networks. AI and machine learning will make the 6G intelligence network management system vulnerable to AI/ML-related attacks.

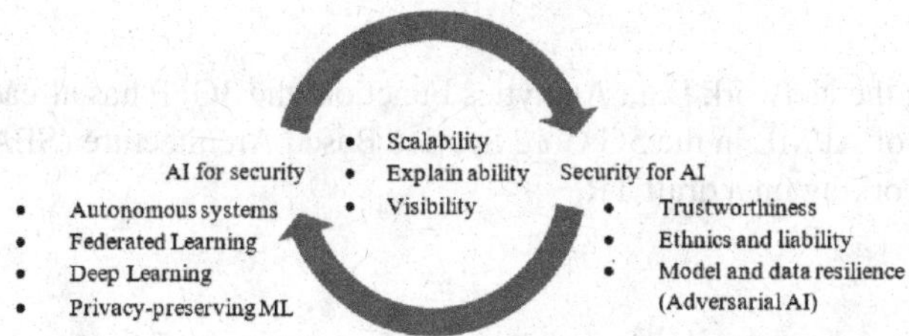

Fig. 4. 6G and AI in security aspect [12]

The compromise of AI frameworks to exploit flaws in such artefacts or traditional attack vectors against their software, firmware, and hardware parts is a serious concern at the AI middleware layer. API-based attacks are another form of attack in which an adversary requests and attacks an API of an ML model to get predictions on input feature vectors which have model inversion, model extraction, and membership inference attacks as a result of it. The potential solution for these challenges are as follows:

- Adversarial training and defensive distillation
- Input validation and control of the information (Provided by ML APIs to the algorithms against evasion attacks and adversarial attacks.)
- Protection of data integrity and authentication of the data origin
- Input validation and moving target defense against poisoning attacks.
- Control the information provided by ML APIs to the algorithms (i.e. add noise to ML prediction to prevent model inversion attacks)

3.2 Standardization in Security and Privacy

The standardization for 6G security and privacy discuses in architecture, technical specification and core protocols, risks and recommendations (see Fig. 5) and covers through different standards and struggles to work more and precise to cover all aspect of 6G Networks.

3.2.1 ETSI

ETSI has created various Industry Specification Groups (ISG) to look into 5G component technologies including NFV (ETSI NFV), AI, and network automation. Also, ETSI ISG ENI was established to develop a Cognitive Network Management architecture that would leverage AI methods and context-aware rules to adapt offered services.

3.2.2 ITU-T

The ITU-T Focus Group on Machine Learning for Future Networks (FG-ML5G) has been created by ITU to work on technical standards for machine learning for future networks, such as interfaces, network topologies, protocols, algorithms, and data formats.

3.2.3 3GPP

By establishing the Network Data Analytics Function, the 3GPP has already addressed the application of AI/ML in the 5G Core Service Based Architecture (SBA). Presently, 3GPP SA3 is working on a draft TR.

3.2.4 NIST

The National Institute of Standards and Technology is in charge of standardizing post-quantum cryptography methods.

3.2.5 IETF

The IETF Security Automation and Continuous Monitoring (SACM) Architecture RFC specifies an architecture for a cooperative SACM ecosystem.

3.2.6 5G PPP

The 5G PPP Security Work Group was formed as a collaborative effort to address 5G security threats and issues, as well as provide insights on 5G security and how it should be addressed.

3.2.7 NGMN

The NGMN 5G End-to-End Architecture Framework v4.3 (2020) lays out the requirements for end-to-end framework capabilities, including security, in terms of network entities and functions.

3.2.8 IEEE

The IEEE P1915.1 Security Standard for Software Defined Networking and Network Function Virtualization (SDN/NFV) aims to offer a framework for constructing and operating secure SDN/NFV environments [12].

3.3 High Bandwidth Demands and Accessibility

Since new technologies like holographic apps and the ongoing increase in connected things will place high demands on 6G networks, it is necessary to find ways to extend network coverage and increase efficiency. This includes researching solutions to increase energy efficiencies, such as low energy utilization and elongated battery charge life duration. Cost efficiency is another vital factor, particularly in network deployment and expansion. This is especially crucial in covering more remote areas. On top of that, high intelligence applications can hurt user costs. Since new technologies like holographic apps and the ongoing increase in connected things will place high demands on 6G networks, it is necessary to find ways to extend network coverage and increase efficiency. This includes researching solutions to increase energy efficiencies, such as low energy utilization and elongated battery charge life duration. Cost efficiency is another vital

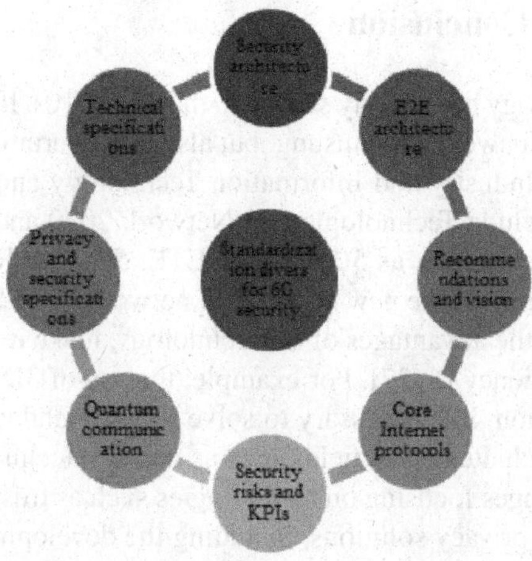

Fig. 5. 6G Security Standardization landscape

factor, particularly in network deployment and expansion. This is especially crucial in covering more remote areas. On top of that, high intelligence applications can hurt user costs.

One way to improve the efficiency of wireless communication systems is the exploitation of the high-frequency spectrum. Bandwidth can be broadened with new spectrum technologies such as mmWave (millimetre wave) technologies [2, 6, 23]. However, mmWave can cause severe non-linear distortions and has a limited transmission range, therefore it must be used with caution and complemented by another technology. One possible addition to mmWave is THz, which has a broader transmission range but is prone to high path loss. As far as energy efficiency is concerned, different wireless charging techniques should be compared. Furthermore, network efficiency can be increased with the use of NG-RAN architecture. Whereas it is expected to support a massive amount of RAN slice subnets, further research is needed to create a virtualized and slicing-aware RAN for 6G mobile networks. Blockchain technology can also increase network efficiency.

As far as network coverage is concerned, non-terrestrial areas, in particular, 6G networks have to be deployed as an ISTN (integrated space and terrestrial network). This network is predicted to carry with it the ground-based layer constructed by terrestrial base stations, the airborne layer empowered by HAP and UAV, and therefore the space borne layer implemented by satellites. So as to expand network reach, LEO satellites are used successfully. Additionally, the reusable rocket Falcon 9 developed by SpaceX helps decrease launching costs for LEO satellites, which may be helpful in increasing network coverage. Some alternatives to LEO satellites are HAP (high altitude aerial platform), which has lower maintenance costs and therefore the possibility of repairing, and UAV (unmanned aerial vehicles), which are more flexible than the satellites and offer the chance of re-planning the RAN dynamically [6].

4 Discussion and Conclusion

Research on 6G technology has already started in the late 2010s. It is not only conducted by companies such as Huawei and Samsung, but also by governmental institutions such as China's Ministry of Industry and Information Technology and the EU [1]. Specialized research groups include Technologies for Network 2030 and the Next Generation Mobile Networks. Projects such as 5G-COMPLETE, 5G-CLARITY, and ARIADNE aim to explore the potential of the new beyond 5G networks. Further research is needed in order to fully exploit the advantages of 6G technology, make it widely accessible and increase its energy efficiency [6, 27]. For example, the use of 3D networks needs to be researched [1]. In addition, it is necessary to solve security and privacy issues, considering multidisciplinary challenges in fields such as politics, technology and ethics. This leads to research challenges focusing on technologies such as trust networking, security architectures, PLS, and privacy solutions, including the development of frameworks to understand the trade-offs between privacy and trust in 6G systems. For these research challenges, legal factors, such as regulation and standardization of privacy and personal identity preservation, as well as workers' rights must be taken into account. Protection against malicious cyber activities, which will be more likely to directly endanger property and human life, is of particular interest [9].

Many research papers focus on one specific aspect of 6G networks. The topics covered in these papers include possible 6G use cases, possible technological trends, and ML technologies to be used in 6G networks. The key technologies discussed in the current 6G research include THz, AI, green networks, use cases, ML, and VLC. A holistic overview of security and privacy challenges and potential solutions is discussed. In order to provide secure and efficient 6G networks, both general and more specialized studies must be conducted so existing key technologies can be refined and new enabling technologies can be developed. That way, the idea of 6G as a supercomputer-like network can be realized in the next years, which will not only benefit the industry but academia and private users as well.

References

1. Alsharif, M.H., Kelechi, A.H., Albreem, M.A., Chaudhry, S.A.: Zia, M.S., Kim, S.: Sixth generation (6G) wireless networks: vision, research activities, challenges and potential solutions. Symmetry **12**(4), 676 (2020)
2. Shahraki, A., Abbasi, M., Piran, M., Taherkordi, A.: A comprehensive survey on 6G networks: applications, core services, enabling technologies, and future challenges. arXiv preprint arXiv: 2101.12475 (2021)
3. Akyildiz, I.F., Kak, A., Nie, S.: 6G and beyond: the future of wireless communications systems. IEEE Access **8**, 133995–134030 (2020)
4. Han, B., Jiang, W., Habibi, M.A., Schotten, H.D.: An abstracted survey on 6G: Drivers, requirements, efforts, and enablers. arXiv preprint arXiv.2101.01062 (2021)
5. Ikram, M., Sultan, K., Lateef, M.F., Alqadami, A.S.: A road towards 6G communication—a review of 5G antennas, arrays, and wearable devices, Electronics **11**(1), 169 (2022)
6. Jiang, W., Han, B., Habibi, M.A., Schotten, H.D.: The road towards 6G: a comprehensive survey. IEEE Open J. Commun. Soc. **2**, 334–366 (2021)

7. Zhao, Y., Zhao, Zhai, W., Sun, S., Niyato, D., Lam, K.-Y.: A survey of 6G wireless communications: emerging technologies. In: Arai, K. (ed.) FICC 2021. AISC, vol. 1363, pp. 150–170. Springer, Cham (2021). https://doi.org/10.1007/978-3-030-73100-7_12
8. Wang, J., Ling, X., Le, Y., Huang, Y., You, X.: Blockchain-enabled wireless communications: a new paradigm towards 6G. Natl. Sci. Rev. **8**(9), nwab069 (2021)
9. Ylianttila, M., et al.: 6G white paper: research challenges for trust, security and privacy. arXiv 2020, arXiv preprint arXiv:2004.11665 (2020)
10. Alsabah, M., et al.: 6G wireless communications networks: a comprehensive survey. IEEE Access **9**, 148191–148243 (2021)
11. Solyman, A.A., Yahya, K.: Key performance requirement of future next wireless networks (6G). Bull. Electr. Eng. Inform. **10**(6), 3249–3255 (2021)
12. Porambage, P., Gür, G., Osorio, D.P.M., Liyanage, M., Gurtov, A., Ylianttila, M.: The roadmap to 6G security and privacy. IEEE Open J. Commun. Soc. **2**, 1094–1122 (2021)
13. Aslam, M.M., Du, L., Zhang, X., Chen, Y., Ahmed, Z., Qureshi, B.: Sixth generation (6G) cognitive radio network (CRN) application, requirements, security issues, and key challenges. Wirel. Commun. Mob. Comput. **2021** (2021)
14. He, J., Yang, K., Chen, H.-H.: 6G cellular networks and connected autonomous vehicles. IEEE Netw. **35**(4), 255–261 (2020)
15. Nguyen, V.-L., Lin, P.-C., Cheng, B.-C., Hwang, R.-H., Lin, Y.-D.: Security and privacy for 6G: a survey on prospective technologies and challenges. IEEE Commun. Surv. Tutor. **23**(4), 2384–2428 (2021)
16. Siriwardhana, Y., Porambage, P., Liyanage, M., Ylianttila, M.: AI and 6G security: opportunities and challenges. In: 2021 Joint European Conference on Networks and Communications & 6G Summit (EuCNC/6G Summit), pp. 616–621. IEEE (2021)
17. Raj, V., CA, A.: Understanding the future communication: 5G to 6G. Int. Res. J. Adv. Sci. Hub **3**, 17–23 (2021)
18. Yang, B., et al.: Edge intelligence for autonomous driving in 6G wireless system: design challenges and solutions. IEEE Wirel. Commun. **28**(2), 40–47 (2021)
19. Nguyen, D.C., et al.: 6G internet of things: a comprehensive survey. IEEE Internet Things J. (2021)
20. Yang, Z., Chen, M., Wong, K.-K., Poor, H.V., Cui, S.: Federated learning for 6G: applications, challenges, and opportunities. Engineering (2021)
21. Slalmi, A., Chaibi, H., Chehri, A., Saadane, R., Jeon, G.: Toward 6G: understanding network requirements and key performance indicators. Trans. n Emerg. Telecommun. Technol. **32**(3), e4201 (2021)
22. Matinmikko-Blue, M., Yrjölä, S., Ahokangas, P., Ojutkangas, K., Rossi, E.: 6G and the UN SDGs: where is the connection?. Wirel. Pers. Commun. **121**(2), 1339–1360 (2021)
23. Ozpoyraz, B., Dogukan, A.T., Gevez, Y., Altun, U., Basar, E.: Deep learning-aided 6G wireless networks: a comprehensive survey of revolutionary PHY architectures. arXiv preprint arXiv: 2201.03866 (2022)
24. Basharat, S., Hassan, S.A., Pervaiz, H., Mahmood, A., Ding, Z., Gidlund, M.: Reconfigurable intelligent surfaces: potentials, applications, and challenges for 6G wireless networks. IEEE Wirel. Commun. (2021)
25. De Alwis, C., et al.: Survey on 6G frontiers: trends, applications, requirements, technologies and future research. IEEE Open J. Commun. Soc. **2**, 836–886 (2021)
26. Tariq, F., Khandaker, M.R., Wong, K.-K., Imran, M.A., Bennis, M., Debbah, M.: A speculative study on 6G. IEEE Wirel. Commun. **27**(4), 118–125 (2020)
27. Letaief, K.B., Shi, Y., Lu, J., Lu, J.: Edge artificial intelligence for 6G: vision, enabling technologies, and applications. IEEE J. Sel. Areas Commun. **40**(1), 5–36 (2021)

Cybersecurity and Society

Building Cross-language Corpora for Human Understanding of Privacy Policies

Francesco Ciclosi[1(✉)], Silvia Vidor[1], and Fabio Massacci[1,2]

[1] University of Trento, Trento, Italy
{francesco.ciclosi,silvia.vidor}@unitn.it, f.massacci@vu.nl
[2] Vrije Universiteit Amsterdam, Amsterdam, The Netherlands

Abstract. Making sure that users understand privacy policies that impact them is a key challenge for a real GDPR deployment. Research studies are mostly carried in English, but in Europe and elsewhere, users speak a language that is not English. Replicating studies in different languages requires the availability of comparable cross-language privacy policies corpora. This work provides a methodology for building comparable cross-language in a national language and a reference study language. We provide an application example of our methodology comparing English and Italian extending the corpus of one of the first studies about users understanding of technical terms in privacy policies. We also investigate other open issues that can make replication harder.

Keywords: Privacy Policies · Comparable corpora · Methodology · Evaluation · Cross-language corpora

1 Introduction

A well-developed literature exists in relation to the analysis of privacy policies (e.g., [27,28,31]), particularly concerning the development of tools to improve the writing [9] and clarity of the policies themselves [8].

Specific studies on users' understanding of privacy policies are instead less frequent (e.g. [13,19,25]). While the assumption that existing privacy policies are excessively long and complex is at the foundation of the majority of works on the topic [1,20,28,30], the details of users' misunderstanding of policies are less studied (e.g. [24,26]). For example, Tang et al. [24] are the first to focus specifically on misconceptions related to technical terms used in privacy policies.

Yet, the ability of citizens to understand what they accept (e.g., 'are they waving their rights without even understanding it?') is a critical issue to gauge the actual success of privacy legislation initiatives such as the European Union General Data Protection Regulation (GDPR) [18]. The introduction of the GDPR in the EU has increased organizations' focus on complying with data protection principles. This privacy-driven approach progressively has grown the complexity of cybersecurity implementation and consequently their costs [12],

A. Skarmeta et al. (Eds.): CyberSec4Europe 2022, CCIS 1807, pp. 113–131, 2023.
https://doi.org/10.1007/978-3-031-36096-1_8

encouraging the development of GDPR's compliance tools [3], and introducing security workers such as the Data Protection Officer [5] (already existing in the past, but now well-defined and mandatory in all the EU member states). Because an organization must write and comply with privacy policies, it is crucial to assess whether the alleged beneficiaries of the protection granted by these policies (i.e., citizens) can actually understand what they are protected from (and what they are *not* protected from).

A critical issue in this respect is that most studies use English and are based on the U.S. reality (e.g. [21,24,27,29]), which has a different culture as well as differently constructed legislation.

European Union policies are typically written in the national language of a country, and any study that is based on the English language would not accurately reflect the proper understanding of the users: we would be probing at the same time their understanding of English *and* their understanding of the privacy issues. Still, using English as the reference language has advantages, particularly in ensuring that researchers from different countries can access and compare the work.

Given these premises, our main goal is to provide a methodology on how to generate comparable privacy corpora when dealing, on the one hand, with the English language and, on the other hand, with a National language (in this case, Italian).

In this work, we describe how we created such corpora and how to quantify the diversity within the corpora as well as a number of other open issues that makes replication studies way harder than one can initially think of.

2 Related Work

Privacy policies have long been the subject of detailed scientific studies; with the advent of the Internet, online privacy policies have proliferated [2,29] - often in the form of long, complex and, easily misunderstandable statements - in tandem with the necessity to explain users' data treatment for each online service. This, situation has led, to the necessity (that under some legislation, as in the EU, also became an obligation) to identify and develop methods to write privacy policies more easily, but also to make them more accessible to users of all backgrounds. Within the literature on privacy policies, two major issues are at the forefront of the discussion: the construction of adequate corpora for future analyses, and the development of automated tools for the analysis of existing policies and the drafting of future policies on the basis of a continuously evolving legal environment.

Privacy Policies' Corpora Selection. One of the main issues identified by the literature in proceeding with the (automated) analysis of existing privacy policies for their overall improvement is the lack of appropriate datasets from which to start such analysis [1,21]. Specifically, the problem for practitioners lies in the selection of policies that represent adequately the great variety in length, complexity and service coverage present among online privacy policies. The situation is further complicated by the presence of different legal backgrounds concerning privacy, for example between the European Union (where the content of privacy policies is mainly determined by the GDPR [18]) and China (where the Personal Information Protection Law (PIPL) sets similar requirements [16]) or the United States (where applicable laws vary between different States or circumstances). These differences can result in different policy structures and contents. As a consequence, the privacy policy of the same company can vary significantly depending on the country from which it is read. An additional factor of variety is the dimension of the company which the privacy policy is referred to, an element which generally impacts both the length of the policy and the frequency with which it is updated [27].

The methods used for policy selection vary between different works. Two main approaches emerge from the literature: the identification of criteria for the manual selection of representative policies (e.g. [27]); and the development of web crawlers to extract the highest possible number of policies available online (e.g. [1]). The two approaches seem to reflect the distinct priorities of different studies conducted on privacy policies, which tend to focus either on the characteristics of the selected policies (a preference for "quality") or on the sheer amount of considered policies (a preference for "quantity"). The second approach seems to be the most common in the literature, though a combined method – establishing a set of quality criteria, often starting from a manual selection and analysis of a few policies generally selected on the basis of popularity, and using such criteria as a basis of action for a crawler – is also employed often.

Tools for Analysis. A thriving strand of literature is then dedicated to automated tools aimed at, among others, analysing, creating, synthesizing, verifying the compliance or extracting specific elements of interest from privacy policies. The automated analysis of privacy policies has become a necessity both for the organizations writing the policies and for supervising authorities, but also for users requiring new manners to identify and understand the highlights of such policies [6]. Situated at the intersection between legal and technical domains, such analysis has recently turned to machine learning and text mining in order to automate and potentially improve a process that still relies heavily on human contribution [21].

Automatic privacy policy analysis is generally performed through natural language processing (NLP) techniques, which remain the dominant approach in the area. As reported by Del Alamo et al. [6], NLP techniques can be divided into symbolic (or classic) and statistical (or empirical). The first starts from human-developed rules to process the policy's text and model natural language; the second, instead, applies mathematical techniques to previously-created corpora of policies to develop generalized linguistic models. The attention of practitioners is mostly directed to the statistical approach and to the creation of tools enabling its execution in an automatic manner [30,31].

Readability and Users' Misconceptions. The academic interest over privacy policies is not limited to the manner in which they can be composed. In fact, the efficacy of a privacy policy does not depend only on its adherence to the legal

requirements established by the countries of reference – though that is indeed an important and necessary element – but also on how understandable it is by the final recipient of the policy: the concerned website's user.
The capability of users to understand the content of privacy policies is analyzable in more than one way. The majority of the literature focuses on the measure of so-called "readability" [7,11], which can be calculated according to a series of mathematical formulas or characteristics such as length, language complexity and univocal meaning.

Though definitely less studied throughout the years, a significant portion of scholarly investigation related to privacy policies has concerned users' misconceptions about the policies' meaning and function [19,25].

3 A Reference Corpus in English

To start a reference corpus, we used the study by Tang et al. [24], who tried to investigate the understandability of privacy policies from the users' perspective, focusing in particular on specific technical terms commonly used in data use policies in the context of the USA.

To achieve such an aim, the authors of [24] ran three different studies:

1. A qualitative pilot study to identify commonly misunderstood technical terms;
2. A large-scale main study to test the respondents' understanding of the selected terms and their comfort with some data use practices;
3. A small-scale follow-up study to support the main study's results.

To select the 22 terms to be included in the main study, the authors of [24] created a preliminary list of 57 terms obtained from manual analysis of the Alexa top 10 U.S. websites as of June 2020 (a common practice in studies on privacy policies [19]) and some selected apps from the Android Play Store. The list was then validated through an automated analysis of a 3609 English-language policies corpus to verify the frequency of use of the selected terms. The 57 terms were also divided into 11 categories based on the macro-area they belonged to (e.g., crypto, storage, tracking). From the original study's authors, we have obtained a spreadsheet including the technical terms (58 since one of them was missing from the original appendix) and the categories used in the pilot study. We also received the authors' original notes, where the policies in which they found the technical terms, the contexts of use, and a link to (the current version of) the relevant privacy policies are specified.

In the study by Tang et al. [24], the 57 terms, shown randomly based on their category, were included as part of the pilot study. In the pilot study, respondents from Amazon Mechanical Turk were asked to define the term they were shown. Based on the pilot results, 20 technical terms that were misunderstood the most (of which ten belong to the set of high-frequency terms commonly misdefined, while the others belong to the set of terms that the participants significantly misunderstood) were selected for the main study, together with two mostly well-understood terms. The main study was divided into two sections, asking respondents to answer multiple-choice questions defining some of the 22 terms and rate their comfort with some data use practices on a five-point Likert scale. The ratio of misunderstood to understood technical terms used for the survey is highly unbalanced (20-to-2), which may affect Tang et al. [24] study's validity. From our perspective, we use them only as control elements to make the study comparable.

Due to the uncertainty connected to the definition of comfort, the follow-up study was then used to verify whether users' attitudes to policies changed using technical versus descriptive terms.

4 Methodology

This section describes a usable methodology to build comparable privacy policies' cross-language corpora by mapping the policies of a corpus taken from a reference study into a new one that adopts the language of a future replication study. Figure 1 represents this methodology's diagram summarizing inputs, outputs, main characteristics considered, and transformations steps involved. Indeed, a cross-national replication study needs to consider a new corpus of privacy policies comparable with the original one because it will probably not be available or existent in a hypothetical parallel corpus. Hence, in this case [10], verifying the comparability of the two corpora is a precondition for using the new one.

The comparability check requires at least three different arguments. The first is the object to be compared, the second is another object to compare the first with, and the third is the respect used to compare these two objects. Hence, the third element is crucial, and its choice influences the comparison's result. Therefore, it is necessary to identify some properties concerning which they compare the corpora in comparing two corpora. There is the need to assess the comparability of a corpus with another that is not available since it will be composed of privacy policies used to replace some that are not available in the language of the future replication study. Therefore, before selecting policies based on the appropriate and specific criteria described below, it will be necessary to consider three data features [10]. These are representativeness, homogeneity, and homoscedasticity. The first feature relates to sharing a property between the two privacy policy corpora. The second feature requires that the data be homogeneous concerning the variables relevant to the purpose of the corpus. The third feature is related to the equal variance of the data across all classes.

Before a researcher can replicate a considered study, it is necessary to ensure that the corpora are comparable. Indeed, constructing multilingual corpora of privacy policies requires considering three different corpora: the *original corpus* in the original study and in the original study's language, a *source corpus* in the original study language and *replication corpus* in the replication language. Hence, it is necessary to make three different comparisons between three distinct corpora:

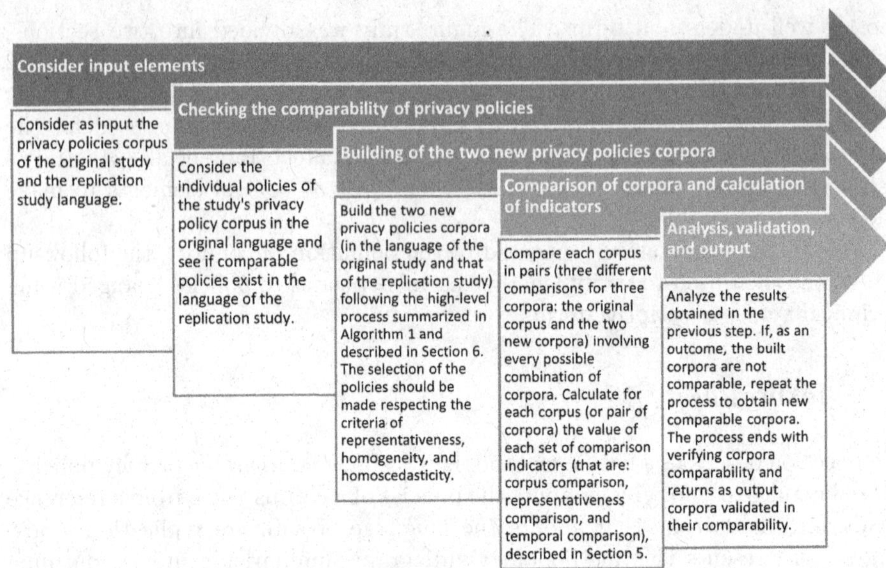

Fig. 1. The methodology to build comparable privacy policies' cross-language corpora

1. between the original study's corpus and the new source corpus in the language of the original study;
2. between the original study's corpus and the new replication corpus in the language of the replication study;
3. between the new source corpus in the original study's language and the new replication corpus in the languages of the replication study.

Identifying a new source corpus in the original language study is necessary because not all policies are usable/present in the replication language, and therefore, there might not be a correspondence between some/several policies in the original language and some policies in the replication language. As we illustrate here, this may happen because a company or institution in the original corpus does not exist in the replication country, or the company does exist but only have a policy in some languages and not the replication language. Only in very particular cases the original corpus and the new source corpus will coincide.

Usually, the availability of comparable corpora is more significant than parallel ones because they have the only requirement that their component documents cover related content in different languages [15]. Many works in the literature have demonstrated the usability of comparable corpora in various areas; for example, in improving CLIR systems [23] or in bilingual vocabulary extraction [4]. [14,22] have shown that an increase in the quality of a comparable corpus offers better performance to applications that refer to it. Moreover, [15] highlighted the need to adopt methods that can qualitatively assess the quality of a corpus. This method allows moving beyond a naive approach based only on reasoning, which can lead to an a priori unpredictable level of performance.

Because of the problems highlighted in comparing different corpora [10], we make use of solutions for measuring the distance between comparable corpora across languages derived from the one described in [17].

In our instance, we built new corpora of privacy policies (in Italian and English) from the privacy policies considered in the study taken as an example. These policies are accessible from the sites of the organizations that make them available through an interlanguage link (i.e., a link that relates documents on the same topic but written in different languages). This reflection allows us to extend to our case the considerations made in [17] regarding retrieving comparable Wikipedia documents. Furthermore, a manual evaluation of the privacy policies retrieved and included in our new corpora (source and replication) showed that, in many cases, the privacy policies in the language of replication were created from a simple translation of the analogous source policies written in English. Indeed, as is evident from Table 1, most companies come from states whose native language is English.

Note that in our case, because the privacy policies are retrieved from the same website (simply choosing the correct language) or from different regional websites of the same company, it is probable that the considered corpora are parallel. However, this is not sure because, due to different legislation (from U.S. and EU), it is not taken for granted that a policy text is the translation of another policy text. Hence, we must assume the only certain fact that, in this situation, the two individually considered corpora are similar in some aspects; that is, they are comparable.

In our case, as suggested in [17], we focused on finding policies with a similar length (difference in word count less than 20%) to increase the probability that they are comparable; that is, they are similar in structure and content. Although most of the policies found have a similar length, there are some exceptions where this condition is invalid. Examples are in the policies of Yahoo, Amazon (IT and U.S., while the state is verified between the IT and NL-EN versions), and the USPS-Poste and Teamsystem-Force pairs (of which there is only one language version of the policies).

A replication gap between the referred example study and the replication study will always exist because some time has passed. This gap has to be manageable and acceptable. To this extent, we identified three groups of indicators to quantify such a gap and which we discuss in more detail in the next section. Then, we analyzed the outcomes provided by these three groups of indicators and qualitatively discussed the real comparability of the corpora.

Finally, having verified the corpora's comparability, we focused on mapping the policies' terms. This activity was made manually and revealed some criticalities described in Sect. 8 which is the ground for future work.

5 Comparison Indicators

Based on the discussion in [10,17], and [15], we propose to use three groups of indicators: *corpus comparison*, *representativeness comparison*, and *temporal comparison*, to qualitatively measure the privacy policies' corpora comparability.

The first indicators' group (*corpus comparison*) measures whether the policies of the original study corpus are comparable with the corresponding (if they exist) policies in the cross-national study language. To compare corpora, we are mainly interested in quantifying how many policies are comparable, replacement (or complementary), and destructured. The indicator *Number of Comparable Policies* measures the number of privacy policies referred to the same company for which there is both a text in the original and replication language. These texts must have a similar (comparable) structure.

The *Number of Replacement Policies* indicator measures the number of policies in which the company from which the original study's policy is extracted does not exist in the replication country language. In contrast, the *Number of Complementary Policies* indicator measures the number of policies for which does not exist a localized version of the policy the original study considered. In the first case, if a product or service of a comparable company exists from the same industrial sector, the policy can be replaced with a new policy of these comparable companies. In the second case, if a localized privacy policy text of a *comparable* company's product or services exists, this policy will be used.

A privacy policy is considered complementary when it is added to a corpus to reflect any updates to a website rankings list (e.g., Alexa TOP10 U.S. or IT) that have occurred since the date of the original study.

The *Number of Destructured Policies* indicator estimates how many policies where a policy in the target language exists; still, this text is not immediately comparable with the text in the original study language due to a significantly different structure. The more destructured policies, the harder any replication study is. To ensure better replicability across languages of a study, the number of comparable policies must be as high as possible.

The second set of indicators measures the representativeness of the corpora. It provides qualitative criteria to follow in determining how to replace policies in the original corpus that are not usable in the replication study corpora (source corpus and replication corpus).

To measure the corpora's representativeness, we propose to do first a qualitative comparison using a table to compare the rank sources for each corpus. Indeed, it is crucial that the process used to build the new corpora be the same. Analogously, the rank sources used by the different corpora must be distinct from each other (because they are based on the constituent policies' language) and homogeneous (they must use the same source as, for example, Alexa Top10). One possible replacement policy criterion is to investigate if a TOP web ranking used in a study carried out in a particular language also exists in a different language, such that both policies talk about the same terms.

For example, it is possible to consider the Alexa TOP10 website list in both languages. Another example is considering the ranking of top companies in a specific industry (e.g., the top banks) for each state to which the language used in the studies refers.

Finally, to consider the replicability of the original study, it needs to assess the temporal comparability of the corpora (third indicators' group). We evaluated qualitatively three indicators to measure this comparability: the *Temporal Internal Consistency*, the *Temporal Replication Gap*, and the *Qualitative Replication Gap*.

We used the *Temporal Internal Consistency* indicator to ensure that the source and replication corpora policies are all in the same narrow interval. This indicator measures within the same body of privacy policies the number of months between the publication date of the most recently updated policy and the one of the least recently updated policy. The *Temporal Replication Gap* indicator aims to highlight if the policy has changed. It measures the average number of months of the update time of policies in the source and replication corpora vs. the ones in the original corpus. This value is calculated only for the comparable or destructured policies because it has no sense for the other ones (complementary or replacement). Indeed, these policies are added contextually to the new source and replication corpora and are absent from the original one. Since the study may give different results because time has passed and many things have happened (e.g., changes in laws), the *Qualitative Replication Gap* indicator is used to mark if major events happened from the original study and its replication.

6 Reconstruction of Policy Corpus

In the initial phase, we focused on looking for the correspondence between the Italian and English policies of the new cross-national source and replication corpora and the English policies of the original corpus we took from the example study of Tang. et al. [24]. Hence, excluding the case in which the policies are comparable, we identified three cases that require attention.

1. Missing policy: there is no Italian policy; however, there is a corresponding Italian app or website.
2. Missing company: there is no corresponding Italian app or website.
3. Destructured policy: there is a corresponding Italian version of the original privacy policy, but we found that this has an entirely different structure.

Henceforth, a team of two researchers analyzed the original corpus of policies and found correspondence rules to build comparable replication and source corpora of Italian and English ones. After defining our policy replication corpus for the Italian study, we concentrated on analyzing whether its policies were structurally similar to those in English of the original corpus. The high-level process to build the new replication and source corpora is presented in Algorithm 1. All the operations listed in the algorithm are done manually by humans. When in Algorithm 1, the condition *ItalianCompanyMissing* is verified, there is a case of a replacement policy. Analogously, if the condition *ItalianPolicyMissing* is satisfied, there is no Italian policy, but there is a corresponding Italian app or website. Hence, this is a case of a complementary policy. Instead, if the condition *ItalianPolicyDestructured* is verified, an Italian policy exists for a specific company. However, it has an entirely different structure from the original English policy (case of destructured policy).

If we need to substitute the English company with another of the same type (for example, another bank will replace a bank), we choose one that operates globally. Analogously, in case we need to substitute the missing privacy policy, we look for another related to a comparable company for the business sector, market segment, and type of product or service. With these choices, we have favored companies operating in the USA and Italy.

Algorithm 1. Look for the corresponding Italian privacy policy entry

```
procedure ITALIAN POLICY CHECK(EnglishPolicyURL)
    Retrieve English privacy policy text from EnglishPolicyURL
    Read English privacy policy text
    Retrieve English company from EnglishPolicyURL
    Read English company
    Search for the correspondent Italian company
    if ItalianCompanyMissing = True then
        Choose a new company with the same type as the original company and a privacy policy in Italian and English
        Retrieve URL and text of Italian policy of new company
        Retrieve URL and text of English policy of new company
        Add new company's English policy to new English corpus as replacement
        Add new company's Italian policy to Italian corpus as replacement
    else
        Search for the corresponding Italian privacy policy of the original Company
        if ItalianPolicyMissing = True then
            Choose another privacy policy in Italian related to a company comparable to the original company
            Retrieve the URL and the text of the Italian policy of the new comparable company
            Add the original company's English policy to the new English corpus
            Add the new comparable company's Italian policy to the Italian corpus
        else
            Retrieve the URL and the text of the original company's Italian policy
            Add the original company's English policy to the new English corpus
            Add the original company's Italian policy to the Italian corpus
            Analyze the Italian privacy policy structure
            Compare the Italian policy structure with the English one
            if ItalianPolicyDestructured = True then
                Operate a manual measures activity of the privacy policy
            else
                Classify the Italian privacy policy as comparable
```

We performed a manual analysis of the Alexa top 10 Italy websites as of November 2021, and analogously, we analyzed selected apps that, in the same period, had ranked better in the "most profitable games" category of the Play Store for Italy. After that, we compared these lists with the analogous ones (that refer to June 2020) in the original study for the U.S. privacy policies. To overcome the 17-month time gap between the establishment of the original corpus and the replication corpus, we made a further comparison by considering the content of the Alexa Top 10 U.S. ranking in the language of the original study as of November 2021.

From the original study, we considered 58 URLs obtained from 17 different companies' privacy policies. After this review phase, we removed six companies' privacy policies; however, we added twelve. This addition allowed us to improve the size of our corpus of policies, especially its specialization in the Italian reality and its focus on EU GDPR [18] concepts. We summarized these activities in Table 1. Our process in detail was as follows

a) the privacy policies of the apps *Infinite Word Search* and *Woody Puzzle* have been replaced by those of the apps *Coin Master* and *Empires & Puzzles* that, in addition to having an Italian privacy policy, respectively (on November 23, 2021) ranked first and fourth in the "most profitable games" category of the Play Store for Italy;
b) the privacy policy of the app *Signal* is replaced respectively by the policy and by the FAQ documentation of the apps *Whatsapp* and *Telegram*. The *Signal* app has an Italian version but not an Italian privacy policy, so we have chosen to replace it with other messaging apps with similar characteristics, such as support for end-to-end encryption. Moreover, because for the app *Telegram* there is not an Italian privacy policy but only an Italian FAQ documentation section in which the considered technical terms are present, we referred to this documentation;
c) the privacy policy of the website *Bank of America* is replaced by the *Unicredit* one, that is a company of the same category and operating worldwide;
d) the privacy policies of the *Reddit* and *Verizon* websites are replaced by the *Vodafone* one, that is a company that provides analogous services;
e) starting from one of the top 10 Alexa U.S. websites on November 2021, we added both the privacy policy of the related company and the one connected to a comparable Italian company (in particular the *Force* U.S. company and the *Teamsystem* Italian one);
f) starting from one of the top 10 Alexa Italian websites on November 2021, we added both the privacy policy of the related company and the one connected to a U.S. comparable company (in particular the *Poste* Italian company and the *USPS* U.S. one);
g) we added the privacy policies of the companies *Zoom* and *Microsoft* which have a website that appears both in Alexa top 10 Italian and in Alexa top 10 U.S. We chose policies from websites that appeared in the Alexa top 10 rankings for IT and U.S. to maintain equivalence between the original corpus, the new source corpus of English policies, and the new replication corpus of Italian policies. The original study's authors built their English technical terms corpus by manually analyzing the Alexa top 10 U.S. websites.

7 Results and Comparison

In our example, we made three different comparisons between three different corpora to determine their comparability level. The first corpus is the English-language corpus, the original used in the study by Tang et al. [24]. The other two are cross-language corpora built (one, the source corpus, in English, and the other, the replication corpus, in Italian, which is the language of a potential replication study) from the first corpus. We aim to use them for a potential replication study on how humans understand privacy policies.

Table 1. Composition of privacy policies corpus (This table describes the compositions of the original privacy policies corpus and the new English and Italian source and replication corpora. Columns named *Orig. Tang et al.*, *New US*, and *New IT* refer to different privacy policies corpora. The first entry refers to the English-language privacy policies corpus analyzed in the original Tang. et al. [24]study, while the second and third entries refer to the new privacy policies source and replication corpora in English or Italian, respectively. The *Referred company* field shows the company (and eventually their product) whose privacy policy we considered. Finally, the *Notes* field summarizes the rationale behind our choices in selecting the privacy policies.)

Referred company	Orig. Tang et al.	New US	New IT	Notes
Yahoo	√	√	√	We maintained it from initial study.
King Games (app Candy Crush)	√	√	√	
LinkedIn	√	√	√	
Amazon	√	√	√	
Google	√	√	√	
Apple	√	√	√	
Facebook	√	√	√	
Wikipedia	√	√	√	
Twitter	√	√	√	
Ebay	√	√	√	
Firefox (documentation)	√	√	√	
Random Logic Games (app Infinite Word Search)	√			We substituted policies because they do not exist in their Italian version.
Athena FZE (app Woody Puzzle)	√			
Moon Active (app Coin Master)		√	√	Companies added from the PlayStore's rank on Nov. 2021.
Zinga (app Empires & Puzzles)		√	√	
Signal	√			We substituted the policy because it does not exist in its Italian version
Telegram (FAQ doc.)		√	√	Companies added to replace the *Signal* one.
WhatsApp		√	√	
Bank of America	√			We replaced the policy because the respective Italian companies do not exist
Unicredit		√	√	Company added to replace the *Bank of America* one
Reddit	√			We substituted companies with new ones focused on Italian reality.
Verizon (cookie policy)	√			
Vodafone		√	√	Company added to replace the *Reddit* and *Verizon* ones
Zoom		√	√	Policies added from the top 10 Alexa Italian and U.S. on Nov. 2021.
Microsoft		√	√	
USPS (only US)		√	√	It was added because it is a U.S. company with similar features and products to the Italian *Poste*
Poste (only IT)		√	√	Company added from the top 10 Alexa Italian on Nov. 2021
Teamsystem (only IT)		√	√	It was added because it is an Italian company with similar features and products to the U.S. *Force*
Force (only US)		√	√	Company added from the top 10 Alexa U.S. on Nov. 2021

Comparing the English-language original corpus from Tang et al. [24] with the source corpus built by us in the same language, we have 52,38% comparable policies, 38,10% complementary policies, 9,52% replacement policies, and no destructured policies. The results are worst when comparing the original English-language corpus and the new replication one in Italian. In that case, we have 47,62% comparable policies, 38,10% complementary policies, 9,52% replacement policies, and 4,76% destructured policies.

In contrast, comparing the two new source and replication corpora in Italian and English, we find these are well aligned. We have 85,72% comparable policies, 9,52% complementary policies, 4,76% destructured policies, and no replacement policies. In all comparisons, the number of destructured policies is low, if not wholly absent.

Hence, rather than using Tang et al.'s [24] privacy policies' source corpus for a cross-language comparison, we compare the two new source and replication corpora (built from the original one) that are more closely aligned.

Moreover, internal temporal consistency exists in the new source and replication corpora policies. Indeed, these policies are all in the same narrow interval because their release varied from June 2020 to September 2021. Furthermore, with few exceptions, the Italian and English versions of our policies were published simultaneously. The exceptions to this are Amazon (where the Italian version is December 2020 while the English version is February 2021), Facebook (with versions varying from August 2020 to January 2021), WhatsApp (varying from January 2021 to November 2021), or Vodafone (varying from July 2021 to November 2021).

For a correct calculation of the value of the "*temporal replication gap*" indicator, it is essential to know the version and date of each privacy policy considered (both in the original corpus in the original study and those in the source and replication corpora in the replication study). Knowing the number of intermediate versions of privacy policies for each company is also helpful. In our example, there are many problems, and this indicator is not helpful. The original study [24] did not specify the version and date of policy updates. We deduced the date of the considered policies by cross-referencing the updating date of the policy with the date of consultation of the TOP 10 of Alexa U.S. (June 2020). We know that this date is incorrect, but it still gives us an indicative idea. Moreover, considering that not all companies expose the historical archive of policy versions, we can obtain a policy date to calculate the indicator in only 7 out of 11 cases. Other companies have made some intermediate versions of the privacy policy disappear from their website (for example, on the Facebook website, the previous versions are no longer available between September 9, 2016, and January 4, 2022). This fact generates another interesting problem because users have given their consent based on a no longer existing policy. We have not considered the case of Facebook because it presents an outlier value. Therefore, we used 6 out of 11 policies in calculating the indicator. Interestingly, with only one exception (Google, for which there were four different versions in the face of a 17-month time gap), between the two studies, there was at most one version gap in the privacy policies considered. We calculated the temporal replication gap value only for the comparable or destructured policies because it has no sense for the other ones (complementary or replacement). Indeed, these policies are added contextually to the new source and replication corpora and are absent from the original one. The final value obtained for this indicator shows that the average number of months of the update time of the policy (comparable or destructured) is 16,5. This result is good because it shows that from the policies version available in the example study's original corpus and the new ones (source and replication corpora) built by us, there is only one version difference and a time lag between updates of just over a year.

Considering the qualitative replication gap indicator, it shows that in the time between the construction of the original corpus and of the pair source and replication corpora (June 2020 - November 2021), there have been no significant regulatory developments. For example, both the *GDPR* and the *California Consumer Privacy Act (CCPA)* predate the construction of the original corpus, while other laws, such as the *Connecticut Data Privacy Act (CDPA)*, the *Utah Consumer Privacy Act (UCPA)*, and the *Virginia Consumer Data Protection Act (VCDPA)* was not yet in effect. Despite this, there have been some changes at the corporate level (e.g., the corporate change from *Facebook* to *Meta*) or at the policy level (e.g., additional information added regarding data retention in the Yahoo policy).

8 Open Problems: Technical Terms May Not Match

After building a privacy corpus in a different language, the next step is replicating different studies. For example, the authors in [24] arranged a survey based on 22 key terms derived from the pilot study's results to investigate the understanding of technical terms.

We experienced many cases of technical terms that do not match and occur with extremely different frequencies.

The most egregious case are the English terms "*personal information*" and "*personally identifiable information (PII)*" (that were distinct in the considered study). Hence, we used a syntactic criterion both to be sure of their overlapping and overcoming it in a single Italian term, "*dati personali.*" In practice, we used a syntactic rule to identify the possible syntactic distinction of these terms. Hence, they are distinguishable if there is no correspondence between the two policies (English and Italian) or if there are orphans or widows. Otherwise, it is possible to conclude that they are the same thing and are codifiable with the same term in Italian.

To understand if the terms PII@US (*personally identifiable information*) and PI@IT (*informazioni personali, personal information*) are equivalent, we manually looked for widows' or orphans' presence related to these technical terms. An *orphan* is a term that appeared in the Italian policy without a match in the corresponding clauses or sections of the English policy. A *widow* is any occurrences in the English policy in which the term PII@US (or the term SPI - *sensitive personal information* -) appears without the term PI@IT in the Italian policy.

We also looked for implicit terms or pronouns that refer to technical terms. We found very few occurrences of those cases.

Other critical issues occur when technical terms do not appear or are rare in our corpora. For example, the term *fingerprinting* does not appear in the Italian corpus and is useless for an Italian language survey. Instead, *public information* and *browser web storage* terms are rare in our corpora, but for an Italian survey, they are significant and can be used.

We illustrate these issues by considering the 22 terms from [24]:

- two high-frequency terms that most users in the pilot study correctly defined;
- ten high-frequency terms that the study's participants commonly misdefined;
- ten additional terms for which the study's participants exhibited significant misunderstandings.

Using our new source and replication corpora of Italian and English policies, we investigate the differences between the frequency of occurrences in privacy policies of the most common Italian and English technical terms (the TOP 10 and the TOP 22 lists). More details are listed in Table 2.

The correspondence between the TOP 10 English list and the TOP 10 Italian one is generally reasonable. 80% of the terms included in the TOP 10 English list also belong to the TOP 22 Italian one (with a peak of 70% of terms also included in the Italian TOP 10). Hence, only 20% of terms in the TOP 10 English list do not belong to the TOP 22 Italian one. The correspondence between the TOP 22 English list and the TOP 22 Italian list is acceptable. 58,33% of terms in the TOP22 English list belong to the Italian one, and 16,66% of them also belong to the TOP10 Italian list. Hence, only 41,67% of terms in the TOP22 English list are outside the TOP22 Italian one.

Out of 22 terms used in the Tang et al. [24] example study's privacy policies English original corpus, ten of these (45,46% of the total) appear in one of the TOP English lists of our new English source corpus (specifically, five in the TOP 10 and the other five in the TOP 22). While the remaining 12 terms (54,54% of the total) are outside our source corpus TOP 22 English list. This outcome means that referring to our source corpus of privacy policies, more than half of the technical terms considered in the study taken as an example are rare. This result is crucial because our source and replication corpora are more focused on EU reality.

The situation is worse, considering the terms used in Italian policies. Only 7 (31,82% of the total) of these terms appear in one of the TOP Italian lists (in particular, five in the TOP 10 and the other two in the TOP 22). The remaining 15 terms (68,18% of the total) are outside the TOP 22 Italian list.

Hence, the technical terms used in the example study's survey by Tang et al. [24] are rarely used in the privacy policies in Italian. This consideration is a crucial point that shows the need first to map technical terms and, secondly, to adapt the survey for replicating it to Italian-speaking respondents. These activities will be the subject of future research work.

Table 2. TOP 10 and TOP 22 lists of more frequent terms in the new Italian source corpus of privacy policies (This table describes the TOP10 and TOP22 lists of terms that appear most frequently in the new Italian source corpus of privacy policies. We used boldface to represent the terms belonging to the TOP 10 list. The order (*Rank IT* column) of technical terms in the table follows the terms that appear most frequently in Italian language privacy policies. The table also shows the ranking of the most frequent technical terms in English language privacy policies (*Rank U.S.* column). Corresponding to the Italian-language term (*Term IT*) is the corresponding English-language term (*Term US*). Finally, the table shows the cardinality with which we detected the term in the new replication and source corpora of Italian-language (*#Freq IT*) and English-language (*#Freq US*) privacy policies, respectively.)

Rank IT	Rank US	Term IT	Term US	#Freq IT	#Freq US
1	1	**Dati Personali**	**Personal information**	1523	1430
2	12	of which	**Personally identifiable inform.**	1012	79
3	2	**Cookie/Marcatori**	**Cookies**	645	784
4	4	**Terzi/Terze parti**	**Third parties**	618	360
5	3	**Informativa sul trattamento dei dati personali**	**Privacy policy**	471	540
6	14	**Rettificare**	**Correct**	170	60
7	7	**Indirizzo IP**	**IP address**	136	153
8	26	**Disattivare**	**Deactivate**	128	25
9	9	**Cifratura/Crittografia**	**Encryption**	86	113
10	5	**Dati sull'account**	**Account information**	60	324
11	56	Hash crittografico	Cryptographically hashed	52	2
12	36	Transferimento di dati	Data transfer	50	15
13	10	Affiliate	Affiliates	48	87
14	6	Pubblicità mirata	Targeted ads	47	157
15	15	Identificatori univoci	Unique identifiers	45	54
16	20	API/SDK	API/SDK	44	44
17	16	Dati relativi all'ubicazione	Location-related information	42	50
18	18	Informazioni sui pagamenti	Payment information	41	47
19	40	Resi anonimi	Anonymize	40	13
20	46	Operazioni del dispositivo	Device operations	39	6
21	29	Categorie particolari di dati personali/Dati sensibili	Sensitive personal information	34	19
22	19	Dati di utilizzo	Usage data	28	45

9 Conclusion and Future Works

The first conclusion of our work is that a strict replication study in a different language is possible only up to a certain extent because some elements do not transfer from the original study to the new one.

Therefore, our contribution is to discover and describe how elements (for example, the original corpus used in the survey) can be adapted from an original study to a new one to understand what is needed to maintain relative comparability of the components of the study, such as the privacy policy corpora.

Still, the results obtained in our case study confirm that by taking due care, it is possible to build cross-language source and replication corpora of privacy policies usable for research purposes, such as investigating how humans understand their content.

The outcomes of this work will be the base for further research activities. Future interesting work is to investigate the validity of automated analysis approaches, i.e. whether just looking for term occurrences in a policy would yield a correct analysis. Precision and recall values achievable in the automated coding of technical terms should be compared from those derived by manual coding. A second aspect is mapping technical terms in different language corpora privacy policies. Our preliminary analysis has already shown that this is not so obvious. Future work could define some indicators to identify the irrelevant, infrequent, overlap, and unreliable technical terms that must be removed or replaced according to the case. This information will help, for example, to replicate the understandability questions from Tang et al. [24] to Italian-speaking people who interact with Italian privacy policies.

Acknowledgement. The authors would like to thank Eleanor Birrell and Ada Lerner for providing us their raw privacy corpus used in their paper [24]. Without their time and expertise this paper would not have been possible. This work was supported in part by the EU under the H2020 Leadership in Enabling and Industrial Technologies program under grant agreement 830929 (CyberSec4Europe).

Data Availability. The datasets generated and analyzed during the study are archived on Zenodo at https://doi.org/10.5281/zenodo.7729546.

CRediT statements. *Conceptualization:* FC, FM, SV; *Methodology:* FC, SV; *Software:* SV, FC; *Validation:* FC, SV, FM; *Investigation:* FC, SV; *Data Curation:* FC, SV; *Writing - Original Draft:* FC, SV; *Writing - Review & Editing:* FC, SV, FM; *Visualization:* FC; *Supervision:* FM; *Project administration:* FM, SV; *Funding acquisition:* FM.

References

1. Amos, R., Acar, G., Lucherini, E., Kshirsagar, M., Narayanan, A., Mayer, J.: Privacy policies over time: curation and analysis of a million-document dataset. In: WWW 2021: Proceedings of the Web Conference 2021, pp. 2165–2176 (2021)
2. Cecere, G., Le Guel, F., Soulié, N.: Perceived internet privacy concerns on social networks in Europe. Technol. Forecast. Soc. Change **96**, 277–287 (2015)
3. Chatzipoulidis, A., Tsiakis, T., Kargidis, T.: A readiness assessment tool for GDPR compliance certification. Comput. Fraud Secur. **2019**(8), 14–19 (2019)
4. Chebel, M., Latiri, C., Gaussier, E.: Bilingual lexicon extraction from comparable corpora based on closed concepts mining. In: Kim, J., Shim, K., Cao, L., Lee, J.-G., Lin, X., Moon, Y.-S. (eds.) PAKDD 2017. LNCS (LNAI), vol. 10234, pp. 586–598. Springer, Cham (2017). https://doi.org/10.1007/978-3-319-57454-7_46
5. Ciclosi, F., Massacci, F.: The data protection officer: a ubiquitous role that no one really knows. IEEE Secur. Privacy **21**(1), 66–77 (2023)
6. Del Alamo, J.M., Guaman, D.S., García, B., Diez, A.: A systematic mapping study on automated analysis of privacy policies. Computing **104**, 2053–2076 (2022)
7. Ermakova, T., Fabian, B., Babina, E.: Readability of privacy policies of healthcare websites. In: Wirtschaftsinformatik Proceedings 2015 (WI 2015) (2015)
8. Fabian, B., Ermakova, T., Lents, T.: Large-scale readability analysis of privacy policies. WI 2017: Proceedings of the International Conference on Web Intelligence, pp. 18–25 (2017)

9. Hosseini, M.B., Breaux, T.D., Slavin, R., Niu, J., Wang, X.: Analyzing privacy policies through syntax-driven semantic analysis of information types. Inf. Softw. Technol. **138**, 106608 (2021)
10. Köhler, R.: Statistical comparability: methodological caveats. In: Sharoff, S., Rapp, R., Zweigenbaum, P., Fung, P. (eds.) Building and Using Comparable Corpora, pp. 77–91. Springer, Heidelberg (2013). https://doi.org/10.1007/978-3-642-20128-8_4
11. Krumay, B., Klar, J.: Readability of privacy policies. In: Singhal, A., Vaidya, J. (eds.) DBSec 2020. LNCS, vol. 12122, pp. 388–399. Springer, Cham (2020). https://doi.org/10.1007/978-3-030-49669-2_22
12. Layton, R., Elaluf-Calderwood, S.: A social economic analysis of the impact of GDPR on security and privacy practices. In 2019 12th CMI Conference on Cybersecurity and Privacy (CMI), pp. 1–6. IEEE (2019)
13. Leicht, J., Heisel, M.: A Survey on privacy policy languages: expressiveness concerning data protection regulations. In: 2019 12th CMI Conference on Cybersecurity and Privacy (CMI), pp. 1–6 (2019)
14. Li, B., Gaussier, E.: Improving corpus comparability for bilingual lexicon extraction from comparable corpora. In Proceedings of the 23rd International Conference on Computational Linguistics (Coling 2010), pp. 644–652 (2010)
15. Li, B., Gaussier, E.: Exploiting comparable corpora for lexicon extraction: measuring and improving corpus quality. In: Sharoff, S., Rapp, R., Zweigenbaum, P., Fung, P. (eds.) Building and Using Comparable Corpora, pp. 131–149. Springer, Heidelberg (2013). https://doi.org/10.1007/978-3-642-20128-8_7
16. National People's Congress of the People's Republic of China. Personal Information Protection Law of the People's Republic of China (2021)
17. Paramita, M.L., Guthrie, D., Kanoulas, E., Gaizauskas, R., Clough, P., Sanderson, M.: Methods for collection and evaluation of comparable documents. In: Sharoff, S., Rapp, R., Zweigenbaum, P., Fung, P. (eds.) Building and Using Comparable Corpora, pp. 93–112. Springer, Heidelberg (2013). https://doi.org/10.1007/978-3-642-20128-8_5
18. Parliament EU and Council EU. Consolidated text: Regulation (EU) 2016/679 of the European Parliament and of the Council of 27 April 2016 on the protection of natural persons with regard to the processing of personal data and on the free movement of such data, and repealing Directive 95/46/EC (General Data Protection Regulation) (2016)
19. Reidenberg, J.R., et al.: Disagreeable privacy policies: mismatches between meaning and users' understanding. Berkeley Technol. Law J. **30**(1), 39–68 (2015)
20. Robillard, J.M., et al.: Availability, readability, and content of privacy policies and terms of agreements of mental health apps. Internet Intervent. **17**, 100243 (2019)
21. Sarne, D., Chler, J., Singer, A., Sela, A., Bar Siman Tov, I.: Unsupervised topic extraction from privacy policies. In: WWW 2019: Companion Proceedings of The 2019 World Wide Web Conference, pp. 563–568 (2019)
22. Skadiņa, I., Vasiļjevs, A., Skadiņš, R., Gaizauskas, R., Tufiş, D., Gornostay, T.: Analysis and evaluation of comparable corpora for under resourced areas of machine translation. In: The 5th Workshop on Building and Using Comparable Corpora, p. 17. CiteSeer (2012)
23. Talvensaari, T., Laurikkala, J., Järvelin, K., Juhola, M., Keskustalo, H.: Creating and exploiting a comparable corpus in cross-language information retrieval. ACM Trans. Inf. Syst. (TOIS), **25**(1), 4-es (2007)
24. Tang, J., Shoemaker, H., Lerner, A., Birrell, E.: Defining privacy: how users interpret technical terms in privacy policies. Proceedi. Priv. Enhan. Technol. **3**, 70–94 (2021)

25. Turow, J., Hennessy, M., Draper, N.: Persistent misperceptions: Americans' misplaced confidence in privacy policies, 2003–2015. J. Broadcast. Electron. Media **62**(3), 461–478 (2018)
26. Vail, M.W., Earp, J.B., Antón, A.I.: An empirical study of consumer perceptions and comprehension of web site privacy policies. IEEE Trans. Eng. Manage. **55**(3), 442–454 (2008)
27. Wilson, S., et al.: The creation and analysis of a website privacy policy corpus. In: Proceedings of the 54th Annual Meeting of the Association for Computational Linguistics, vol. 1, pp. 1330–1340 (2016)
28. Zaeem, R.N., et al.: PrivacyCheck v2: a tool that recaps privacy policies for you. CIKM 2020. In: Proceedings of the 29th ACM International Conference on Information & Knowledge Management, pp. 3441–3444 (2020)
29. Zeadally, S., Winkler, S.: Privacy policy analysis of popular web platforms. IEEE Technol. Soc. Mag. **35**(2), 75–85 (2016)
30. Zimmeck, S., Bellovin, S.M.: Privee: an architecture for automatically analyzing web privacy policies. In: 23rd USENIX Security Symposium (USENIX Security 14), pp. 1–16, San Diego, CA. USENIX Association (2014)
31. Zimmeck, S., et al.: MAPS: scaling privacy compliance analysis to a million apps. Proceed. Priv. Enhan. Technol. **2019**(3), 66–86 (2019)

Governance Foundations for the European Cybersecurity Community

Afonso Ferreira[1(✉)], Christina von Wintzingerode[2], Dirk Müllmann[2], Abdelmalek Benzekri[3], Pierre-Henri Cros[4], Indra Spiecker gen. Döhmann LL.M[2], and Elvire Prochilo[5]

[1] CNRS, Institut de Recherches en Informatique de Toulouse – IRIT, Toulouse, France
Afonso.ferreira@irit.fr

[2] Goethe-Universität Frankfurt am Main, Frankfurt, Germany

[3] Université Paul Sabatier, Institut de Recherches en Informatique de Toulouse – IRIT, Toulouse, France

[4] Université Paul Sabatier, Toulouse, France

[5] Pragma-Consult, Toulouse, France

Abstract. While Regulation EU 2021/887 of 20 May 2021 established the European Cybersecurity Industrial, Technology and Research Competence Centre and the Network of National Coordination Centres, it has not addressed in any detail the identification, structuring, or coordination of the cybersecurity actors in Europe. This paper proposes their structure and input, extending on work done in the project CyberSec4Europe, which was funded by the European Commission to design, test, and demonstrate potential governance structures for the European Cybersecurity community.

Keywords: Cybersecurity · Community · Governance

1 Introduction

Regulation EU 2021/887 of 20 May 2021 established the European Cybersecurity Industrial, Technology and Research Competence Centre and the Network of National Coordination Centres. With this, the European legislator intends to end the fragmentation of efforts in research and development of cybersecurity products in the EU.

However, in comparison to the rules regarding the establishment, structure and tasks of the European Competence Centre and the national coordination centres, the establishment, governance structure and tasks of what the regulation termed the "Community" are rather vaguely described in the Regulation.

It is against this background that the European Commission decided to fund four pilot projects to help build and strengthen cybersecurity capacities across the EU, as well as provide valuable input for the set-up of the Cybersecurity Competence Network with a European Cybersecurity Research and Competence Centre. These projects are Concordia, CyberSec4Europe, ECHO, and Sparta.

A. Skarmeta et al. (Eds.): CyberSec4Europe 2022, CCIS 1807, pp. 132–148, 2023.
https://doi.org/10.1007/978-3-031-36096-1_9

The pilot CyberSec4Europe designed, tested and demonstrated potential governance structures for a future European Cybersecurity Competence Network using best practice examples derived from well-proven concepts like, e.g., CERN (for more examples see [1, pp. 21–33] [2, pp. 4–25, 29–32]), as well the expertise and experience of partners.

With a focus on community-building and thus bottom-up approaches to identify and solve cybersecurity-related problems, the CyberSec4Europe pilot project proposed the installation of additional regional, sectoral and cross-border networks at the Community level. As one element to achieve this goal, CyberSec4Europe envisioned the introduction of Community Hubs of Expertise in Cybersecurity Knowledge (CHECKs) into a future form of the regulation. The network would be significantly strengthened and advanced into a true structure that would ensure efficient flows of information that are implemented swiftly and occur within the most efficient layers.

Accordingly, this paper contributes to the foundations of a framework facilitating the emergence of bottom-up communities of knowledgeable cybersecurity experts that would also integrate potential users and their needs, including from the civil society.

2 Legislative Framework–Regulation (EU) 2021/887

With Regulation (EU) 2021/887 of 20 May 2021[1] the European legislator intends to end the fragmentation of efforts of the industrial and research communities in cybersecurity and to pool and network the existing wealth of expertise and experience in the EU instead.[2] Building sufficient technological and industrial capacities and capabilities shall enable the Union to autonomously secure its economy and critical infrastructures and become a global leader in the area of cybersecurity.[3] For the implementation of these goals the Regulation provides for the interaction of different relevant stakeholders[4] from public entities, Member States and the Union as well as from industry, academia, research and other civil society entities. The Regulation established the European Cybersecurity Industrial, Technology and Research Competence Centre and the Network of National Coordination Centres.

2.1 Categories of Actors

The Regulation divides the different stakeholders into three categories of actors. The European Cybersecurity Competence Centre and its tasks, organisation and funding are the main regulatory object. Its mandate is to support the Union in strengthening capacities and capabilities in all areas of cybersecurity and improve the EU's competitiveness in cybersecurity[5] by pursuing objectives like the promotion of cybersecurity research,

[1] Hereinafter "the Regulation". All Articles and Recitals referred to in this chapter are those of the Regulation, unless explicitly named otherwise.

[2] Recital (7).

[3] Recital (12).

[4] Recital (10).

[5] Art. 3.

innovation and implementation, the creation of capacities, skills, knowledge and infrastructure in this field and the bringing together of stakeholders in a common European cybersecurity ecosystem[6]. Its tasks are divided into strategic and implementation tasks.[7]

As a second category of actors the Regulation provides for the National Coordination Centres and the Network of National Coordination Centres.[8] Their tasks[9] include the provision of expertise, the functioning as a national contact point and the support of the Competence Centre in its assignments. In particular, that includes the coordination and involvement of stakeholders, the improvement of knowledge about cybersecurity in the Member States and the promotion and dissemination of the results of the Network's work.

Finally, the Regulation provides for the Cybersecurity Competence Community.[10] The Community supports the Competence Centre and the Network of National Coordination Centres and shall enhance, share and disseminate cybersecurity expertise across the Union. It shall consists of a broad variety of cybersecurity stakeholders from industry, research, politics and civil society and is thus intended to bring together these key players with other national and European cybersecurity institutions.

2.2 The Cybersecurity Competence Community

The Competence Community is the largest and most diverse group of actors subject to the regulation. Notwithstanding, its establishment, governance structure and tasks are rather vaguely described in comparison to those of the European Competence Centre and the National Coordination Centres. The following analysis focuses on the strengths and weaknesses of this approach in the light of the goals the Regulation is aiming at.

Members and Membership. A community can be characterised as a group of individuals or individual entities with a mutual bond and/or pursuit of common goals (translated definition [3]). The compound term "Competence Community" in the Regulation thus suggests that potential members must not only have a certain affinity, but above all must also have certain competences in the field of cybersecurity.

The broad variety of potential members from industry, including SMEs, academic and research institutions, civil society, European standardisation organisations, public bodies dealing with operational and technical cybersecurity issues, and stakeholders from sectors with an interest in cybersecurity and facing cybersecurity challenges[11] serves the stated objective of bringing together the main stakeholders in the field of cybersecurity in the European Union. However, by whom and according to which criteria the importance is to be determined remains completely open. Due to the lack of normative standards in this regard, it cannot be evaluated at all whether or not the stated goal of bringing together the "most important" stakeholders has been successfully achieved.

---

[6] Art. 4.
[7] Art. 5.
[8] Rules for their establishment are laid down in Art. 6.
[9] Art. 7.
[10] Art. 8.
[11] Art. 8(2).

Obtaining membership takes place in two steps. First, the National Coordination Centre of the Member State in which the respective institution is established must check whether the institution fulfils the membership criteria. If this is the case, the institution can, in a second step apply for registration as a member of the Community with the European Competence Centre.[12]

The criteria for the membership are a combination of capacity requirements and a catalogue of areas of expertise in the field of cybersecurity. An entity wishing to become a member of the Community must demonstrate that it can contribute to the mission of the Competence Community and has expertise in at least one of the specified areas.[13] The intention to establish a multidisciplinary Competence Community by including as many types of institutions as possible by listing a wide range of areas of cybersecurity expertise becomes very clear from the membership criteria.

The weak point, however, is how possible members who are not already well networked and informed should learn about the possibility of application and registration and, vice versa, how the Community gets to know about new members. Ensuring not only that all possible members get to know about the Competence Community and the possibility of a membership, but also to keep the Community updated on new members will therefore be crucial to establish an agile Community and to exploit its full potential.

Possible Role of the Community. How the Community can contribute to the success of European cybersecurity does not only depend on the recruitment of members but also on the role the Regulation assigns to the Community. The Regulation is very concise when it comes to an explicit description. However, the tasks assigned to the Community as well as its integration into the structure of the European Competence Centre and intended cooperation with the National Coordination Centres and the Network offer valuable clues on that.

Tasks. In the literal sense, a distinction can be made between the Community's own tasks and support tasks. The Community (as a whole) has the broadly described assignment of promoting, sharing and disseminating cybersecurity expertise throughout the Union.[14] The Regulation does not specify, how or by which means this task is to be accomplished. In addition, the Community has a supporting role in fulfilling the missions of the Competence Centre and the Network by involving both in its work[15] and by providing advice through its working groups and the Strategic Advisory Group in the Competence Centre on issues related to the agenda, the annual and multi-annual work programme[16].

The tasks of the members of the Community are laid down separately in Art. 9 of the Regulation. These tasks assign the members a supporting role in the fulfilment of the tasks of the Competence Centre and the Coordination Centres and provide for participation in certain activities and the working groups established by the Governing Board. An independent performance of tasks by the members is only envisaged to a very limited extent. The members' own tasks could only arise indirectly through the Community's

[12] Art. 8(4).

[13] Art. 8(3).

[14] Art. 8(1).

[15] Art. 8(2), e.g., refers to the National Coordination Centres.

[16] Art. 8(9).

tasks regarding the promotion, sharing and dissemination of expertise. Due to the lack of an internal structure of the Community, however, an organised division and execution of these tasks is just as little possible, at least within the framework of the Regulation, as a subsequent self-monitoring with regard to the success or failure of the performance of tasks and possible need for improvement. Thus, the Regulation does not encourage the formation of a Community through the organised joint performance of tasks.

Integration into the organisational structure of the European Competence Centre. Members of the Community may attend meetings of the Governing Board as observers only, without voting rights, at the invitation of the Chairperson of the Governing Board.[17] Permanent observer status is not envisaged for the Community. Neither the Regulation nor the Rules of Procedure of the Governing Board contain any arrangements on the selection criteria for which member(s) of the Community should be invited to a meeting. In this respect, it is important to ensure equal distribution of participation opportunities for representatives of different groups of stakeholders and within these groups. Even if the participating members of the Community do not have voting rights, the position as observer possibly conveys impressions and information that other Community members do not receive at all, only incompletely and/or with delay and which in turn could e.g. be important for their own strategic or economic decisions. Even the appearance of favouring certain members or interest groups needs to be avoided.

In addition to the Governing Board and the Executive Director a Strategic Advisory Group is also part of the permanent structure of the Competence Centre.[18] The selection of members for the Strategic Advisory Group is provided for in the Single Programming Document 2022–2024 of the Governing Board in the period up to and including 2023 [4, p. 14]. This group consists of a maximum of 20 members, which are selected by the Governing Board from among the representatives of the members of the Competence Community upon the proposal of the Executive Director.[19] The Competence Community itself is neither involved in the proposal nor the selection process. Thus, the Strategic Advisory Group is explicitly not a representation of the members of the Community to the Competence Centre in the sense of democratic participation. At least the rules on the composition of the group are intended to ensure a balanced reflection of the Community.[20] Nevertheless, the procedural rules for appointing the members of the Advisory Group[21] [5] still show room for improvement. For example, there are no rules for the case that more than 20 equally suitable member representatives respond to the call of the Executive Director and whether or how extensively the decision for the selection of the listed members would have to be justified and published. It must also be ensured that the call is made equally accessible to all members of the Competence Community.

[17] Artt. 12(6), 14(5).

[18] Art. 11(2)(c).

[19] Art. 18(1)(2).

[20] Cf. Art. 18(1).

[21] Art. 18(3) Regulation i.c.w. Art. 20 of the Rules of Procedure of the Governing Board.

The mode of operation of the Advisory Group is only roughly determined in the Regulation.[22] Once established, the Advisory Group shall adopt its own rules of procedure.[23] As its name suggests, the Strategic Advisory Group has only an advisory-supporting role in the Competence Centre[24]. It may e.g., decide on and organise public consultations, but these require the approval of the Governing Board.[25] The Governing Board may, but is not obliged to, invite a representative of the Advisory Group to its meetings.[26] The Advisory Group, unlike ENISA,[27] does not have a permanent observer status on the Governing Board and the Group members have thus no obligatory right to attend the Governing Board meetings. They have also no voting rights in Board decisions. Furthermore, the Governing Board does not have to follow the recommendations of the Strategic Advisory Group, nor does it have to justify or at least give reasons for deviations.[28] Overall, the degree of participation of the Advisory Group in the work and decisions of the Board is remarkably weak.

Despite that, it is still to be welcomed that the Council's position in the legislative process to not integrate a body of the Competence Community into the structure of the Competence Centre at all was ultimately not able to prevail[29]. The Strategic Advisory Group is at least one permanent point of contact between the Competence Centre and the Community. However, with the decision not to design the Strategic Advisory Group as a representation of the Competence Community and to create very limited opportunities for its participation, an opportunity was missed,[30] [6, p. 483] [7, p. 693] to create a real incentive not only for the participation in the Advisory Group, but also for a membership in the Competence Community in general.

Another field of activity for the members of the Community are working groups, established by the Governing Board under consideration of the recommendations of the Strategic Advisory Group.[31] Where necessary, the coordination of the working groups is carried out by one or more members of the Strategic Advisory Group.[32]

---

22 The Governing Board has so far only made a provision in Art. 20 of its Rules of Procedure for the appointment procedure, but has not defined and published the working methods of the Strategic Advisory Group. It is quite conceivable that the rules of procedure will be supplemented after the advisory group has been established.

23 Art. 19(5).

24 Cf. Art. 20.

25 Art. 20(c).

26 Art. 12(7).

27 Unlike ENISA, the Strategic Advisory Group is not a permanent observer in the meetings of the Governing Board, cf. Art. 12(7).

28 Neither does the Regulation provide for a duty to state reasons, nor is there a voluntary commitment by the Governing Board in its Rules of Procedure.

29 Council of the European Union, Mandate for negotiations with the European Parliament, 9 March 2020, proposal and remark 27, Interinstitutional file 2018/0328(COD), Doc. No. 7616/19, 26.03.2019.

30 The criticism towards the limited role of the Scientific-Technical Advisory Board in the analysis of the Regulation Proposal is in this respect transferable almost unchanged to the Strategic Advisory Group.

31 Art. 13(3)(n) i.c.w. Artt. 8(9), 9(b).

32 Art. 19(2).

Unlike the Strategic Advisory Group, the working groups are not permanent structural elements in the Competence Centre with specific tasks of their own. Specific working groups can be set up to collaborate on issues relevant to the work of the Competence Centre[33] and to provide advice on the agenda, the annual and multi-annual work programme[34]. This is a quite narrowly defined assignment of tasks on a case-by-case basis by the Governing Board to individual members of the Community. Unfortunately, neither the Regulation nor the Rules of Procedure of the Governing Board[35] provide for procedural rules or criteria for the selection of these Community members. Such rules would be desirable not only from a rule of law perspective, but also for community building. Ensuring a certain plurality and diversity of the working groups can indirectly lead to new contacts and exchange between Community members, who are not already networked. This, in particular, would promote the dissemination of expertise and could give rise to new impulses for research and development.

Cooperation with the National Coordination Centres and the Network. The Regulation assigns tasks to the National Coordination Centres and the Network, among others, related to the Community and its members.[36] The Network, like the Competence Centre, shall cooperate with the Community as appropriate.[37] The National Coordination Centres shall serve as main contact points for the Community at national level and shall assist the Competence Centre in particular in coordinating the Community through coordination of its members.[38] The promotion and dissemination of relevant work results of the Network, the Community and the Competence Centre at national, regional or local level is also one of the tasks of the National Coordination Centres.[39] It also has to promote, facilitate and encourage the participation of civil society, industry, in particular start-ups and SMEs, academia and research and other stakeholders in cross-border projects and cybersecurity activities at national level.[40] While this task is in fact not directly related to the Community, it does also not explicitly exclude its members. In addition, National Coordination Centres can help stimulate interest in a membership and encourage appropriate institutions to join the Competence Community.

In return, the Community shall e.g., involve the National Coordination Centres in its work[41]. Its members shall work closely with the National Coordination Centres to

[33] Cf. Wording in Art. 19(2).

[34] Cf. Wording in Art. 8(9).

[35] Art. 14 of the Rules of Procedure of the Governing Board deals with "working groups", but the Regulation does not refer to the working groups in the Regulation. In terms of content, it deals with "*ad hoc* working groups", the necessity, formation and composition of which seem to be conceived differently from the working groups mentioned in the Regulation. A clearer description in the Rules of Procedure (and, if necessary, a definition of the terms) would be desirable.

[36] Cf. Art. 7(1).

[37] Art. 3(2).

[38] Art. 7(1)(a).

[39] Art. 7(1)(h).

[40] Art. 7(1)(c).

[41] Art. 8(2).

assist the Competence Centre in fulfilling its mission[42] and shall assist the National Coordination Centres in promoting specific projects[43].

Opportunities and Barriers for Community Building. The Regulation, thus, creates possible touching points between the Coordination Centres as public actors and the Community or its members as predominantly private law actors. The role of the National Coordination Centres "in the middle of the action" offers a suitable starting point for the creation of national, regional or local communities and networking within the Community, if designed actively and purposefully. The complementary mandate for the Community to work closely with the Coordination Centres supports this approach. However, the Regulation does not lay down structures for practical task implementation and cooperation. Thus, it is left to the National Coordination Centres and the Competence Community to design these. The resulting freedom of design offers both sides the opportunity to take national, regional or local, thematic and sector-specific circumstances into account for the cooperation design. A realistic approach must of course still be aware of the danger that the individual efforts in the Member States fail and that no cooperation at all or no sufficient cooperation for the promotion of European cybersecurity is achieved. While the National Coordination Centres, as public institutions, have an internal structure "by order" and can use traditional forms of action under their national legal systems, the *Competence Community,* contrary to its name, is not yet a structured unit that can revert to such common organisational or financial resources. Whether and how the cooperation will succeed in practice therefore remains to be seen.[44] [1, 2, 8].

Considering that the Competence Community - despite or precisely because of the thematic affinity of its members - will include competitors with opposing interests, e.g. with regard to political influence, funding opportunities or expansion of market shares, an "automatic" or "natural" formation of a Community seems far-fetched. Although the Regulation lays down the criteria and procedure for becoming a member of the Community, it does not contain any explicit rules on how to build the Community from the registered members and which structures it can actively use to fulfil its tasks. Thus, the tasks of the Community and its members as well as their integration into the governance structure of the Regulation, can give at most only clues as to what kind of Community the legislator had in mind. As demonstrated, however, the Regulation alone does not contain powerful enough community-forming factors.

The broadly chosen community concept is the best approach to cover as many areas and existing competences in the field of cybersecurity in the European Union as possible. Another question, however, is whether the broad notion of a Community in theory can be brought to practical life at all. The participation design is one decisive element in this regard. Studies on private standardisation organisations, which could also be described as communities, demonstrate that regularly only those stakeholders with the necessary

42 Art. 9(a).

43 Art. 9(c).

44 According to Recital (17), with regard to the management of the Community and its representation in the Competence Centre, e.g. the experience of the 4 pilot projects CONCORDIA, ECHO, SPARTA and CyberSec4Europe, which were launched at the beginning of 2019 within the framework of Horizon 2020, shall be drawn upon. CyberSec4Europe has extensively addressed governance design issues for the Competence Community.

financial, time, and human resources can exert active influence, because this is what makes active participation possible in the first place. Not all interests therefore have the same chances of assertion [9, p. 174], even if in principle everyone can participate [9, p. 117] [10, p. 38 et seqq.]. The resulting work therefore only reflects the contributions of the actively involved, assertive stakeholders and is not a consensus of all stakeholders. This effect cannot be ruled out for the Competence Community. The organisational efforts that come with an involvement of Community members within Community networks, in working groups or in the Strategic Advisory Group may exceed the organisational possibilities of smaller members, no matter how much expertise and experience they have. Particularly in the field of cybersecurity, with rapid technical developments and effects that reach into every area of society and government, it is undesirable to leave existing competences unused only due to structural deficits of the participation design in the Regulation.

3 Organising the Community

As discussed above, it is essential to activate and effectively use the potential that lies within the concept of a Competence Community. The Regulation's top-down approach and the limitation of Community members to observing or advisory roles without real opportunities for influence do not offer much incentive for an active involvement, while the exclusive participation design makes it even more difficult to exploit existing competences. Opportunities for the cooperation, collaboration and knowledge exchange within the Community as well as funding opportunities for its members have to be ensured in order to reach this goal.

Therefore, the fact that the Regulation does not offer sufficient instruments for the establishment and governance of the Community should be seen as an opportunity. The absence of strict rules leaves space for the development of a true bottom-up approach for the Community building. The power of bottom-up approaches results from their possibility to provide broad expertise and knowledge of industry, academia and stakeholders in specific areas by organising information gathering and distribution. It is, thus, an appropriate way of activating research and development capacities.

One way to establish and organise the Community could therefore be the introduction of hubs in which different stakeholders could join their efforts, accumulate special expertise, promote scientific exchange and facilitate research or development of solutions. These Community Hubs of Expertise in Cybersecurity Knowledge (CHECKs) would be low-level, easy-to-access points of accumulation of regional, sectoral or topical interests and information, and they can serve as accelerator to demands and problem identification as well as solution mechanisms.

We note that CHECKs are different from the Digital Innovation Hubs (DIHs) launched by the European Commission in fundamental ways. DIHs were launched by European Commission in the scope of the Digitising European Industry initiative in 2016, in order to coordinate with Member States and regions towards common goals to help companies to become more competitive with regard to their business/production processes, products or services using digital technologies. In the new programme Digital Europe (2021–2027), they are called European DIHs (EDIHs) and defined as one-stop shops supporting companies to respond to digital challenges and become more competitive. They provide access to the latest knowledge, expertise and technology to support their customers with piloting, testing and experimenting with digital innovations [11, 12].

As a first step it is necessary to further develop the idea of CHECKs. Their optimal design requires answering a variety of questions, such as the organisation, composition, tasks and funding of CHECKs as well as their relationship to each other, to the national coordination centres and the European Competence Centre. The answers should be based on practical experience gained in the pilot projects, analysis of legal frameworks, expediency and teleological considerations, and stakeholder feedback [13, 14].

Therefore, the CyberSec4Europe pilot project proposed the installation of additional regional and cross-border networks at the Community level [1, 2, 8]. As one element to achieve this goal, CyberSec4Europe envisioned the introduction of CHECKs into a future form of the regulation. The network would be significantly strengthened and advanced into a true structure that would ensure efficient flows of information that are implemented swiftly and occur within the most efficient layers. It has to be noted that also from the point of the Community membership it can be advisable to establish different decision-making processes, which will not always include all partners on all issues.

3.1 Our Use-Case

Two types of CHECK emerged after the preliminary analyses, namely one that is an economic actor in the cybersecurity landscape and must be sustained by a sound business model, and another that is part of the public administration and financed as a public good. The case described here, namely the CHECK-T pilot, in Toulouse, France, that is used to validate a specific governance model, is an example of the former type.

In view of the implementation of CHECK-T, interviews were conducted with stakeholders in order to learn about their needs and requirements regarding CHECKs, e.g., which details make the concept of CHECKs attractive for them to participate and contribute to the cybersecurity Community. These results together with possible changes in the governance structures may constitute the basis for the improvement of the European cybersecurity governance in future revisions of the regulation.

The interview campaign was carried on in order to identify the main needs and expectations, types of financially sustainable activities and a multidisciplinary pool of actors that would be willing to participate in the creation and development of the CHECK-T, aiming at:

- Mobilise communities of actors with different but complementary challenges
- Project a common vision
- Identify a consensus on the expected missions within the consortium

Highlight the benefits for each stakeholder by sharing, contributing, and financing in common.

3.2 Needs and Expectations

The interview campaign included a total of 40 stakeholders from four large community groups (cybersecurity end users, cybersecurity solutions providers, technology centres, and economic development accelerators). The expressed needs and expectations were divided in six main categories, as follows.

- **Capacity building**: Guarantee the sharing of data, sensitive information, and technological research with other partners on all types of incidents and on the responses provided.
- **Transfer of uses, sharing of R&D&I costs**: implementing methodological processes transferable from one sector to another, at lower costs.
- **Technological leadership**: Sharing expertise and general know-how, infrastructure, and investment costs by obtaining R&D funding.
- **Trust-building**: Building a local and European base of trust, promoting cooperation and coopetition between members (ethical framework, protection of freedoms, dissemination of trust).
- **Business Return On Investment (ROI)**: facilitate the obtaining of funding in Cybersecurity Innovation and accelerate the maturation of projects and products to the market and awareness-raising, co-innovation activities.
- **Usability by design**: Eliminate barriers by studying use cases and demonstrating scientific and technological know-how before large-scale deployment towards industrial products.

Such analysis is summarised as follows.

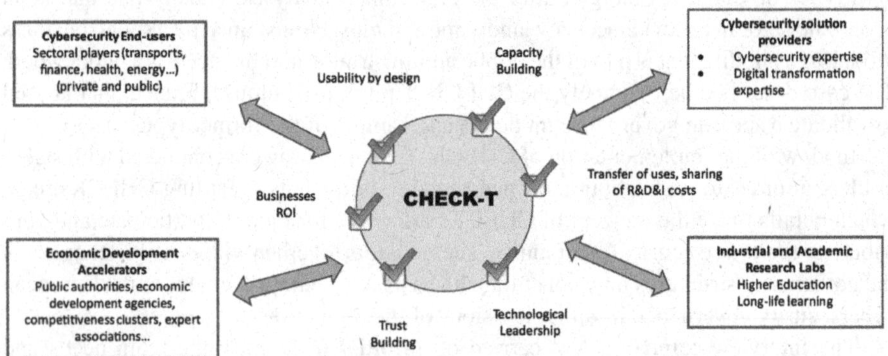

Fig. 1. Community groups and mission classes for a CHECK

3.3 Main Findings

In each of the six categories described above, possible interactions between the actors (from one community group to another and peer-to-peer by highlighting the concept of coopetition) were further explored. Some remarkable examples by category include:

- **Capacity building**: Information sharing, including common interpretation of cybersecurity legal texts.
- **Transfer of uses, sharing of R&D&I costs**: Here again information sharing was central, e.g. about best practices.

- **Technological leadership**: Pooling of lobbying activities.
- **Trust-building**: Agreeing and publishing a common ethical framework of cooperation.
- **Business Return On Investment (ROI)**: Very important point, that includes networking, market access, and the identification of funding opportunities.
- **Usability by design**: Elicitation of requirements that may be common to many members.

A comprehensive synthesis of the main findings is given in the figure below.

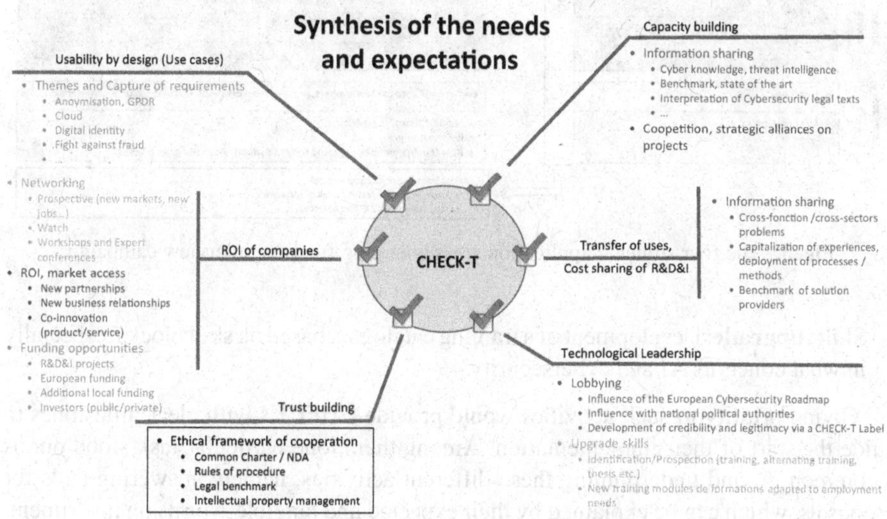

Fig. 2. Synthesis of the needs and expectations

The next step defined four strategic application areas, which must be implemented in order for the stakeholders to take an interest in the creation of a CHECK:

- **R&D&I funding**
- **Services**
- **Market access**
- **Skills upgrade**

In each of these areas, several priority and evolving activities have been identified and are described below.

Finally, the following activities emerged as foundational in order to increase the likelihood of success of a CHECK.

- **R&D&I funding**: Exploration of the opportunities to participate in European and national calls for projects in AI and cybersecurity.
- **Services**: Networking and lobbying in order to influence cybersecurity roadmaps, e.g. within the CyberSec4Europe project.
- **Market access**: Fight against banking fraud as a first use-case, based on the decompartmentalization of business data.

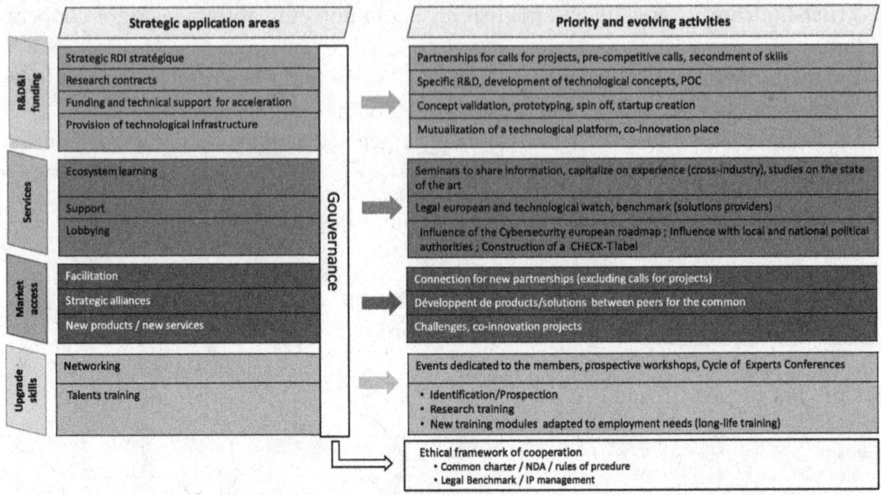

Fig. 3. The four strategic application areas emerging from the interview campaign

- **Skills upgrade**: Development of a training catalogue, based on skill blocks, especially in what concerns AI and cybersecurity.

Giving priority to such activities would provide CHECKs with clear milestones to guide the start of their implementation. Among them, one particular task stood out as a common ground underpinning these different activities, namely answering calls for proposals, which can be explained by their expected and tangible returns on investment. As a consequence, this common feature was chosen as a first working basis for defining the financial value that CHECKs should have, in order to bring its potential members to join and work towards effectively implementing and developing the above four activities.

Following this line of reasoning, a CHECK may propose itself as a tool for its members to target regional, national, and European calls for proposals, for instance by selecting specific calls for proposals and then identifying and coordinating its competent members that are best fit for answering them. In such a case, CHECKs' role would be either to build and coordinate appropriate skills consortia to respond to calls for projects, or to identify and orchestrate the available skills necessary to join, as a partner, larger consortia preparing to respond to calls for projects. This could also be done by considering that the CHECK, as the representative of the community of competence of its territory, would be the legal entity participating in the response submitted to the call, on behalf of its subset of selected members.

Both the coordination of proposals and the participation in consortia imply that a CHECK must be in possession of a complete and up-to-date inventory of the skills and the knowledge available among its members in the field of cybersecurity, and be informed of their availability and intention to participate in the implementation of such collaborative projects.

4 Recommendations

The analysis carried out reveals potential for improving the role of the Community in various areas. For a successful exploitation of the existing knowledge and expertise of the Community, the current regulation lacks instruments and incentives for their involvement, and this has to be overcome. In this section we give recommendations pertaining to these aspects, in order to remediate missing features of the regulation. Legal as well as organizational and financial aspects have to be taken into account.

4.1 The Review of the Cybersecurity Regulation

A revision of the regulation by the European legislator should consider at minima the following points.

Potential Community members or already existing networks need to be approached systematically to inform them about the possibility of application and registration and, even more important, about the benefits and added values of a membership in the Community. It needs to be clear why a stakeholder should decide to apply for the Community and put efforts into the tasks that come with a membership.

The participation of Community members should be strengthened, e.g. in the Strategic Advisory Group. The Group should be given a permanent observer status in the meetings of the Governing Board and the Board should be obliged to give an explanatory statement in case of full or partial non-consideration of advice given by the Strategic Advisory Group. It should also be considered to give the Community a voice in the decision which of its members join the Strategic Advisory Group. Participation and representation in decision-making processes are benefits that should not be underestimated.

The Community needs a governance structure, which allows for an organised approach on the existing cybersecurity challenges while offering the necessary flexibility as an answer to the diversity of stakeholders and circumstances in the Member States.

More obvious, but not less important than participatory or organisation instruments, is the dedication of funds to certain tasks or projects to encourage research and development activities in the Community. This can either encourage the collaboration of members in already existing connections as well as the establishment of new ones, e.g. for specific tasks.

4.2 Governance of CHECKs

As indicated above, governance issues are transversal to the strategic application areas and depend on the specific activities to be implemented. The appropriate governance model to be chosen depends a great deal on decisions needed to implement the inventory described above, as it can be considered the capital on which a CHECK must be based. In order to carry out such an inventory as efficiently and comprehensively as possible, it is necessary to quickly determine the group that will participate in the foundation of the CHECK, i.e. whether or not it will be composed only by representatives from the End User, Cyber Security Solution Providers, Technology Centres, and Economic Development Accelerators communities that have been consulted in order to define the strategic axes and the priority activities.

Accordingly, the first decision of the group of founders should be to agree on the subject matter of CHECK, and therefore its role, in particular with respect to the calls for proposals. This is because both subject and role would delimit the appropriate legal status that is required for a CHECK to become a legal entity. The choice of a legal status will also help to determine the contractual nature of the inventory, which may be a simple directory of territorial competences in the area or a database of relevant persons, staff or not, from the communities that constitute the CHECK, and on which it will rely to participate in calls for proposals and to fulfil its contractual commitments once the project is implemented. It is worth noticing that one of the main added-values of a CHECK to the current cybersecurity regional landscape in the EU is exactly this capacity to coordinate and orchestrate exogenous and diverse skill resources in the form of a cooperative with a legal status.

Therefore, the governance model should be discussed by the founders of CHECKs in order to establish an internal organisation that is conducive of the role to be implemented, but, crucially, cannot create competition to their own members. This last point needs particular attention, as it directly impacts the economic model of a CHECK, as discussed in the following.

4.3 Funding and Sustainability

The abstract concept of a CHECK is very attractive and all interviewed stakeholders were very positive about its priorities, membership, activities, and so forth. However, questioning starts immediately once aspects related to the funding of such activities come to fore, as very few stakeholders are eager to embark in such a journey if they are not first shown how their financial investment would enable the generation of income for themselves and in a near future, through such activities. This is why the orchestration of skill resources emerged as a priority task for a CHECK, as it makes CHECKs primarily a source of revenue for its members, which may then be complemented with activities around lobbying, sharing good-practices and information, and capacity building.

In this sense, if a CHECK is established as a cooperative means for its members to target regional, national, and European calls for proposals, and to coordinate the corresponding responses, then funding should normally be implemented through a mix of (i) membership fees paid by its constituting members, (ii) access fees for consultation of its directory, (iii) consultancy fees related to the facilitation of participation in calls for proposals, as well as through (iv) bonus schemes on the results.

We note that if the decision is to establish the CHECK as the legal entity that is to be contracted in successful responses to calls of proposals, on behalf of its members, then the funding would also include the collection of overheads and administrative budget of projects won. On the other hand, such a decision should be dependent on the satisfactory resolution *ex-ante* of thorny IPR issues. As a matter of fact, this should not be considered as an impediment, since very successful examples of this kind of organisation exist, notably IMEC in Belgium.

Another important point of attention for CHECKs as legal entities is the fact that calls for proposals usually come with stringent rules on the financial capacity of bidders. Therefore, a CHECK bidding in calls for proposals should be able to demonstrate that the amounts for which it bids represent a fraction of its financial capacity, which is given by its capital and turnover. It is likely that the amount of equity allocated to a CHECK will be the result of the discussions with the founders as it will reflect the level of their ambition. The turnover could be based on the combination of the membership, access, and consultancy fees and bonuses alluded above.

As a result, in order to quickly ensure the feasibility and relevance of the approach chosen for a territory, it is recommended to go through a phase where the formal "pre-configuring" of the organisation to be established is funded. Its effective implementation implies favouring legal support by an actor in the territory with a certain notoriety in the targeted ecosystem. By thus incubating a CHECK, such an actor would enable the CHECK to attract funds to deploy a first structuring project prototype that would demonstrate the robustness and sustainability of its economic model, whereby kickstarting the legitimacy and the added-value of the CHECK in the eyes of its stakeholders.

Finally, as part of such a partnership logic, this model based on a seed legal support by a third party should favour a structure with mainly public capital. Indeed, the production of common deliverables by a multidisciplinary ecosystem requires an environment of trust from the outset that only public authorities can guarantee at that point.

5 Conclusion

The case of the CHECK-T pilot that was tested by CyberSec4Europe, through its partner UPS-IRIT, contributed notable insights based on day-to-day implementation experiences, including the existence of some mistrust from the part of public administrations themselves, because of issues related to their perimeter of action and influence.

In view of the installation of additional European regional and cross-border networks at the Community level, CyberSec4Europe already envisioned the introduction of CHECKs into a future form of the Regulation while the legislative procedure was still in progress. Unfortunately, this has not been considered by the legislator and if it will be considered in case of an amendment, cannot be foreseen. However, despite the missing support of the CHECK concept, there are at least no limitations in the Regulation for the Community to organise itself.

For stakeholders to take an interest in CHECKs, four strategic application areas must be implemented, namely access to funding in R&D&I, capacity building, market access, and dedicated services. Such services to be offered could then contribute to the economic security of the so-called essential sectors of the territory and would have as primary vocation to support the rise in the capacities of SMEs / SMIs and subcontractors of these sectors, in their approach to crisis management, in particular related to cybersecurity. The development and deployment of services related to the establishment of a CHECK would be done in close partnership with solution providers and the research and higher education communities in the region.

Finally, Member States and, wherever necessary, their regions, should provide dedicated funds to kick-start contractual Public-Private partnerships with the CHECKs in order to increase their attractivity in the eyes of stakeholders. As described in this paper, our interview campaign elicited the needs from potential stakeholders and highlighted services expected from such an organisation. The needs and potential services detailed here are meant to serve as a basis upon which to build the CHECKs' business models in future. Public seed-funds are crucial in that they would help to create a virtuous circle, where the return-on-investment in joining one such CHECK becomes more evident.

Acknowledgments. This work was based on very rich conversations with the members of Work Package 2 of CyberSec4Security, whom the authors warmly thank. This work was partially supported by the European research projects H2020 CyberSec4Europe (GA 830929) and LeADS (GA 956562) and Horizon Europe DUCA (GA 101086308), and by the CNRS IRN EU-CHECK.

References

1. CyberSec4Europe H2020 Project. D2.1 Governance Structure (2020)
2. CyberSec4Europe H2020 Project. Deliverable D2.3: Governance Structure v2.0 (2021)
3. Duden online. https://www.duden.de/Rechtschreibung/Gemeinschaft. Accessed 25 Oct 2022
4. European Cybersecurity Competence Centre. https://cybersecurity-centre.europa.eu/system/files/2022-08/GB%20decision%20No%202022_6_ECCC%20SPD%202022-2024_Budget%202022.pdf. Accessed 25 Oct 2022
5. European Cybersecurity Competence Centre. https://cybersecurity-centre.europa.eu/system/files/2021-11/ECCC%20Decision%20No%20GB20211%20RoP_final.pdf. Accessed 25 Oct 2022
6. von Wintzingerode, C., Müllmann, D.: Ein europäisches Netzwerk für Cybersicherheit, in Den Wandel begleiten - IT-rechtliche Herausforderungen der Digitalisierung, Edewecht, pp. 475–492 (2020).
7. von Wintzingerode, C.G., Müllmann, D., Spiecker gen. Döhmann, I.: Ein Netzwerk für Europas Cybersicherheit, Neue Zeitschrift für Verwaltungsrecht (NVwZ), pp. 690–695, 2021
8. CyberSec4Europe H2020 Project, Deliverable D2.2: Internal Validation of Governance Structure, 2021
9. Bolenz, E.: Technische Normung zwischen "Markt" und "Staat" Bielefeld (1987)
10. Hartlieb, B., Hövel, A., Müller, N.: Normung und Standardisierung, Berlin (2016)
11. Foray, D., et al.: Guide on Research and Innovation Strategies for Smart Specialisation
12. Digital Innovation Hubs, European Commisison. https://s3platform.jrc.ec.europa.eu/digital-innovation-hubs. Accessed July 2022
13. Nai-Fovino, I., Neisse, R., Lazari, A., Ruzzante, G.: European Cybersecurity Centre of Expertise - Cybersecurity Competence Survey. Publications Office of the European Union, Luxembourg (2018)
14. Penchev, G., Shalamanov, V.: Architecture and Process Oriented Approach to Institution. Inf. Secur. Int. J. **46**, 99–113 (2020)

Building a Cybersecurity Awareness Program: Present and Prospective Aspects

Sunil Chaudhary[1(✉)] and Vasileios Gkioulos[2]

[1] European Center on Privacy and Cybersecurity, Faculty of Law, Maastricht University, Bouillonstraat 3, 6211 LH Maastricht, The Netherlands
sunil.chaudhary@maastrichtuniversity.nl

[2] Department of Information Security and Communication Technology, Norwegian University of Science and Technology, Teknologivegen 22, 2815 Gjøvik, Norway
vasileios.gkioulos@ntnu.no

Abstract. This chapter discusses present and prospective aspects of cybersecurity awareness (CSA) initiatives. Concerning the first, it presents practices suggested by numerous past research studies that involve both CSA and other relevant fields of study in order to build a more effective CSA program. The second segment recommends leveraging the capabilities of artificial intelligence (AI) and machine learning (ML) to design and deliver a more customized and personalized experience to CSA program audiences. This utilization of AI and ML will presumably contribute to making CSA programs more effective and efficient.

Keywords: Cybersecurity Awareness · Good Practices · Customized and Personalized Experience

1 Meaning of Cybersecurity Awareness

Cybersecurity awareness (CSA) is about making people mindful of security risks and threats applicable to them, aiming to motivate them to adopt good security practices in their personal and professional lives. More specifically, it entails *cognition* (i.e., acquiring knowledge and comprehension of cybersecurity challenges), *attitude* (i.e., leading to positive changes in attitudes and interests toward cybersecurity), and *behavior* (i.e., ultimately making the needful cybersecurity behavioral adjustments). For a CSA program to achieve this objective, *the communicated information, the medium of delivery, the timing, and the periodicity of it must be adjusted to the target audience* [1]. In terms of content, the delivered information must be of sufficient depth to alert the audience to relevant security issues, enhancing their understanding of both the potential ramifications and the suitable adaptations to their security posture.

The rest of the chapter is structured and organized as follows: Sect. 2 describes the various stages of CSA initiatives, along with good practices for each stage that could help execute them in the most effective ways possible. Section 3 discusses the how AI and ML can be utilized to enhance the effectiveness of CSA initiatives. Finally, Sect. 4 contains the conclusions of the chapter.

A. Skarmeta et al. (Eds.): CyberSec4Europe 2022, CCIS 1807, pp. 149–160, 2023.
https://doi.org/10.1007/978-3-031-36096-1_10

2 Stages of Cybersecurity Awareness Initiatives

In general, a CSA program consists of three phases. They are the pre-implementation phase, implementation phase, and post-implementation phase, in accordance with the National Institute of Standards and Technology (NIST) framework [2]. The phases are similarly listed in the European Union Agency for Cybersecurity (ENISA) framework [3] as plan, assess, and design; execute and manage; and evaluate and adjust. Regardless of how the phases are classified, the first phase is a preparatory stage where awareness needs are identified and all program preparations are made. During the second phase, the awareness program is run and managed according to the plan. The awareness program's effects and impacts are assessed/measured in the final phase in order to determine the value received from organizing it as well as what needs to be adjusted or updated in subsequent iterations. Each phase is further divided into several sub-phases, each of which includes a number of activities. Figure 1 depicts a conceptual framework for a CSA program with its different phases, sub-phases, and activities derived from the review and consolidation of nine past frameworks [1]. Additionally, some good practices that could help execute each phase, sub-phase, and activity effectively are discussed next.

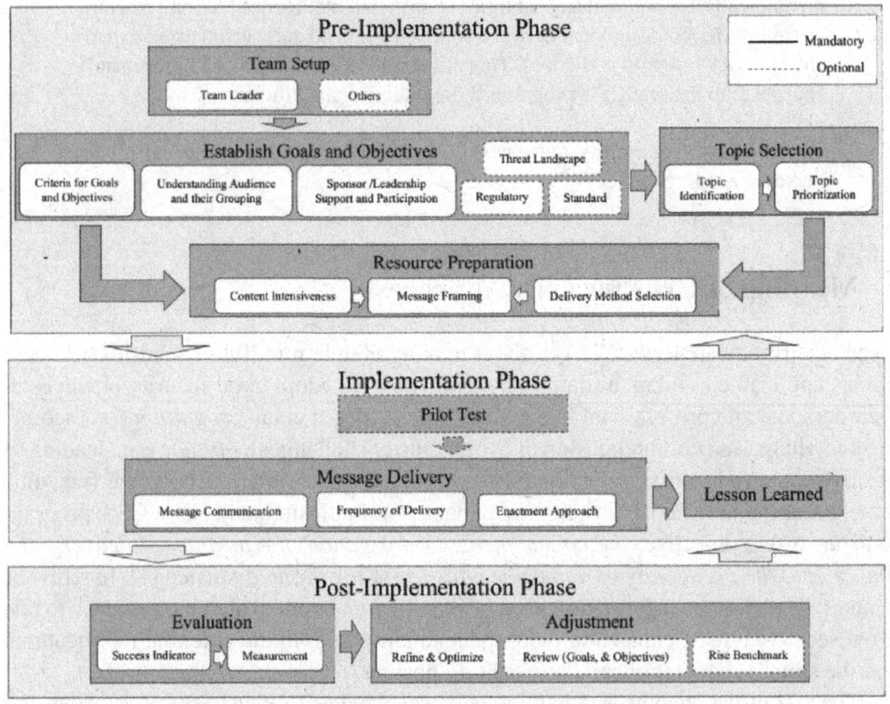

Fig. 1. CSA Framework [1].

2.1 Pre-implementation Phase

Team Setup. The team should be *inclusive* (i.e., comprise people from different expertise areas or departments of the organization) [4] with clearly defined roles, responsibilities, and accountabilities for each member [3]. An inclusive team would facilitate the awareness activities in many ways, such as by avoiding resistance to making awareness mandatory, aiding in audience comprehension, and possibly obtaining additional resources. Generally, it is advisable to have two full-time CSA professional members [5], but one full-time CSA professional is a must [6] in order to enhance the prospects of achieving CSA maturity [7]. The full-time CSA professional should lead the team, be equipped with both *technical* and *soft skills* [5], and be *context aware* (i.e., acknowledge that each group has its own unique set of values, challenges, and strengths) [8]. Communication skills, familiarity with learning concepts, knowledge of awareness tools and techniques, personal attributes, career and collaborative attributes, and the people skills required to persuade the audience to learn and practice cybersecurity are examples of soft skills [5, 8].

Criteria for Goals and Objectives. The goal and objective support the rationale behind developing a CSA program, i.e., what the program wants to achieve, and can be exclusive to a target group. The needs (or baseline) for a CSA program can be identified by conducting a *needs assessment* [3, 9]. Criteria-wise, the goal set should be clear and simple, and its objectives should be SMART (Specific, Measurable, Attainable, Relevant, and Time-bound) [10]. These objective characteristics are required to determine whether or not a CSA program produces the expected results. For example, a goal can be – *to identify and manage human risks to an acceptable level*, whose respective objectives can be – *to reduce accidental data loss incidents by 75% and improve incident reporting to 100%*.

Understanding the Audience and their Grouping. To effectively design, develop, implement, assess, and update a CSA program, it is vital to understand the target audience and their security behavior. Furthermore, it may need to group the audience, preferably based on their cybersecurity beliefs and expertise [11], and organizational roles and responsibilities [4]. This segmentation of the audience is essential to tailoring and personalizing the awareness materials and delivery so as to effectively serve their needs.

Sponsor/Leader Support and Participation. A CSA program can become sustainable only if it receives an appropriately high priority in terms of support and participation from the top management in an organization [12, 13]. CSA programs that have received top management support have proven to be more successful [14]. Their support and participation are critical for several reasons: first, they possess budgetary authority and so can ensure the required budget and resources for CSA initiatives; second, they usually have access to sensitive information and cyber assets and are therefore high-value targets of cyber criminals and attackers; and finally, their commitment to CSA programs will send a positive message to employees and also motivate them to take CSA initiatives seriously [15, 16].

Topic Identification. To identify relevant CSA topics that are useful and interest the target audience, a range of strategies, such as surveys, interactions, and others, could be used. In the case of micro and small organizations, relying on a small sample of qualitative or even informal staff interviews [2] could be adequate and cost-effective. However, in the case of medium and large organizations, a range of sources can be used for *need assessment*, including but not limited to conducting interviews with various relevant groups, examining existing CSA programs, analyzing cyber incidents in the organization or industry trends, making technical or infrastructure changes in the organization, and so forth [3]. The identified CSA topics should encompass common threats, threats that are prevalent and relevant to the organizations and the target audience [12], as well as reactive and proactive security measures in reaction to new events and situations, such as changes in security laws and the implementation of new technologies [2].

Topic Prioritization. The CSA team may not be able to cover all specified CSA topics at the same time, and it becomes necessary to categorize cyber threats and prioritize those that pose an imminent risk and have the potential to cause significant harm. For example, topics relevant to critical security roles and controls [17], specific to the organization's role and risk profile, relevant to critical projects, neglected by the audience, and with readily available resources [2] should be given high priority.

Resource Preparation. Designing and developing every resource for a CSA program is not always required. A variety of awareness and related materials available on the Internet can be incorporated [2, 3]; many sources that distribute CSA materials for free have been listed in [18, 19]. However, before using such resources, they must be assessed to determine whether they meet the needs of the program or whether they need to be tailored. In general, the CSA materials should be inexpensive to develop, fit the target organization's culture and infrastructure, and not necessitate time-consuming actions to utilize.

Content Intensiveness and Complexities. The content intensity and complexity should be appropriate for the target audience in order to pique their interest in CSA programs and increase participation [2]. CSA content can be classified as *general* (i.e., suitable for everyone), *intermediate* (i.e., suitable for management, decision-makers, and some specialized roles), and *in-depth* (i.e., suitable for specialized roles and some management) [20]. Depending on the audience type, the content's intensity and complexity should be adjusted from general to in-depth.

Message Framing. Effective CSA content is more than just what is conveyed; it is also about how the information is received, interpreted, and assimilated by the audience. A message can be framed and communicated in several ways without changing its facts but differing in its impacts on people. Framing has a considerable impact on, for example, how an individual processes information, makes decisions [21, 22], and is persuaded [23]. Psychological factors, such as *loss aversion, the bandwagon effect,* and *confirmation biases,* can be leveraged during message framing to improve the persuasiveness of the CSA message [1]. Similarly, properties like *information quality* (credible and consistent information, up-to-date information, complete information), *message framing* (direct, positive), *suggestion quality* (doable, convenience), and *content presentation* (clarity, well-structured, using multiple representations, understandability of the main message, and localization) (see [1, 24]) should be considered to influence the message reception and interpretation of the audience.

Delivery Method Selection. CSA programs use a multitude of delivery methods to disseminate awareness messages, for example, workshops, newsletters, posters, screensavers, emails, games, videos, audios, simulations, online quizzes, and so on. These methods can be broadly categorized into three types: *instructor-led*, *computer-based*, and *text-based* [25]. As is obvious, each category has its own advantages and disadvantages [1]. Therefore, the following criteria could be used to determine their eligibility for use: are cost-effective; have a broad outreach; support diversity and inclusiveness; are easy and simple to develop, operate, manage, and update; include standardized assessment and feedback features; support information richness; require minimal additional requirements; and interest and motivate the audience [3, 26–28]. It is often suggested to use *multiple methods* that could cover the needs of a diversified audience for CSA purposes [29, 30].

2.2 Implementation Phase

Pilot Test. A small-scale preliminary test with the target audience could be conducted to assess the efficacy of prepared or upgraded awareness resources [31]. This type of test will aid in finding flaws in resource design that must be fixed before they can be used for the intended CSA program. A pilot test is not required for an existing or ongoing small-scale CSA program, but it can be important for a new (or first-time) large-scale (or mass) CSA program. A pilot test is an additional stage in the CSA process (or a resource drain) with no certainty that it will identify and help prevent any difficulties. However, if the CSA program is intended for a large number of people, the benefits of a pilot test may outweigh the time and money spent on it.

Message Communication. The CSA message might address one or more related topics at the same time. In practice, the awareness message should reach everyone in the target audience. However, simply reaching the target audience does not guarantee that the awareness message will be received, read, and taken seriously. As a result, it is critical that an awareness message reaches the intended audience and has a positive impact on them (i.e., influence or motivate them to adopt the good security practices and advice in the message). There are two critical factors in effectively communicating security messages: the *messenger* and the *communication approach*. The messenger or source of information should be someone whom the audience is most likely to *listen to* and *trust* [32]. Such an individual could be someone with authority or someone with similar characteristics, such as peers. Regarding communication, it should consider the psychological and other influencing factors that increase the audience's participation and drive them to practice (or translate into actions) the security knowledge they learn from the program (see [33, 34]).

Enactment Approach. The ultimate objective of CSA is behavior change. In general, two approaches are used for the purpose: a soft approach (i.e., persuasion techniques) and a hard approach (i.e., coercive techniques) [35]. It is often recommended in CSA to use a soft approach to encourage security behavior change [35–37]. Some rationales behind this recommendation are as follows:

- organization cannot afford to continuously monitor employees' behavior and to dismiss or discipline a large number of skilled staff needed for a tough approach [38],
- treating employees as enemies and using forceful enforcement can increase tension between enforcers and the rest of the organization [37],
- in order to keep up with the ever-changing digital landscape and constantly changing cybersecurity, a long-term behavioral change is required, which can be possible through a soft approach [39], and
- feelings of fear or anxiety in cybersecurity are considered to be counterproductive, especially in the absence of clear communication and efficacious information about how to respond to the threat [40].

However, there are also some research studies that put forward contrary views and advocate for a level of fear in cybersecurity to produce a positive effect [41]. Their reason for this is that through persuasion, the probability of compliance is improved, whereas evoking fear by highlighting the unpleasant consequences of non-compliance makes people care about compliance [41]. The debate on which approach is better, soft or tough, has no end unless other conditions are considered. Finally, the major challenge in using either a soft approach or a tough approach is determining the critical factors that can motivate employees to comply or deter them from non-compliance, respectively. More importantly, due to various intervening factors, it is difficult to prove unequivocally that a certain persuasive factor has motivated compliance behavior or punishment has prevented non-compliance behavior. The views on these critical factors often vary with no common ground; different experts may offer different perspectives based on their personal experiences. Therefore, it is suggested that the enforcement approach used to address non-compliance should be a soft approach (mainly using intrinsic incentives) unless a specific need arises for a tough approach.

Frequency of Delivery. To remain up-to-date and relevant to the intended audience, CSA programs should be periodically updated [42]. Furthermore, the effects of CSA programs attenuate over time, resulting in the forgetting of knowledge that is no longer used. As a result, CSA programs should be periodically organized, and the shorter the time between two successive programs, the more effective CSA will be [43]. This is why a CSA program should be organized on a regular enough basis to retain its effectiveness while also updating and reinforcing security knowledge. However, the CSA program incurs costs and takes time, which should be considered when determining its frequency.

A question that requires an answer is, "*How often should CSA programs be organized?*" The simple answer would be that the frequency is adequate to maintain the topic in the minds of individuals [42]. According to the *Curve of Forgetting*, if we assume 100% of the information learned at the end of a lecture and there is no attempt made to retain the information, we remember only 30%–50% of the information by day 2, and this dwindles to only 2%–3% by day 30. However, this trend of forgetting information can be changed by applying *Dale's Cone of Experience Model* to information delivery [44]. The model conveys that people retain information told, shown, and experienced (done) to them in ascending order, i.e., the information shown remains longer than the information told, and the information experienced remains longer than the information shown. Therefore, by utilizing delivery methods that support perceptual learning styles, information retention can be improved. Memory retention can be improved further by reducing *cognitive overload* [45]. However, a study has shown that in general the effect of a CSA program decreases at an unacceptable level after six months [46], thus it should be organized at least once every six months, except if it is about responding to new events and situations.

Lessons Learned. The CSA program's effectiveness can be improved in the following or future initiatives by combining feedback from audiences and lessons learned from the program's implementation [9]. Furthermore, in terms of materials and expertise, advice and lessons learned from colleagues and/or organizations in charge of other awareness projects could be quite beneficial [3]. For example, one department can share its experiences with other departments in an organization, allowing them to plan ahead of time to avoid making the same mistakes. But for this, the lessons learned during the different phases of the program should be properly captured, debriefed, and documented for the effective transfer and use of information [3].

2.3 Post-implementation Phase

Evaluation. CSA is an iterative process that focuses on continuous improvement [2, 42]. In each iteration, CSA programs are reviewed and evaluated for their effectiveness and to determine areas for improvement in future iterations. Many past studies used a variety of quantitative and qualitative approaches, such as surveys, interviews, tests, and others, to measure positive changes, namely, in security knowledge, attitude, and behavior, for evaluation purposes. However, these studies do not perform a holistic evaluation but limit themselves to measuring only a few factors [47]. More importantly, several of them created their own questionnaires while employing questionnaires for surveys and tests, which are frequently non-standardized. Worse, some studies that supply security solutions or propose a framework conduct an evaluation solely to establish and prove that their work is relevant and useful. To address these challenges in CSA evaluation, ENISA proposed measuring a combination of four key performance indicators (KPIs): process improvement, attack resistance, efficiency and effectiveness, and internal protection [42]. Similarly, Chaudhary et al. [47] proposed metrics for CSA evaluation. The metrics suggested measuring all four KPIs (impact, sustainability, accessibility, and monitoring) to determine the overall effectiveness of a CSA program. Furthermore, the measurable parameters selected for each indicator should be economical to gather, consistent to measure, expressible in cardinal numbers and units, and contextually specific. Finally, it is recommended that when designing and using questionnaires, either a recognized security standard should be followed or a standardized questionnaire like the Human Aspects of Information Security Questionnaire (HAIS-Q) [48], Security Behavior Intentions Scale (SeBIS) [49], and SA-6 scale [50] should be used.

Adjustment. Cybersecurity threats are dynamic in nature, constantly changing with emerging and evolving technologies. Moreover, in order to address them, cybersecurity measures (e.g., technological measures, laws/regulations, and policies/ procedures/

standards) are always evolving, with new measures being developed and existing ones being updated. As a result, in order to remain relevant and effective, a CSA program must be adjusted by considering and incorporating these shifting cybersecurity landscapes and scenarios. Furthermore, the lessons learned and weaknesses revealed by the monitoring and evaluation processes should also be utilized to improve the effectiveness of the program.

3 Artificial Intelligence/Machine Learning Assisted Cybersecurity Awareness

In recent times, almost every discipline is exploring artificial intelligence (AI) and machine learning (ML) as the means for increased efficiency and higher levels of automation. Cybersecurity is no exception and widely utilizes AI and ML methods to achieve various objectives, for example, security incident pattern extraction [51], intrusion detection [52], malware classification and detection [53], spam detection [54], and so on. Alarmingly, the usage of AI and ML methods has not been limited to constructive purposes; cybercriminals and other malicious actors are also misusing and abusing them for ill gain. Deepfake, AI-supported password guessing, human impersonation on social networking platforms, AI-supported hacking, and so on are a few examples of the misuse and abuse of AI and ML methods by cybercriminals [54].

In the context of CSA, AI and ML are also finding potential uses, primarily through accelerating the transition from traditional computer-assisted CSA training to computer-based CSA training. In this computer-based CSA training, AI and ML methods can be applied to automate its various crucial activities so that a more personalized, customized, and optimized CSA training could be offered to a mass audience easily and effectively. Some potential CSA activities in which AI and ML methods can be applied are mentioned next.

3.1 Identification of Vulnerable Audience Groups

Cyber risks change over time within an organization. As a result, identifying the vulnerable employee group for the given cyber threats on time is critical for effective CSA training. This information is important for CSA training planning and for determining security topics and focus groups that need to be prioritized. Analyzing relevant data such as the history of compromises, employee knowledge and expertise, and role-specific risks by using ML algorithms can help with tailoring the message and medium of delivery to selected groups. Similarly, such analysis can assist not only with determining the probability of employees being targeted but also with inferring the probability of such an attack succeeding.

3.2 Personalization and Customization of CSA Training

According to current best practices, the content and procedures used for CSA training must be tailored to the needs and preferences of the audience. This has been proven to improve the impact of the training and extend the period of adherence to a more robust security posture. However, with limited resources available for CSA purposes, this recommendation is often not adhered to.

Every audience is diverse. In the same organization, employees can be different in their nature of work, age group, education, work experience, national culture, and so on. Moreover, the employees can have different levels of security expertise and attitudes toward security. These variances also determine the employee's needs and expectations from a CSA program. For example, some employees may prefer short video training, while games with relatable characters may appeal to others, and some may thrive on task-based learning and simulations. In meeting the individual needs and expectations of employees in a CSA program, ML can play a vital role.

With the use of ML algorithms, it is possible to comprehend and, to some degree, predict the audience's requirements and expectations from CSA training. Furthermore, these algorithms can be applied to estimate what each audience member knows, what s/he needs to learn, and how s/he learns best or prefers to learn. This information can be utilized to design more personalized and customized CSA content and training approaches that best fit the audience's roles, responsibilities, and challenges. The training contents will be more *relevant* (up-to-date information on the security issues suitable to the audience), *relatable* (engaging characters and real-world scenarios that the audience can relate to), and *fitting to the audience's expertise and knowledge level*. Similarly, the delivery approach will be adjusted according to the learning curves (attention spans and retention) of the audience and how s/he uses the training materials (time availability for the training).

3.3 Projection of Future Threats

It is preferable to have CSA initiatives that prepare the audience for both existing and evolving cyber risks and threats. But cyber risks and threats are dynamic in nature, and keeping pace with them is naturally difficult for any organization. Moreover, raising awareness of every evolving cyber risk and threat through the traditional approach can be resource-taxing.

In this case, ML techniques can be used to analyze past cyber threats to uncover patterns in their evolution, and then use that knowledge to forecast how the threats will evolve over time and generate potential future threats. These machine-generated threats can be used to teach the audience about the future course of attacks and how to stay protected from them.

4 Conclusions

The ultimate goal of CSA is to change people's cybersecurity behaviors for the better. And changing behavior is not an easy feat; many things must be considered. The good practices presented in this chapter can help CSA professionals and organizations that plan to design, develop, and implement a CSA program effectively. They will also assist the individuals in monitoring and evaluating CSA programs.

Finally, AI and ML methods can become very effective means to automate various crucial activities of CSA training, for example, identification of vulnerable groups; projection of future threats; personalization, customization of training content and approach; and others. By automating these activities, we can avoid the *"one size fits all"* approach that is prevalent in CSA training [55] and instead provide the audience with more optimized, customized, and personalized CSA training [1, 56]. It can assist in closing the gaps and providing high-quality CSA training, or more specifically, delivering the right CSA content to the right audience at the right time in the right way.

Funding. This work has been financially supported by the CyberSec4Europe project (Proposal No. 830929). This chapter is a combined, revised, and shortened version of the deliverable report D3.19 [1] from CyberSec4Europe's WP3- Blueprint Design and Common Research, and a short paper presented in CyberSec4Europe–Research to Innovation: Common Research Framework on Security and Privacy.

References

1. Chaudhary, S., Pape, S., Kompara, M., Kavallieratos, G., Gkioulos, V.: D3.19 Guidelines for enhancement of societal security awareness. CyberSec4Europe (2022)
2. Wilson, W., Hash, J.: Building an information technology security awareness and training program. National Institute of Standards and Technology (2003)
3. ENISA: The new users' guide: How to raise information security awareness. European Union Agency for Cybersecurity (2010)
4. PCI: Information Supplement: Best Practices for Implementing a Security Awareness Program. PCI Security Standards Council (2014)
5. Spitzner, L., deBeaubien, D., Ideboen, A.: The rising era of awareness training. SANS Institute (2019)
6. Voss, B.: The ultimate defense of depth: security awareness in your company. SANS Institute (2021)
7. SANS Institute: Maturity model, https://www.sans.org/security-awareness-training/resources/maturity-model/ last accessed 21 October 2022
8. Haney, J.M., Lutters, W.G.: Skills and characteristics of successful cybersecurity advocates. In: Workshop on Security Information Workers, Symposium on Usable, Santa Clara, California, USA (2017)
9. Hueca, A., Manley, B., Rogers, L.: Building a cybersecurity awareness program. Software Engineering Institute (2020)
10. Mustaca, S.: Define S.M.A.R.T IT security goals. https://blog.isc2.org/isc2_blog/2013/02/define-smart-it-security-goals.html. Accessed 21 October 2022
11. Bottomley, E., Munnelly, C., Tryl, L., Wride, S.: What makes a successful campaign? Wellcome Trust and the Campaign for Science and Engineering (2020)
12. Vroom, C., von Solms, R.: A practical approach to information security awareness in the organization. In: Ghonaimy, T.A. (eds.) Security in the Information Society, pp. 19–37. Springer (2002)
13. Manke, S., Winkler, I.: The habits of highly successful security awareness programs: a cross company comparison. Secure Mentem (2014)
14. Coventry, L., Briggs, P., Blythe, J., Tran, M.: Using behavioral insights to improve the public's use of cyber security best practices. Government Office for Science (2014)

15. Jones, C., Mccarthy, R.V., Halawi, L.: Utilizing the technology acceptance model to assess the employee adoption of information systems security measures. Int. J. Inf. Technol. Manage. **19**(2), 43–56 (2010)
16. Andrew Valentine, J.: Enhancing the employee security awareness model. Comput. Fraud Secur. **2006**(6), 17–19 (2006)
17. Chaudhary, S., Gkioulos, V., Goodman, D.: cybersecurity awareness for small and medium-sized enterprises (SMEs): availability and scope of free and inexpensive awareness resources. In: 8th Workshop on The Security of Industrial Control Systems & Of Cyber-Physical Systems, Copenhagen, Denmark (2022)
18. Chaudhary, S., Gkioulos, V., Goodman, D.: D9.11 SME cybersecurity awareness program 2. CyberSec4Europe (2021)
19. Caballero, A.: Security education, training, and awareness. In: Vacca, J.R. (ed.) Computer and Information Security Handbook, pp. 497–505. Morgan Kaufmann (2017)
20. Vessey, I.: Cognitive fit: a theory-based analysis of the graphs versus tables literature. Decis. Sci. **22**(2), 219–240 (1991)
21. Kelton, A.S., Pennington, R.R., Tuttle, B.M.: The effects of information presentation format on judgment and decision making: a review of the information systems research. J. Inf. Syst. **24**(2), 79–105 (2010)
22. Smith, S.M., Petty, R.E.: Message framing and persuasion: a message processing analysis. Pers. Soc. Psychol. Bull. **22**(3), 257–268 (1996)
23. Chaudhary, S., Kompara, M., Pape, S., Gkioulos, V.: Properties for cybersecurity awareness posters' design and quality assessment. In: 17th International Conference on Availability, Reliability, Vienna, Austria (2022)
24. Stockhardt, S., et al.: Teaching phishing security: Which way is best? In: 31st International Conference on ICT Systems Security and Privacy Protection, Ghent, Belgium (2016)
25. Shaw, R., Chen, C.C., Harris, A.L., Huang, H.-J.: The impact of information richness on information security awareness training effectiveness. Comput. Educ. **52**(1), 92–100 (2009)
26. González-González, C.S., Izquierdo, F.B., Delgado, P.T.: Integrating the principles of dgbl, cscl, and playability in the design of social videogames: a case study. In: Student Usability in Educational Software and Games: Improving Experiences, pp. 293–304. IGI Global (2013)
27. Mabitle, K., Kritzinger, E.: Schoolteacher preference of cyber-safety awareness delivery methods: a South African study. In: Silhavy, R. (ed.) CSOC 2020. AISC, vol. 1225, pp. 268–283. Springer, Cham (2020). https://doi.org/10.1007/978-3-030-51971-1_22
28. Bada, M., Nurse, J.R.: Developing cybersecurity education and awareness programmes for small- and medium-sized enterprises (SMEs). Inf. Comput. Secur. **27**(3), 393–410 (2019)
29. Gattiker, U.E.: Can an early warning system for home users and SMEs make a difference? a field. In: International Workshop on Critical Information Infrastructures Security, Samos Island, Greece (2006)
30. Ghazvini, A., Shukur, Z.: A framework for an effective information security awareness program in healthcare. Int. J. Adv. Comput. Sci. Appl. **8**(2) (2017)
31. Dolan, P., Hallsworth, M., Halpern, D., King, D., Vlaev, I.: MINDSPACE: Influencing behaviour through public policy. Institute for Government (2010)
32. Chaudhary, S.: D9.18 Awareness Effectiveness Study 2. CyberSec4Europe (2022)
33. Chaudhary, S., Gkioulos, V., Kompara, M.: D 9.26 Awareness effectiveness study 3. CyberSec4Europe (2022)
34. Kirlappos, I., Parkin, S., Sasse, M.A.: "Shadow security" as a tool for the learning organization. SIGCAS Comput. Soc. **45**(1), 29–37 (2015)
35. Bawazir, M.A., Mahmud, M., Molok, N.N.A., Ibrahim, J.: Persuasive technology for improving information security awareness and behavior: literature review. In: 6th International Conference on Information and Communication Technology for The Muslim World (ICT4M), Jakarta, Indonesia (2016)

36. Adams, A., Sasse, M.A.: Users are not the enemy. Commun. ACM **42**(12), 40–46 (1999)
37. Kirlappos, I., Beautement, A., Sasse, M. A.: "Comply or Die" Is dead: long live security-aware principal agents. In: International Conference on Financial Cryptography and Data Security, Okinawa, Japan (2013)
38. Kyonka, E.G.E.: Law of Effect. In: Naglieri, J.A. (eds.) Encyclopedia of Child Behavior and Development, pp. 868–870. Springer (2011)
39. Lawson, S.T., Yeo, S.K., Yu, H., Greene, E.: The cyber-doom effect: the impact of fear appeals in the US cyber security debate. In: 8th International Conference on Cyber Conflict (CyCon), Tallinn, Estonia (2016)
40. Renaud, K., Dupuis, M.: Cyber security fear appeals: unexpectedly complicated. In: New Security Paradigms Workshop, San Carlos, Costa Rica (2019)
41. ENISA: Information security awareness initiatives: Current practice and the measurement of success. European Union Agency for Cybersecurity (2007)
42. Wang, Y., Qi, B., Zou, H.-X., Li, J.-X.: Framework of raising cyber security awareness. In: IEEE 18th International Conference on Communication Technology (ICCT), Chongqing, China (2018)
43. Davis, B., Summers, M.: Applying Dale's Cone of Experience to increase learning and retention: a study of student learning in a foundational leadership course. In: Engineering Leaders Conference 2014 on Engineering Education, Doha, Qatar (2014)
44. Paas, F., van Merriënboer, J.J.G.: Cognitive-load theory: methods to manage working memory load in the learning of complex tasks. Current Directions Psychol. Sci. **29**(4), 394–398 (2020)
45. Reinheimer, B., et al.: An investigation of phishing awareness and education over time: When and how to best remind users. In: Sixteenth Symposium on Usable Privacy and Security, Virtual (2020)
46. Chaudhary, S., Gkioulos, V.: Katsikas, S: Developing metrics to assess the effectiveness of cybersecurity awareness program. J. Cybersecur. **8**(1), 1–19 (2022)
47. Parsons, K., McCormac, A., Butavicius, M., Pattinson, M., Jerram, C.: Determining employee awareness using the Human Aspects of Information Security Questionnaire (HAIS-Q). Comput. Secur. **42**, 165–176 (2014)
48. Egelman, S., Peer, E.: Scaling the security wall: developing a security behavior intentions scale (SeBIS). In: 33rd Annual ACM Conference on Human Factors in Computing Systems, Seoul, Republic of Korea (2015)
49. Faklaris, C., Dabbish, L., Hong, J.I.: A self-report measure of end-user security attitudes (SA-6). In: USENIX Symposium on Usable Privacy and Security (SOUPS), Santa Clara, CA, USA (2019)
50. Sarker, I.H., Kayes, A.S.M., Badsha, S., Alqahtani, H., Watters, P., Ng, A.: Cybersecurity data science: an overview from machine learning perspective. J. Big Data **7**(1), 1–29 (2020). https://doi.org/10.1186/s40537-020-00318-5
51. Abdullahi, M., et al.: Detecting cybersecurity attacks in internet of things using artificial intelligence methods: a systematic literature review. Electronics **11**(2) (2022)
52. Gibert, D., Mateu, C., Planes, J.: The rise of machine learning for detection and classification of malware: research developments, trends and challenges. J. Network Comput. Appl. **153** (2020)
53. Musser, M., Garriott, A.: Machine learning and cybersecurity: hype and reality. Center for Security and Emerging Technology (2021)
54. Stone, M.: How to optimize security awareness training for different groups. https://securityintelligence.com/articles/how-to-optimize-security-awareness-training-for-different-groups/. Accessed 26 September 2019
55. Alruwaili, A.: A review of the impact of training on cybersecurity awareness. Int. J. Adv. Res. Comput. Sci. **10**(5) (2019)

Building European Cybersecurity Ecosystems: Lessons from the Past

Aljosa Pasic(✉)

Atos Spain, Albarracin 25, 28037 Madrid, Spain
aljosa.pasic@atos.net

Abstract. The European Commission proposed to set up the European Cybersecurity Competence Centre (ECCC), together with the Network of National Coordination Centres (NCCs), and Competence Community (CC), which together can be considered as a specific type of a multi-organisational structure or ecosystem aiming at strengthening cybersecurity community capacities. The challenge here is to identify commonly found issues to be solved, as well as decide on governance of new ecosystem, while using "lessons learned" from similar structures, both from the past EU cybersecurity initiatives, as well as from the other IT areas. In this paper we give such an overview of similar initiatives, such as cybersecurity communities, forums, innovation hubs, or public private partnerships. We conclude this part with an overview of lessons learned, before bringing forth concrete activities and results produced by four EU pilot projects to build a cybersecurity ecosystem. Then we postulate ways in which these can be extended to the benefit of the ECCC/NCC/CC ecosystem approach by the EU, and that could be considered for the future governance model and strategic directions.

Keywords: Cybersecurity · Governance · Community · Ecosystem

1 Introduction

The European Union has articulated its ambition to maintain its digital sovereignty and become a global leader in the digital economy, which is closely linked to challenges in the area of cybersecurity. These include the lack of cooperation between Member States, industries and academia, leading to fragmented efforts in research and development (R&D), insufficient investment in cybersecurity at EU level, increased demand for cybersecurity skills, know-how and infrastructure, or (in)consistencies in policies, legal frameworks and actual practice. To meet these challenges, the European Commission proposed to set up the European Cybersecurity Competence Centre (ECCC), together with the Network of National Coordination Centres (NCCs), and the Competence Community (CC), which together can be considered as a specific type of multi-organisational structure or ecosystem aiming at strengthening the cybersecurity community capacities in the EU.

The current regulation [34] still leaves many uncertainties open, and the four pilot projects of the Cybersecurity Competence Community (ECHO, SPARTA, CS4E and

A. Skarmeta et al. (Eds.): CyberSec4Europe 2022, CCIS 1807, pp. 161–174, 2023.
https://doi.org/10.1007/978-3-031-36096-1_11

CONCORDIA, see [27]) are continuously providing their feedback on these open issues. At this stage, for example, not many details about the governance of financial provisions are revealed about the ECCC, which will be located in Bucharest [35], or the other two layers (NCC, CC), so this paper is based on an analysis of lessons learned from other similar value co-creation experiences, as well as the feedback collected in the four pilot projects.

The Cybersecurity4Europe project report [17], for example, proposes a governance structure, with an overview of the inputs on which it is based, while a later deliverable [18] is bringing some experiences and experimentations with the governance structures of cybersecurity ecosystems from various EU Member States. In October 2021 ENISA, ECSO and the four pilot projects (CONCORDIA, SPARTA, CS4E, ECHO) submitted their draft recommendations to the ECCC, following a consensus process about the future priorities. Besides these recommendations, representatives of these projects and institutions elaborated a "concept on the way forward" with 11 strategic directions where the "competence community" cold make a significant contributions. These strategic directions are not presented here, as they need to be further enhanced and maybe fine-tuned for specific target stakeholders. However, stimulating cost-efficient instruments for growth, transfer, or creation of value networks, should also be considered in the future revisions.

In order to have a cybersecurity ecosystem capable of addressing such a diversity of identified challenges, it is essential to take into account stakeholder views and current best practices. The four pilot projects have already gathered views from more than 80 stakeholders via surveys, interviews, and workshops. In this paper, we additionally present some of the previous lessons learned and best practices in different kinds of cybersecurity initiatives, networked organisations or "cybersecurity ecosystems", as they are called in the CONCORDIA project.

In this context, we define ecosystem as "a system of people, practices, values, and technologies in a particular environment" [25]. The ecosystem includes roles, tasks, and relationships, which could be customized for different layers or even different Member States [26]. Unlike the concept of network, ecosystems also bring dynamicity, since different alternatives need to be considered from the economic perspective (e.g., reuse of software components, shared resources such as labs, scale-up of new solutions etc.).

2 Related Work

Network effects that increase the value are also studied in the context of internet platforms, which often enable single companies to take large market shares [3], with well-recognized internet services such as advertising, social networks and search engines being the most prominent examples. As a result, so-called scaling benefits within "platform economy" or "multi-sided markets" arise. Depending on the type of application, the added value benefits users in different ways and depends on openness and centralisation [4]. In the more open examples, the value should grow for everyone, although smaller entities experience more difficulties. Although some elements could be applicable to the cybersecurity ecosystem and the CC, for example lessons from multi-sided market for the e-identity services, these platforms are not directly related to the CC model.

Business ecosystems [1, 2] are structures where large companies can co-evolve their skills together with academic partners and smaller, more agile companies. Unlike the CC, these are centred around one large company, although it also builds upon an idea of value creation by putting together different assets and skills. This process is often non-linear as in the CC, but the configuration is not that complex, and stakeholders are mainly partnering from supply side. These partners are expected to complement each other, while in the CC we will certainly have to deal with overlapping and competing supply side stakeholders.

A similar notion (but applied exclusively to digital technologies) is termed Digital Business Ecosystem (DBE) and it has been defined [9] as "a collaborative environment made up of different entities that co-create value through information and communication technologies (ICTs)". The concept of Digital Business Ecosystem was coined initially in the context of the implementation of the eEurope 2002 action plan, and the projects funded by the 6th Framework Programme of the European Commission and clustered under the name "Technologies for Digital Ecosystems", presented their main research and empirical achievements in a book [12].

According to [10], the DBE comprises two main tiers, digital and business, where this second tier refers to an economic community of stakeholders that operate outside their traditional industry boundaries. It does not, in comparison to the envisaged cybersecurity ecosystem or the CC, consider academic research or regional economic development, for example. On the other hand, similarity lies in the fact that the DBE relies on synergy between different stakeholders, and value co-creation as an important driver.

The main characteristics of DBEs are platform, symbiosis, co-evolution and self-organisation [11]. Here we find further differences with the ECCC/NCC/CC approach. In the four pilot projects for the cybersecurity ecosystem and the CC, "platform" vaguely refers to a collection of tools, innovations and/or services, but its focus differs from federated cyber-range platforms to research testbeds. Symbiosis and synergy between stakeholders in pilot projects are also common elements, but the instruments for governance support are still lacking. Finally, co-evolution and self-organisation are characteristics that might be desirable, but impossible to evaluate and validate in the four pilot projects. What seems inevitable is that different categories of relationships will co-exist in the ECCC/NCC/CC, including organised and ad-hoc collaborations among stakeholders. Organised collaborations might include long-term strategic relationship networks, e.g., between ECCC and NCC, or inside of regional hubs, while informal and ad-hoc collaborations might be desirable on cross-border level, for example in R&D consortia.

Digital Innovation Hubs (DIHs) are a kind of ecosystem that exists with this name from 2016. Originally, they were linked to the Digitising European Industry (DEI) initiative [21]. Afterwards, the DIH concept was also evolving towards the European DIH and outside of the industry sector, and has also been suggested as a model for cybersecurity ecosystems. This also caused divergence from the original vision and there was an attempt [22] to establish a shared common conceptual framework of a DIH within the European DIH community. This included five different building blocks as the backbone of the European DIH network, roughly described around competences, services, economies and finance and finally collaborations and networks. One of the distinctive features of "DIH-like ecosystem" is the focus on SMEs and mid-caps that are faced with a "valley of death", term that in innovation denotes the period between prototype and market-ready solution. Elevated economic risks and market failures are also common in cybersecurity, while "economies of scale", one of the main DIH assumptions, are also very important for the cybersecurity ecosystem.

Given that DIHs also have a regional focus, synergy was established with a mechanism called "Smart Specialisation Platform". This European Commission initiative exists since 2011, in order to facilitate mutual learning, networking opportunities and other activities for regions. Thematic Smart Specialisation platforms have also been created and while digital technologies are considered as a transversal priority in most regional S3 across Europe, DIHs started to be used as a policy instrument to boost these priorities [23]. Synthesis of empirical research and the analysis of the governance arrangements underpinning Smart Specialisation strategies were published in 2021 [24], but there is no specific analysis yet of DIH synergy and its impact on economy and policy objectives.

Some experiences in what can be labelled as "cybersecurity ecosystem" in Europe already exist, and those should also be taken into account when shaping governance and evolution of the forthcoming ECCC/NCC/CC ecosystem. Although related communities (IT, network, information security and others) existed before, we look at the period of the last 13 years and focus only on EU initiatives sponsored or co-funded by the European Commission or agencies of the European Union. We leave out of scope associations of professionals, such as (ISC)2, ISACA or ISF, communities that grew around training or traditional technical conferences (such as SANS in US, that was founded in 1989), as well as the purpose-built communities that deal with specific issues, such as international confederation of computer incident response teams FIRST.

The EP3R (European Public-Private Partnership for Resilience) was established in 2009 and shut down in April 2013. ENISA [29] described it as "the very first attempt at Pan-European level to use a Public-Private Partnership (PPP) to address cross-border Security and Resilience concerns in the Telecom Sector". This statement might be questionable, since it was not a contractual PPP, and because different working groups with information security focus already existed in several European initiatives ([30, 31] and [32]), co-funded by the European Commission within the Sixth Framework Programme (2002–2006).

The EP3R had an important support from ENISA that initiated, supported and participated in many discussions. The PPP approach was judged to be particularly appropriate for addressing complex cooperation problems and the model was even proposed for Information Sharing and Analysis Centres (ISACs) and similar initiatives.

Initially, the EP3R was facing challenges and value propositions such as team building, trust, joint objectives and action plan identification and others, but stakeholders soon lost interest and in a related survey they mentioned a couple of shortcomings, such as the need for smaller working groups, focused and limited in time, the need to improve motivation and incentives of demand side stakeholders, simple but formal rules and governance etc. In 2011, ENISA published a Good Practice Guide on Cooperative Models for Effective PPPs [33] and included some of these opinions in it.

PPPs are a well-known instrument that has been used many times by the Commission, which published Guidelines for Successful Public–Private Partnerships [16] in 2003. The establishment of the network and information security (NIS) Public-Private Platform was announced in the Cybersecurity Strategy of the European Union in 2013 [13]. The NIS Platform was supposed to complement and underpin the proposed NIS Directive, while at the same time its subsections (working groups) were addressing objectives such as input to the secure ICT Research & Innovation agenda at national and EU level, or assessment of Business Cases and Innovation Paths. The Commission has convened the first plenary meeting of the NIS platform on 17 June 2013, but this initiative, similar to the EP3R, was also short-lived. It is also worth noticing that both the EP3R and the NIS platform were "self-proclaimed" or designated PPPs, as opposed to later "contractual" PPPs (cPPPs) [8] that emerged in the H2020 programme.

Nevertheless, the NIS Platform paved the way for the establishment of the first cPPP in cybersecurity in July 2016. The EU was committed to invest €450 million in this cPPP, whose private counterpart was represented by the European Cyber Security Organisation (ECSO). This cPPP was preceded by similar initiatives in other digital technologies, such as photonics, robotics, high performance computing or 5G technologies in 2013, or big data in 2014. It should be noted that the "private" part includes many public stakeholders, such as academia and public sector, and as a such it represents in essence also a kind of ecosystem. In the case of ECSO, many are confused by the differences between cPPP and ECSO itself, which explains in its web page [14] that within its governance the Partnership Board is the actual communication channel between the European Commission and the ECSO. While at the time of writing this paper the role of ECSO in the upcoming cybersecurity ecosystem is still unclear, there is no doubt that there are some useful lessons and elements that could be reused from ECSO and the cPPP that was active during H2020 framework programme.

Finally, we should also mention the cybersecurity ecosystems that have very focused objectives, such as data sharing. ENISA conducted a study on Cooperative Models for Public-Private Partnership (PPP) and ISACs [15], collating information on best practices and common approaches. As for the ecosystems focused on cybersecurity research, there are useful lessons in the EU 7th Framework Programme, where "Network of Excellence" (NoE) was used as the funding scheme. It did so by supporting a "Joint programme of activities" implemented by various stakeholders, although mainly from the academic sector, with a possibility of longer-term cooperation. An example is the NESSOS project [19], focused on secure software and services, or the European Network of Excellence in Cryptology (ECRYPT 2) [20]. Both of these examples are limited in focus and type of stakeholders and, although they could be interesting starting point for specific substructures e.g., working groups within CC, reusability of their conclusions is limited.

3 Stakeholder Analysis

Some stakeholders in cybersecurity ecosystem, similar to what has already happened in the four pilot projects of the Cybersecurity Competence Community (ECHO, SPARTA, CS4E and CONCORDIA, see [27]) will have both contributor and beneficiary role, being present simultaneously on the supply and demand sides (for example, telecommunication use case in CONCORDIA project [28]).

Stakeholder analysis in the cybersecurity ecosystem goes further than only looking at the supply and demand side, or inclusion of "other" external stakeholders, such as policymakers, certification and standardization bodies or legal organizations. Segmentation could and should take into account the current level of maturity, territorial approach, cultural differences, size of organizations, risk-appetite, and many other parameters.

Collaboration and cooperation can be analysed from several perspectives, from co-design (e.g., research project) of solutions to service co-delivery (e.g., coordinated response from security teams from different Member States, see also work on Collaborative Automated Course of Action Operations (CACAO) Security Playbooks in CONCORDIA [5]). Less visible issues and challenges, such as SME networking, where supply-side SMEs could complement each other, should also be investigated from a wider economic angle.

Besides complementarities and cooperation, other value drivers for stakeholder collaboration and cooperation should be considered in the economic models for the cybersecurity ecosystem, including efficiency, avoiding vendor lock-in, or interplay between economics and digital sovereignty. Value network reconfiguration or government intervention through policy might be needed when addressing technology acceptance or user adoption. Growth and evolution of the ecosystem (the CONCORDIA consortium expands every year with new project partners), and the motivation for diverse stakeholders to collaborate and cooperate should also be analysed.

The technology provider group, for example, could be expanded to other providers (external to the current participants of four pilot projects, or the initial CC) that could replace one of the existing technologies or connect them to the different environments. Research groups (universities, institutes) might need to collaborate with members which provide consultancy services to enable the transfer of knowledge to the industry or creation of new start-ups. Open-source and other related EU communities in digital technologies (e.g., GAIA-X [39], ADRA [40], FIWARE [41], AIOTI [42], different European DIHs [43] etc.) could have their role in the adoption and further development and the sustainability of the ecosystem. Standardisation and certification bodies, individual investors, business angels, governmental organisation, incubators, accelerators, innovation centres, professional associations of cybersecurity practitioners, citizens and others should all have clear role and rules of engagement within the ecosystem.

This engagement may adopt various forms, depending on the context. Project or action types could include contracted work, transferring technology, smaller expert and consultancy services, permanent cooperation structures, industry-specific or sector-specific associations or sub-structures, spin-off and start-up companies supported by ecosystem incubators, etc. We might expect that the final ecosystem configuration will strongly depend on the choice of a governance model and the pool of funds and equipment available.

From the pan-European perspective, solutions are not only supposed to be reused, or used in a collaborative and cooperative manner, but also evaluated by the "peers" from the same target audience, as well as by the stakeholders with different perspective. Failure to synchronize activities across member states, pertinent to the second tier of this ecosystem (NCC) would cause excess of effort put into "reinventing the wheel", too much overhead activities, additional challenges of benchmarking, interoperability, matching and reconfiguration, possibility to miss compatible value propositions and others.

4 Governance Model

As mentioned before, the CC governance model is still under construction, but the four pilot projects ECHO, SPARTA, CS4E and CONCORDIA already made proposals in this regard, as well as regarding its strategic directions or set of principles. The ecosystem, for example, should monitor capability for scaling and capacity utilization, rapid identification of members that do not bring in value and can be excluded, reciprocal interdependence between members, members acting as mediators or "glue" for a value proposition, and it should be able to identify gaps and challenges in a collaborative and cooperative manner, taking into account multiple perspectives and multidisciplinary views. While ecosystem objectives are directly related to the long-term digital society and cybersecurity goals, specific stakeholder configurations in sub-structures, e.g., sector or technology-dependent, should be feasible.

While all four projects addressed possible CC governance models in different ways, the CS4E project went one step further by proposing a network of Community Hubs of Expertise in Cybersecurity Knowledge (CHECKs) [17], as a kind of the bottom-up approach to put forward a sub-structure of the cybersecurity ecosystem. There have been several categories taken into account for governance best practice analysis prior to the CHECK proposition. Besides stakeholder analysis and organizational structures, decision-making or coordination mechanism with external bodies have also been discussed. The model and its assumptions were validated in the real-life scenario, namely with cybersecurity stakeholders in Toulouse in an entity named Community Hubs of Expertise in Cybersecurity Knowledge (CHECK Toulouse) [18]. Based on this work, conclusions and recommendations have been provided for the roadmap [36]. These include not only the use of CHECKs to organise the Community and provide flexibility but also a systematic approach to registering communities and hubs, as well as the exploration of practical implications of community decision-making.

SPARTA project deliverables [7] describe the structures, processes and activities that characterize the governance of the SPARTA and their adequacy for the ecosystem under the European Cybersecurity Competence Centre (ECCC). The project uses its own governance model as the case and concludes that there was strong utilization of some committees and processes (e.g., road mapping), while other governance bodies (notably the Certification Task Force, the Ethics Board, and the Advisory Committee) were underutilized, something to be attributed to the early stage of the project. While the first study used a pilot-internal perspective, addressing both management and governance aspects of the pilot during the first work period, later work concerned the applicability of SPARTA's findings about pilot governance objectives, structures and mechanisms to the real-world implementation ECCC. However, SPARTA's internal governance structure, including its success criteria, are not directly applicable to the ECCN/NCC/CC scenario. For this reason, project did re-assessment of recommendations for SPARTA's governance. Main findings were on general governance issues (e.g., interaction with other EC funded projects occurred, without formal cooperations, or consortium extensions), governance model (e.g., SPARTA's T-SHARK program, that used Stage-Gate methodology [38] explored options of including operational capabilities in a competence center at European level), horizontal integration (e.g., the level of integration between components produced within each of their four technical programs was maximized through specific collaboration support) and continuous assessment (e.g., task of continuous monitoring and assessment was made part of operational project management).

The ECHO project formulated the ecosystem as a Collaborative Networked Organisation (CNO) and described development, assessment and selection of the governance model alternatives [26]. It used the Analytic Hierarchy Process (AHP) method to reach consensus among stakeholders, engaging with the European Cyber Security Organisation (ECSO) as well. The alternatives' assessment was done by comparing the governance model performance against each pre-defined criterion. The solution accepted by most stakeholders was to create one "umbrella" alternative, so called Alternative 0 (A0), based on best practices from the other four alternative models. In a later deliverable [6] the overall design framework was described through RACI (Responsible, Accountable, Consulted, Informed) matrix, while key process discovery (e.g., Strategic Planning Process; Partnership Development Process; Catalogue Management and Customer Relations Management process description; Innovation (R&D) Process) was done with the help of the COBIT framework [44]. There is also an assessment of organisational structure similarity of the ECHO Consortium and the future ECHO CNO, with a conclusion that the consortium has similarity to ECHO CNO's Central Hub. The future roadmap was also considered, with possibilities such as a merge of ECSO and the other three pilot projects in one organization (forming ECSCON, in line with the joint Governance White paper agreed by the Commission and other pilot projects). Another option is the establishment of the ECHO Network as an NGO with Chapters and a Central Hub to be the ECHO Cybersecurity Competence Centre after the end of the project. ECHO Governance Consultancy Services (E-GCS) is considered to be one of the project outcomes and was developing its Services Catalogue.

Although governance was not addressed through a separated task or work package in CONCORDIA, this project also provided few lessons about the possible governance issues and models. Growth and evolution of ecosystem was efficient as CONCORDIA consortium was expanding every year with new project partners. So called "Pan-European Cybersecurity Start-Up Community" (PECS-UP) was active in CONCORDIA and linked to agile governance, as well as a vision in technology transfer and market adoption. Start-up support service in CONCORDIA was provided through information, diffusion of best practices and matchmaking, executed in collaboration with entities such as ECSO (European Cybersecurity Organisation) or EIT Digital. CONCORDIA supported creation of cybersecurity investment platform, aimed to coordinate financing resources and instruments to support the maturation of Europe's cybersecurity sector through private investment. Other outcomes that were related to ecosystem collaborative processes include annual ranking of key exploitable results, done by Industrial Strategic Committee (ISC) and an interactive website where professionals from across the EU can contribute and comment on the roadmap for the cybersecurity ecosystem [45] (Table 1).

Table 1. Ecosystem Governance in Four EU projects

Project	Governance Work Package	Main Results
Cybersecurity4Europe	WP2	Model based on CHECKs, bottom-up approach, pilot in Toulouse
CONCORDIA	No WP or task dedicated to governance	Several collaborative processes have been piloted
SPARTA	WP1	Stage Gate methodology and T-SHARK governance model
ECHO	WP3	Service Groups and a Central Hub to form the ECHO Cybersecurity Competence Centre, Pilot National Hub in Bulgaria (NH-BG) and pilot of Service Group

5 Strategic Directions, Gaps, and Challenges

The rationale for the "ecosystem"-based model is also that it fits demands concerning uncertainty and fragility. For example, there is little certainty regarding the window of opportunity, as the cybersecurity technology moves and changes very fast. The length of time that will elapse between the prototype launch and the development of meaningful or scalable demand from EU users is shorter than it is for the other digital technologies. Early-stage users tend to be particularly fragile. Pioneer adopters do not have the testimonials, benchmark or references from the existing operational environment users, or other types of evidence such as proof of value (PoV). Even if such evidence exist, solution might not be easily transferred or reusable from one operational environment to another.

One idea coming from the joint meeting of four pilot projects and ENISA, and related to ecosystem market driven strategic directions, is to use the CC marketplace as the single-entry point with an emphasis on early product and prototype visibility. The value proposition of such a marketplace needs to be worked out, but it could basically create an environment for the conversation and mapping between demand and supply side in EU cybersecurity market, eventually leading to better and more mature products. "Try before buy" or "test before invest" could also be reflected or linked to this marketplace, as well as a range of other free or subsidized services and business processes that could serve as a "hook" to sign up new customers, also outside EU.

Ecosystem-based trials or PoV projects might need innovative instruments, involving the assumption of successful adoption from the demand-side "pioneers" and later scaling-up. However, it is likely that some less profitable research or some cybersecurity segments will need to follow different paths, and this is where governance mechanism should include multiple tiers or substructures with parallel sets of rules or policies, to keep ecosystem aligned with the latest economic, business, but also breakthrough research objectives.

In case of the CONCORDIA pilot project, for example, there are already some services offered for free to the CONCORDIA community, such as the possibility to test technologies or the catalogue of online training offerings. The project also addresses limitations and barriers when it comes to the adaptation of cybersecurity to the needs of SMEs and start-ups, such as the lack of expertise (CONCORDIA training), financial resources (CONCORDIA virtual lab), or optimisation of the solutions to their needs and scale (CONCORDIA experiments). The ranking of exploitable results is done on an annual basis, having in mind the evolution of technology readiness level (TRL), but also market readiness level (MRL), innovation potential and the importance of ecosystem support in its exploitation path.

Cybersecurity4Europe project identified also need for the maturity framework to enable better understanding of different nodes of EU cybersecurity innovation ecosystem, whether these are organized in a Digital Innovation Hubs (DIH), CHECKs or any other "hub"-like format. Framework is based on a set of flexible criteria, which can be used to develop the maturation strategies and further develop cybersecurity innovation ecosystems. Different criteria include size, number and type of members, industry sector or specialization in technology (e.g., Cluster of Industry 4.0 cybersecurity or Community interested in cloud security issues), level of centralization and/or involvement of public administration, monitoring and continuous improvement practices, maturity of collaboration and partnerships, support services, management of memberships, common resources, ecosystem results and outcomes etc. Maturity criteria are not exhaustive and there is a strong interdependence between them, which needs to be reviewed and further finetuned.

Beyond the support for integrating specific cybersecurity technologies in the processes and products created by start-ups and SMEs, there is also significant business potential for European cybersecurity start-ups and SMEs in showcasing their innovations and solutions, and in this way attracting investors, finding better geographical coverage and expanding besides national boundaries, as well as identifying partnerships in value networks, whether it is with larger cybersecurity suppliers or with the other start-up or SME that complements their solutions. The challenge here is to be able to implement the assessment of highly innovative ideas through the community, especially for so called "deep tech" start-ups, without disclosing the idea itself.

The gap in the ecosystem might also appear between the top-down policy or market issues and bottom-up research and innovation. Finally, dynamics of relationships that have a direct impact on trust, and in consequence on economics, should also be addressed as a challenge for the ecosystem.

6 Conclusions

Cybersecurity ecosystems modelling is a topic of particular importance for the future EU cybersecurity policy, as it includes establishment of the EU Cybersecurity Competence Centre (ECCC), the Network of National Coordination Centres (NCCs) and the Cybersecurity Community (CC). Four pilot projects of cybersecurity competence community (ECHO, SPARTA, CS4E and CONCORDIA) have started their work in 2019 and are continuously providing their feedback on a number of issues, including research roadmap, governance model, strategic directions, gaps and challenges.

In this paper we tried to make an analysis of lessons learned from the other similar value co-creation experiences, cybersecurity communities and public-private partnerships, as well as to present some work and the feedback collected in the four pilot projects. Stakeholders in the four pilot projects, which are also representative of the future ecosystem, might have multiple roles, while levels of membership or relationships between are likely to be very dynamic, in both formal and informal dimensions. The EU cybersecurity market's fragmentation is likely to be reduced, therefore increasing the economy of scale, but shaping instruments to enable mapping between demand and supply still needs to find place. The overall benefit is expected to be very positive, but also difficult to assess, as the economic impact attribution to "ecosystem existence" is hard to validate. The inclusion of "ecosystem role" parameters in the exploitation plan descriptions might help, for example by addressing support for the testing, certification preparation, maintenance, data exchange etc.

Although there is an aim to align industrial strategy and policy priorities with the generation of innovative ideas, there is a still a need to improve policy-market-technology-society alignment, as well as embed economic issues in the ecosystem. Further gaps might appear in territorial coverage, capacity, and maturity of cybersecurity landscape in different Member States. The challenges related to the EU cybersecurity ecosystem and stakeholders outside of the EU are also yet to be addressed. Finally, dynamics of relationships that have a direct impact on trust, and in consequence on economics should also be explored. The following recommendations could be derived:

- Make governance "liquid" to address dynamicity of an ecosystem: re-assessment of roles, levels of membership, type of relationships, formal and informal dimensions etc., based on meritocracy and balanced representations of different communities (industry, research, users) and member states of the EU
- Shape "research to market" mechanisms that would enable better mapping between demand and supply, between industrial strategy and research lines, and would address economics of cybersecurity, including economy of scale and the current fragmentation
- Streamline different processes, rules and activities related to collaborative processes inside of cybersecurity ecosystem, including capability-building, policy support, R&D road mapping or joint assessment (of research priorities or exploitable results).
- Strive to address both top-down and bottom-up approaches, leading to a more efficient stakeholder engagement in issues which lie at the intersection. High level policy, for example, should match better demand side needs.
- Build upon different types of existing hubs and communities, including different types of CHECKs. Some of these are financed as a public good, while the other could be self-sustainable. Address mistrust that could exist between different hubs, related to their perimeter of action and influence, through specific mechanisms or transition processes.
- Align EU, national and regional interests, but also different research agendas. Interface mechanisms would thus be necessary to avoid any kind of duplication and overlaps, as well as to make periodic alignment verifications.
- Address capacity to coordinate and orchestrate exogenous and diverse skills and resources. Support and coordination activities for this ecosystem should also improve

the general awareness towards cybersecurity issues and ecosystem itself. The management of research and innovation results, maybe in a form of an online catalogue or marketplace, should be considered.
- Cover mentoring and capital investment strategies for cybersecurity start-ups.
- Address common testbeds and other resource sharing, such as datasets or experimental facilities.

Activities in an ecosystem are characterized by trade-offs and consensus, and process of building it can also be understood as "connecting the dots". It is a challenging task to design governance and ecosystem strategy "by the community" and "for the community", but we do have many lessons learned from the previous initiatives, as well as the four pilot projects. Cybersecurity4Europe is an example of a project where strategy, implementation options and operational execution were well synchronized and evaluated in several community decision making processes. Ranking of project results within the exploitation activities is a good example of community effort to amplify impact and improve research to market transfer. After consideration of several alternative procedures and implementation choices, from marketplace to innovation competitions, tactical choice was to apply the process of filtering and prioritization of the exploitable results by the community, with a posterior selection of the most innovative and market attractive asset by an external jury at the final Cybersecurity4Europe event [37].

Collective transparent assessment can also be applied to many other processes, for example the assessment of the claimed properties of cybersecurity solution (e.g., coverage, ease of integration or effectiveness) or market readiness levels (MRL). These would enable buyers to make optimized purchasing decisions and would give vendors stronger incentives to deliver technology with improved efficacy. "Try before buy" could be used inside of ecosystem, to help start-ups to faster penetrate the market. "Test before invest" scheme would be useful for cybersecurity investors that are not experts in technology.

Ecosystem approach ideas obviously bring some important challenges with it, such as common assessment processes, rules or norms, assessment objectivity and independence, distribution of assessment cost, decision-making process etc. Tyranny of majority, whether this is research (sub)community, or some other group around specific interest, or well-organized minority, that could manage to promote specific solutions or topics thanks to the apathy or lack of interest of others, are also challenges to have in mind. Polycentric governance, like the one described in WP2 of Cybersecurity4Europe is definitely good candidate that could deal with these challenges.

Acknowledgements. This work was partially supported by the European research projects H2020 CyberSec4Europe project (GA 830929) and CONCORDIA (830927).

References

1. Anggraeni, E., Hartigh, E., Zegveld, M.: Business ecosystem as a perspective for studying the relations between firms and their business networks (2007)
2. Wieninger, S., Götzen, R., Gudergan, G., Wenning, K.: The strategic analysis of business ecosystems: new conception and practical application of a research approach. 1–8 (2019). https://doi.org/10.1109/ICE.2019.8792657

3. Noe, T., Parker, G.: Winner take all: competition, strategy, and the structure of returns in the internet economy. J. Econ. Manage. Strategy **14**(1), 141–164 (2005). https://doi.org/10.1111/j.1430-9134.2005.00037.x
4. Arkko, J.: The influence of internet architecture on centralised versus distributed internet services. J. Cyber Policy **5**(1), 30–45 (2020). https://doi.org/10.1080/23738871.2020.1740753
5. Update on Security Playbook Standardization, https://www.concordia-h2020.eu/blog-post/an-update-on-security-playbook-standardization/. Accessed Nov 2022
6. ECHO deliverable D3.3 Governance Model Description (2021)
7. SPARTA deliverable D1.2 Lessons learned from internally assessing a CCN pilot (2020)
8. EC web page Contractual public-private partnerships: https://ec.europa.eu/programmes/horizon2020/en/contractual-public-private-partnerships. Accessed Nov 2022
9. Nachira, F., Dini, P., Nicolai, A.: A network of digital business ecosystems for Europe: roots, processes and perspectives. Digital business ecosystem. Eur. Commission Inf. Soc. Media (2007)
10. Stanley, J., Briscoe, G.: The ABC of digital business ecosystems. Commun. Law J. Comput. Media Telecommun. Law, 15(1) (2010)
11. Senyo, P.K., Liu, K., Sun, L., Effah, J.: Evolution of norms in the emergence of digital business ecosystems. In: Baranauskas, M.C.C., Liu, K., Sun, L., Neris, VPd.A., Bonacin, R., Nakata, K. (eds.) ICISO 2016. IAICT, vol. 477, pp. 79–84. Springer, Cham (2016). https://doi.org/10.1007/978-3-319-42102-5_9
12. EC publications, Digital Business Ecosystems (2007)
13. Cybersecurity Strategy of the European Union: an open, safe and secure cyberspace, JOIN/2013/01 final. https://eur-lex.europa.eu/legal-content/EN/TXT/?uri=CELEX:52013JC0001. Accessed Nov 2022
14. ECSO and cPPP relationship: https://ecs-org.eu/cppp. Accessed Nov 2022
15. ENISA study on Cooperative Models for Public-Private Partnership (PPP) and Information Sharing and Analysis Centers (ISACs). https://op.europa.eu/en/publication-detail/-/publication/597dee0f-2285-11e8-ac73-01aa75ed71a1. Accessed Nov 2022
16. European Commission Guidelines for Successful Public Private Partnerships (2003). https://ec.europa.eu/regional_policy/sources/docgener/guides/ppp_en.pdf. Accessed Nov 2022
17. Cybersecurity4Europe project deliverable D2.3 Governance Structure v2.0 of CS4E available here: https://cybersec4europe.eu/wp-content/uploads/2021/02/D2.3-Governance-Structure-2-submitted.pdf. Accessed Feb 2023
18. Cybersecurity4Europe project deliverable D2.2 Internal Validation of Governance Structure
19. Network of excellence on engineering secure future internet software services and systems. http://www.nessos-project.eu/. Accessed Nov 2022
20. European network of excellence in cryptology - Phase II, https://cordis.europa.eu/project/id/216676. Accessed Nov 2022
21. Digitising European industry imitative report, working group 2, digital industrial platforms (2017)
22. DIHNET.EU project deliverable: defining digital innovation hubs as part of the European DIH network (2020)
23. JRC technical reports, digital innovation hubs in smart specialisation strategies, early lessons from European regions (2018)
24. JRC Policy Insights, the impact of smart specialisation on the governance of research and innovation policy systems (2021)
25. CONCORDIA project deliverable D6.3 Innovation management strategy
26. ECHO project deliverable D3.2 Governance alternatives
27. Joint web site for four pilot projects of cybersecurity competence community: https://cybercompetencenetwork.eu/. Accessed Nov 2022

28. CONCORDIA web site: https://www.concordia-h2020.eu. Accessed Nov 2022
29. EP3R 2010–2013, four years of Pan-European public private cooperation, ENISA report, (2014)
30. Pasic A., NESSI and ESFORS: paving the way towards secure software services, European critical information infrastructure newsletter (2006)
31. Pasic, A.: Building blocks for future internet of services: trust, security, privacy and dependability, MIT Press book on New Architectures for Future Internet, (2009)
32. Pasic, A.: Delivering building blocks for internet of services: trust, security, privacy and dependability. In: Tronco, T., (eds) New Network Architectures. Studies in Computational Intelligence, vol 297. Springer, Berlin, Heidelberg, (2010) https://doi.org/10.1007/978-3-642-13247-6_12
33. ENISA report, good practice guide on cooperative models for effective PPPs (2011)
34. Regulation (EU) 2021/887 of the European Parliament and of the Council of 20 May 2021 establishing the European Cybersecurity Industrial, Technology and Research Competence Centre and the Network of National Coordination Centres. https://eur-lex.europa.eu/eli/reg/2021/887/oj. Accessed Nov 2022
35. Web site of European cybersecurity competence centre and network, ECCC and NCC: https://cybersecurity-centre.europa.eu/. Accessed Nov 2022
36. Cybersecurity4Europe project deliverable D2.4 Roadmap of the Set-Up of the NCC. https://cybersec4europe.eu/wp-content/uploads/2022/12/D2.4-Roadmap-of-the-Set-Up-of-the-NCC_v1.0_submitted.pdf. Accessed Feb 2023
37. Final event of Cybersecurity4Europe project: https://cybersec4europe.eu/event/momentum/
38. Sparta blog about T-SHARK governance model: https://www.sparta.eu/news/2020-10-28-innovation-governance-based-on-the-diversity-of-factors-that-shaped-the-development-of-the-sparta-t-shark-program.html. Accessed Feb 2023
39. GAIA-X website: https://gaia-x.eu/. Accessed Feb 2023
40. ADRA website: https://adr-association.eu/. Accessed Feb 2023
41. FIWARE website: https://www.fiware.org/. Accessed Feb 2023
42. AIOTI website: https://aioti.eu/. Accessed Feb 2023
43. EU DIH website: https://digital-strategy.ec.europa.eu/en/activities/edihs. Accessed Feb 2023
44. COBIT website: https://www.isaca.org/resources/cobit. Accessed Feb 2023
45. CONCORDIA monitor board: https://concordia.monitorboard.nl/roadmap/. Accessed Feb 2023

Author Index

A. Skarmeta et al. (Eds.): CyberSec4Europe 2022, CCIS 1807, p. 175, 2023.
https://doi.org/10.1007/978-3-031-36096-1

Printed in the United States
by Baker & Taylor Publisher Services